Engaging with Ethics in International Criminological Research brings the ethical issues and challenges confronted by the criminological researcher to life. Rather than provide dry guidance on how to navigate institutional ethics review, it contains a wealth of insights – from international scholars at the forefront to contemporary criminology – into the ethical thinking and decision-making involved in all serious criminology. These contributions are full of interesting and thought-provoking discussion of profound moral issues. It will be of interest to anyone researching, studying or teaching criminology.

Gerry Johnstone, *Professor of Law, Law School, University of Hull, UK*

Drawing on scholars studying myriad international sites, *Engaging with Ethics* goes beyond other books that merely criticize the power structure providing a blockade for research, instead offering programmatic statements and examples of how to navigate through these barriers to produce empirically rich, theoretically driven, yet ethical research that honors both those we study and those who write about criminals and criminal justice settings.

Patricia A. Adler, *Professor Emeritus, University of Colorado, USA and*
Peter Adler, *Professor Emeritus, University of Denver, USA*

Universities have defined 'ethics up'. In doing so they have fundamentally reshaped, and are actively reshaping, how research is done. Nowhere is this more evident than in criminology. *Engaging with Ethics* offers insightful reflections on this 'ethical creep' – its history and its implication across geographically dispersed research areas. It calls for an 'ethical imagination' grounded in the 'lived experiences' of active, experienced and sensitive researchers.

Clifford Shearing, *Professor in the School of Criminology and Criminal Justice,*
Griffith University, Australia

Adorjan, Ricciardelli and the contributors have assembled a valuable set of materials on a critical, yet understudied topic. They take the reader inside the dynamics of field research to explore areas not covered in traditional methods texts. A must-read for both experienced and novice field researchers.

Curt Taylor Griffiths, *Professor and Director, Police Studies Centre,*
Simon Fraser University, Canada

ENGAGING WITH ETHICS IN INTERNATIONAL CRIMINOLOGICAL RESEARCH

Despite a voluminous literature detailing the procedures of research ethics boards and institutional ethical review processes, there are few texts that explore the *realpolitik* of conducting criminological research in practice. This book explores the unique lived experiences of scholars engaging with ethics during their criminological research, and focuses on the ethical dilemmas that researchers encounter both in the field and while writing up results for publication. Who benefits from criminological research? What are the roles and impacts of ethics review boards? How do methodological and theoretical decisions factor in to questions of ethical conduct and research ethics governance?

This book is divided into four parts:

- Part I, *Institutional arrangements and positionality*, explores the ongoing and expanding process of ethics protocol and procedures, principles of confidentiality, and the positionality of the researcher.
- Part II, *Trust and research with vulnerable populations*, examines the complexity of work involving prisoners, indigenous peoples and victims of extreme violence, power dynamics between researchers and participants, and the challenges of informed consent.
- Part III, *Research on and with police*, reflects on the importance of transparent relations with police, best practices, and the consequences of undertaking research in authoritarian contexts.
- Part IV, *Emerging areas*, scrutinizes the ethics of carceral tours and suggests possible alternatives, and offers one of the first sociological and criminological examinations of dark net cryptomarkets.

Drawing upon the experiences of international experts, this book aims to provoke further reflection on and discussion of ethics in practice. This book is ideal for students undertaking courses on research methods in criminology, as well as a key resource for criminology researchers around the world.

Michael Adorjan is Assistant Professor of Sociology at the University of Calgary, Canada, and Fellow with the Centre for Criminology, University of Hong Kong, China.

Rose Ricciardelli is Associate Professor at Memorial University of Newfoundland, Canada.

ENGAGING WITH ETHICS IN INTERNATIONAL CRIMINOLOGICAL RESEARCH

Edited by Michael Adorjan and Rose Ricciardelli

LONDON AND NEW YORK

First published 2016
by Routledge
2 Park Square, Milton Park, Abingdon, Oxon OX14 4RN

and by Routledge
711 Third Avenue, New York, NY 10017

Routledge is an imprint of the Taylor & Francis Group, an informa business

British Library Cataloguing in Publication Data
A catalogue record for this book is available from the British Library

Library of Congress Cataloguing in Publication Data
Names: Adorjan, Michael, editor. | Ricciardelli, Rose, 1979– editor.
Title: Engaging with ethics in international criminological research /
edited by Michael Adorjan and Rose Ricciardelli.
Description: First Edition. | New York : Routledge, 2016. |
Includes bibliographical references and index.
Identifiers: LCCN 2015047619 | ISBN 9781138938397 (hardback) |
ISBN 9781138938403 (pbk.) | ISBN 9781315675671 (ebook)
Subjects: LCSH: Criminology–Research. | Research–Moral and ethical aspects.
Classification: LCC HV6024.5.E54 2016 | DDC 174/.9364–dc23
LC record available at https://lccn.loc.gov/2015047619

ISBN: 978-1-138-93839-7 (hbk)
ISBN: 978-1-138-93840-3 (pbk)
ISBN: 978-1-315-67567-1 (ebk)

Typeset in Bembo
by Out of House Publishing

Printed in Great Britain by Ashford Colour Press Ltd., Gosport, Hampshire.

CONTENTS

FIGURES

TABLES

CONTRIBUTORS

Michael Adorjan is Assistant Professor of Sociology at the University of Calgary, Canada. His research and teaching focus on youth crime representations and responses, perceptions of crime and policing, and cyber risk. He is currently primary investigator on a project, funded by the Social Sciences and Humanities Research Council of Canada, examining perceptions of youth towards cyber risk. Conducting research in both Canada and Hong Kong, he is interested in developing a comparative criminological imagination.

Pat Carlen is an internationally renowned criminologist, currently Honorary Professor at the University of Leicester, UK. She has published 19 books and many articles in the areas of criminal and social justice generally and women's imprisonment in particular, underscoring the connections between women, crime and poverty. Carlen was editor-in-chief of the *British Journal of Criminology* from 2006 to 2013, and served as editor of the *Sociological Review*, book review editor of *Punishment and Society* and member of the editorial (or international editorial) boards of journals such as *Legal and Social Studies*, the *Howard Journal of Criminal Justice* and the *International Journal of the Sociology of Law*. In addition, she was founder of the Keele University Criminology Department, and co-founder of the UK campaigning group, Women in Prison.

Hayley Crichton is a PhD student in Sociology at Memorial University of Newfoundland, Canada. Her field of study relevant to her dissertation is corrections, though she actively participates as a research assistant in the project conducted through the partnership established between Memorial University of Newfoundland and RCMP Division B.

Erin Gibbs Van Brunschot is Associate Professor and Head of the Sociology Department at the University of Calgary, Canada. Her primary research interests are in the realms of crime, security and risk, with specific interests in how individuals, organizations/agencies and state orientations to risk both diverge and converge. Erin co-authored two books with Les Kennedy, *Risk Balance and Security* (2008, Sage) and *Risk in Crime* (2009, Rowman and Littlefield). Her current research focuses on offender management and various technologies that are used to enhance public security, including the use of global positioning systems to electronically monitor offenders, and considers the challenges involved in the application of this technology to various types of offending and offender management goals.

Kevin D. Haggerty is a Killam Research Laureate and editor of the *Canadian Journal of Sociology*. He is Professor of Sociology and Criminology at the University of Alberta, Canada. His recent work has been in the area of surveillance, governance, policing and risk. He and his co-author (Aaron Doyle) are currently writing *57 Ways to Screw Up in Graduate School*, a book which conveys a series of professional lessons for the next generation of graduate students.

Tracy Hardy recently retired from her position as Assistant Commissioner and Commanding Officer (B Division) of the RCMP. Since joining the RCMP in 1981, Hardy has held the position of Team Leader/Investigator, Serious Crime Section and Detachment Operations NCO as well as Criminal Operations Officer, Planning Officer, Integrated Security Unit for the 2010 Winter Olympics in Vancouver, BC. She assumed the position of Commanding Officer of L Division and was promoted to Chief Superintendent. In 2012, she became Commanding Officer of B Division. Hardy has been awarded the Queen's Golden Jubilee Medal, Queen's Diamond Jubilee Medal, RCMP Long-Service medal, Bronze and Silver Clasps, two Commanding Officer's Commendations and the Canada 125 Medal. Most recently, she was invested as Officer of the Order of Merit of Police Forces. She is a member of the International Association of Chiefs of Police, the Canadian Association of Chiefs of Police and the International Association of Women Police.

Laura Huey is the Director of the Canadian Society of Evidence Based Policing, the Director of the Canadian Policing Research Network, a member of the Council of Canadian Academies' Expert Panel on the Future of Policing Models, a founding member of SERENE-RISC (a NCE-funded cybercrime research consortium) and a Senior Researcher for the Canadian Network for Research on Terrorism, Security and Society.

Mark Israel is Professor of Law and Criminology at the University of Western Australia. He has a degree in law and postgraduate qualifications in sociology, criminology and education. He has published over 70 books, book chapters and journal articles in the areas of research ethics and integrity, criminology, socio-legal studies, higher education and research policy, political exile and migration. His book on *Research Ethics and Integrity for Social Scientists: Beyond Regulatory Compliance* was published by Sage in 2015. Mark has won teaching and research prizes in Australia, the United Kingdom and the United States. He has undertaken research ethics and research integrity consultancy for, among others, Australian State and Federal governments, the National Health and Medical Research Council, the Commonwealth Scientific and Industrial Research Organisation and a range of higher education institutions, health authorities and NGOs in Australia, New Zealand and Hong Kong. He also acts as an ethics reviewer for the European Research Council.

James Martin is Senior Lecturer and Criminology Program Coordinator at Macquarie University in Sydney, Australia. He has a long-standing research interest in conventional and online drug distribution networks, non-state governance and the global War on Drugs, and he has conducted a variety of original theoretical and empirical studies in these areas. Dr Martin's recent book, *Drugs on the Dark Net: How Cryptomarkets are Transforming the Global Trade in Illicit Drugs*, was the first research monograph in the world published on the topic of cryptomarkets and online drug distribution.

Craig Minogue has survived in prison since 1986. Completing a BA (Honours) in 2005, he was awarded a research PhD in Applied Ethics, Human and Social Sciences in 2012. He is a regular contributor to community legal and health education projects, and has over 50 publications in the fields of education practice, philosophy, criminal law, human rights, health and infection control, and prison-related issues. Craig's work demonstrates that it is possible for academics on the outside to work ethically with an academic inside.

Justin Piché is Associate Professor in the Department of Criminology, University of Ottawa, Canada. His research examines the reproduction of the prison idea as a hegemonic response to criminalized harms in state bureaucracies and popular culture, as well as abolitionist logics, strategies and alternatives. He was awarded the 2012 Aurora Prize from the Social Sciences and Humanities Research Council of Canada 'for excellence, creativity and originality in research and a deep commitment to sharing knowledge that enriches Canada's intellectual and cultural life'.

Rose Ricciardelli is Associate Professor at Memorial University of Newfoundland, Canada. She has published in a range of academic journals including: *British Journal of Criminology*, *Sex Roles*, and *Theoretical Criminology*. Her first book, released in the spring of 2014, entitled *Surviving Incarceration: Inside Canadian Prisons* explores the realities of penal living for federally incarcerated men in Canada. Her current work, in partnership with the RCMP, includes creating and implementing extrajudicial measures in areas policed by the RCMP in the province. Her primary research interests include evolving conceptualizations of masculinity, and experiences and issues within different facets of the criminal justice system. She studies prison culture, desistance, and the coping strategies, risk perception and lived experiences of prisoners, correctional officers and police officers.

Dale C. Spencer is Assistant Professor in the Department of Law and Legal Studies at Carleton University, Ottawa, Canada. His main interests are violence, victimization and the criminalization of marginalized populations, with a specific focus on the homeless and young people. He has published two books, *Reimaging Intervention in Young Lives* (with Karen Foster, University of British Columbia Press, 2013) and *Ultimate Fighting and Embodiment* (Routledge, 2012), and two edited volumes, *Emotions Matter* (with Kevin Walby and Alan Hunt, University of Toronto Press, 2012) and *Fighting Scholars* (with Raul Sanchez Garcia, Anthem Press, 2013), and his work can be found in a number of journals, including *Body and Society*, *Punishment and Society* and *Ethnography*.

Kevin Walby is Associate Professor and Chancellor's Research Chair in the Department of Criminal Justice, University of Winnipeg, Canada. He has co-edited, with R.K. Lippert, *Policing Cities: Urban Securitization and Regulation* (Routledge, 2013) and *Corporate Security in the 21st Century: Theory and Practice in International Perspective* (Palgrave, 2014). He is co-author, with R.K. Lippert, of *Municipal Corporate Security in International Context* (Routledge, 2015).

Maggie Walter is a descendant of the Parerebeenne people from North Eastern Tasmania and is passionately interested in Indigenous methodologies and race relations in settler colonized nation-states. Maggie is a long-term member of the steering committee of the Longitudinal Study of Indigenous Children and has published extensively in the field of race relations, Indigenous inequality and research methods and methodologies. Recent books include *Indigenous statistics: A Quantitative Methodology* (with Chris Andersen, Left Coast Press, 2013), *Inequality in Australia: Discourses, Realities and Directions*, 2nd edition (with D. Habibis, Oxford University Press, 2014) and *Social Research Methods*, 3rd edition (editor, Oxford University Press, 2013).

Jianhua Xu is Assistant Professor in the Department of Sociology at the University of Macau, China, as well as an Honorary Fellow in the Centre for Criminology, University of Hong Kong, China. His research interests include sociology of crime and deviance, crime and victimization related to rural-to-urban migrant workers in China, policing, victimology and urban sociology. His recent publications have appeared in the *British Journal of Criminology*, *Theoretical Criminology*, *International Journal of Offender Therapy and Comparative Criminology*, *Crime, Law, and Social Change* and *Qualitative Sociology Review*, among others.

INTRODUCTION

Michael Adorjan and Rose Ricciardelli

Ethical horizons in criminological research are in a constant stage of emergence, with ethical issues taking often unpredictable forms and decisions made in the field leading to consequences for research participants, criminal justice practitioners and researchers alike. Despite a voluminous literature on research ethics boards and institutional ethical review processes, relatively few scholars have written about their own experiences engaging with ethics during all phases of criminological research: from initial preparation and submission of a proposal for ethical review, to data collection and on to dissemination and publication of findings. Centred on the *realpolitik* of conducting criminological research in practice, this collection is composed of an international scope of expert contributors who unpack the 'ethics' – the issues and dilemmas – of doing research in corrections, policing and on the streets or in any other areas tied to systems, experiences or processes of justice. With ethics as a central organizing concept, the lived experiences at the intersection of ethics and methodology in criminological research are explored throughout the chapters.

Our intention through this collection is to move beyond critiques of institutional ethics review and help inspire an *ethical imagination* (see Adorjan, this volume) regarding ethical decisions that extend well beyond individual research settings and participants. We hope that this volume also inspires further discussion about ethics both among experienced researchers and students seeking to tune their craft. Our contributors reflect upon the various phases involved in conducting research and liaising with various stakeholders, including research participants, ethics review boards, academic publishers and journal reviewers, and practitioners in the criminal justice system. Not only do we address how researchers have experienced and addressed issues at this nexus, including balancing benefits and harms for both researchers and those being researched, we do so from the perspectives of an international scope of contributors who cross methodological orientations and areas of research.

Ethical spaces

The *pro forma* highlighting of current ethics protocols and procedures is always a necessary part of any discussion on research ethics. Indeed, from study conceptualization to research ethics board reviews, into the field and later in published contributions, ethical issues and challenges face each and every researcher. However, our intention here is not to focus on the ins and outs of formalized procedures and processes. We encourage our readers to look to the many admirable sources for insight into why we write formal ethical protocols and the need for 'informed consent', 'debriefing letters' and other such processes that are all too familiar to many, from students to avid researchers (e.g. Israel 2004, Chapter 3; Neuman & Wiegand 2000; Noaks & Wincup 2004, Chapter 3). Most criminological methods textbooks center, justifiably and necessarily, on the broader aspects of research design, including problems of formulation, sampling and the various stages involved in data collection, analysis and publication. Issues related to ethics are addressed, often presented as "help[ing] readers understand their ethical responsibilities as researchers", with reference to "the Nuremberg Code, research sponsorship, rights of human subjects and deception" (Champion 2006). For example, Hagan's (2014) textbook (9th edition) *Research Methods in Criminal Justice and Criminology* explicates a range of "classical and contemporary research in the field" and strives to help "students and professionals better understand the extensive diversity of research available and in progress in criminal justice" (see also Bachman & Schutt 2014; Holt 2012; King & Wincup 2008). Here, however, we take a different approach. Instead of treating ethical considerations as discreet topics or taking a unidirectional and 'top down' pedagogical design (which is useful for new students interested in learning about criminology and what they may anticipate when engaging in criminological research), we examine processes and experiences of ethics in the context of conducting research, including dilemmas encountered during the various phases of entry into the field, engaging with participants and writing up results for publication. Writing is itself an ethical act; especially so when one is writing about ethical realities encountered during the course of producing research. We focus on these realities, which shape the researcher, the work produced and are shaped by the researcher and political realities.

Offering an international scope, with attention paid to the 'friction' (cf. Tsing 2005) of globalizing conventions and practices in ethics as well as local idiosyncrasies, contributors draw on auto-ethnographic reflection, both analytical and evocative, and critical engagement with the *realpolitik* of engaging in criminological research today. Our contributors have a wide range of expertise, including ethnographic research on police in mainland China, victimology and studying those experiencing trauma from victimization, fear of crime and perceptions of police as well as research collaborations with police, the politics and ethical implications of carceral tours, and online illicit drug 'cryptomarkets' in cyberspace. They raise questions about who benefits from criminological research, the role and impact of ethics review boards, and how methodological and theoretical decisions factor into questions of ethical conduct and research ethics governance. Ethical dilemmas are framed as 'mixed investments' (see Gibbs Van Brunschot, this volume) involving multiple audiences (often with differing expectations regarding the purpose and 'payoffs' of research), including academics, criminal justice practitioners and victims. The chapters thus highlight themes and issues salient within a global context of crime and criminological research but are situated by local socio-political conditions across nations: from the United Kingdom to Canada, China (including Hong Kong and mainland China) and Australia.

Chapter overview

The first part of the book focuses on institutional arrangements and positionality, beginning with Kevin Haggerty's article on 'ethics creep'. It has been just over ten years since Haggerty first published his influential article in *Qualitative Sociology*. We open this volume with this article as it establishes both the institutional context of conducting research in universities today and sets up some of the key debates that all authors in this collection respond to either directly or indirectly. Drawing on Weber's (1968) work on rationalization and bureaucracy, Haggerty examines the ongoing and expanding process of ethics protocols and procedures in institutions and areas not originally anticipated. Simply said, universities are 'defining ethics up', drawing increasingly sensitive speculations of prognosticated risk and harm that capture an increasing array of arguably innocuous research designs under their expanding hermeneutic net. The article, as one may expect, examines the often cited disjuncture between the scientific-medical model, upon which institutional ethics reviews were founded, versus the model of ethnographic research, where informed consent is sometimes seen as undercutting access to participants. Indeed, here, defining even what the research 'goal' constitutes, its beginning and end, is deliberately murky for the precise reason that ethnographers seek to establish a long-standing and slowly emerging trust with often difficult or subaltern – and criminal – populations. Haggerty speaks as an insider, drawing on his experiences as a member of his faculty's research ethics board at the University of Alberta.

In the next chapter Michael Adorjan, a Canadian, offers a reflection on his experiences conducting research on perceptions of crime and police in Hong Kong. The chapter examines experiences that are frequently and relatively generically encountered in the field, including acquiring informed consent (i.e. through focus group research), making adjustments during the course of research as findings are accumulated, and finally issues related to the dissemination of research findings. Ethical issues are in some respects comparable to those often encountered anywhere, yet Adorjan relates his experiences as an outsider navigating research in Hong Kong, which lends its own challenges related to an ever-shifting insider–outsider positionality. The chapter encourages readers to more explicitly consider their own positionality during the course of conducting research.

The following chapter, by Pat Carlen, raises insightful and controversial questions framed from her extensive four decades of research experience. Writing directly and candidly about her research on female ex-prisoners and poverty, Carlen challenges readers to think beyond narrow visions of ethical compliance to consider the situational dilemmas that behoove researchers to ask long-standing questions of 'whose side' they are on (i.e. the still salient debate between Becker and Gouldner), and engage in an *ongoing* positioning of the self in relation to the 'other' being researched. As Carlen highlights, the dilemmas criminologists face differ when researching putatively 'subaltern' populations lacking agency and power such as formerly imprisoned poor women, versus criminality among the elite and powerful. In qualitative and ethnographic research, theoretical competence, for Carlen, is simultaneously ethical competence, involving decisions about who to give voice to, and who to silence, as well as decisions post-publication regarding adherence to principles of confidentiality, even when this involves protecting corporate criminal interests. 'Of course' researchers should follow their institutional ethics code, Carlen argues, and 'of course' they should maintain an ethical course while navigating the research process. But what comes across after reading Carlen's contribution here is that ethical struggles encountered decades ago continue to resonate and matter far beyond the submission of a final completion report to a research ethics board.

The second part of the book centers on trust and research with vulnerable populations. The part begins with Mark Israel's examination of research involving prisoners and prisons in the United States. Israel draws on the history of prison-based research and the development of research ethics guidelines and procedures. Rather than protecting prisoners, he shows how, in response to scandal involving medical research, research ethics regulation has enabled prisons to protect themselves against risk while simultaneously limiting the ability for prisoners to benefit from research. The politics of conducting prison-based research is discussed, including how, despite researchers' best intentions, correctional officers may perceive researchers as spies sent to monitor behavior or prisoners may gain the false impression that participating in research will be regarded positively during parole review. Israel also explores the challenges of obtaining informed consent among prisoners, which can easily be compromised by the coercive nature of prison environments and power dynamics. The more 'subtle forms of manipulation' that take unconscionable advantage of the condition of prisoners to encourage prisoners to participate and threaten negative repercussions upon refusal are also factors when acquiring prisoners' consent. Scandals, like those involving pharmaceutical research that debased prisoners' rights and subjected them to direct harm, have led to revised protocols and standards for ethically sound research. Israel, however, documents how requirements for ethics approval may discourage research that is critical of corporate or government interests. There is little space for critical criminology (i.e. a criminology invested in scouring evidence for inequalities, abuse and further victimization as a product of the system itself) when it comes to reforming research ethics regulations. Challenging the 'power' of correctional institutions is an ethical process in and of itself, but one which conflicts with the ethics precepts designed by correctional institutions to 'protect prisoners'. In this light, Israel also offers a case for covert research, which he argues may be required if the power of correctional institutions and their efforts to protect their interests are to be unrobed and demystified.

The following chapter, written by Maggie Walter, shifts the focus to research with Indigenous peoples. Walter argues that conducting ethical research with Indigenous peoples requires going beyond the 'rubber stamp' of institutional ethics approval. The chapter reinforces the ubiquitous social problems facing Indigenous peoples around the world, whose average rates of poverty, unemployment and imprisonment are invariably much higher than the respective settler population. Walter also underscores that, despite these commonalities, Indigenous peoples share similar experiences of colonization and being a minority 'Other' within their first world home nations. Walter then offers a cross-national comparative analysis of first world 'settler states' (the US, Canada, Australia and Aotearoa New Zealand), surveying developments in each regarding ethical guidelines for research on (and, more ideally, with) Indigenous peoples. It becomes clear that 'research ethics' are often conflated with a Eurocentric, biomedical model, and are often ignorant of and/or unsympathetic to the particular exigencies relevant to Indigenous peoples. The comparative survey includes detailed tables delineating between minimum standards, as well as good and best practices, of ethical compliance with Indigenous ethical frameworks. Interestingly, Walter then turns to how some criminologists have actively resisted the development of ethical guidelines for research with Indigenous peoples. She suggests researchers explicitly consider the axiological and ontological positions they bring with them to research – how they see their world and understand it. The ethical risk, Walter argues, is that this position, however unintended, may come to exclude certain ways of knowing and understanding Indigenous standpoints and experiences. She follows by offering a telling case study, based in Australia, to illustrate her arguments, which touches on the inter-related issues of hegemonic power, ethics and criminological research with Indigenous peoples. As Walter argues, in response to myopic (and implied, unethical) research practices and conclusions, asking why Aboriginal and Torres Strait Islander people are incarcerated more often is not an objective question when it is asked in the absence of the context of Indigenous lives.

The final chapter in this part, by Dale Spencer, turns to a post-structural 'ethics of witnessing' geared to ethical research with victims of extreme violence, specifically homeless men. Spencer underscores the 'polyvocality' of victim trauma, requiring researchers to go beyond victimization as a static experience, and to consider how recalling experiences of victimization is itself a way for victims to survive and persevere. He also illuminates how the researcher takes on responsibilities as a witness to violence and how the writing of research becomes an ethically informed "work of mourning" (p. 113). The ethical challenge becomes how researchers write about the experiences of victims without typecasting or diluting the experience. Research here becomes a dynamic encounter which suggests not only the polymorphous nature of vulnerabilities but also how they challenge static power dynamics between researcher and participants.

The third part of the book offers reflections on research on and with police. The ethical challenges faced by researchers aiming to establish partnerships with police are addressed in two chapters, each with a distinct focus. The section begins with Erin Gibbs Van Brunschot's chapter examining collaborations with criminal justice agencies. She argues that all parties must deal with "mixed investments" in research collaborations. Focusing on her research with the police, specifically analyses of the application of Global Positioning System (GPS) electronic monitoring to different types of offenders, Gibbs Van Brunschot explores both successful and unsuccessful efforts at collaboration, offering invaluable pointers regarding best practices both researchers and criminal justice officials may follow in order to produce research 'useful' to all parties. Although quick to point out that what may excite academics about police data may not have the practical focus and outputs policing organizations usually expect, her chapter underscores the value of strong community policing practices. Such practices help facilitate mutually beneficial collaborations with academics and the general public alike. Departments that embrace community policing, she argues, are more likely to be receptive to research questions broader than traditional policing (i.e. crime fighting, crime control) mandates. The chapter proceeds by outlining valuable reasons for both academics and police to collaborate, after which Gibbs Van Brunschot turns to some of the reasons that led to both positive and negative collaborative experiences.

Several useful suggestions are offered to academics aiming to get things off on the right foot, including having discussions prior to commencing research with relevant stakeholders – instead of the funder determining these in advance from the 'top down' – and other team members; building a shared sense of meaning regarding central concepts, including the meaning of collaboration', 'research' and 'outcomes'; and aiming to have support at the executive policing level, which often helps facilitate positive interactions at the 'front line' level. Gibbs Van Brunschot illuminates some of the broader external pressures on police – including those from politicians – that can erode executive-level supports despite best intentions. In addition, various parties may differentially invest resources in collaborations, and expectations, for example of research results, length of time needed, commitment of researchers beyond specific project timelines, and so on, may not always align. Importantly, Gibbs Van Brunschot argues that potentially sensitive findings related to police practices do not necessarily need to lead to a breakdown in the collaboration, so long as mutual trust and transparency is established at the outset, and both researchers and police frame research questions, expectations and possible outcomes in a way that benefits both parties.

The next chapter reflects on a successful collaboration between academics and the Royal Canadian Mounted Police. The chapter is co-written by Rose Ricciardelli and her academic colleagues, along with a former Assistant Commissioner and Commanding Officer of the Royal Canadian Mounted Police. As the authors point out, "Canadian research has generally involved research *on* policing institutions rather than research *with* Canadian police agencies or officers" (p. 145, emphasis in original). Ethical challenges, they present, relate to aligning the interests of upper management, front-line police officers and academic researchers. On the one hand, the police may expect efficiently produced applications of theoretically informed methodology and analysis, and may become frustrated by the sometimes limited 'practical' impact of research or its relatively slow process. Police may also be initially distrustful of often liberally inclined academics who are perceived to be inherently antagonistic to police. Academics, likewise, must appreciate the police's need to maintain confidentiality and that their desire to invite academics to conduct research is based on specific pragmatic goals leading to operational outcomes. Ethical dilemmas are avoided, the authors show, by maintaining transparent relations early on (e.g. through memorandums of understanding) and for the duration of research, which includes the dissemination of findings. Spelling out reasons for participating and related expectations is crucial to build trust and effective collaboration for both parties. The contributors also illuminate ongoing challenges that may strain positive intentions, for example a police officer's concern with how their participation may be viewed by superior officers. The authors conclude by highlighting how memorandums of understanding between police and academics must stipulate what can be done with research findings, including whether some findings may be censored from publication in academic journals.

In addition to contributors who reflect on their collaborations with police, Jianhua Xu writes about his experiences conducting research on policing in mainland China, which reveals issues familiar to qualitative researchers (e.g. access to police, how findings are disseminated), but which are uniquely catered to the Chinese authoritarian context. Xu writes about the need for criminologists to be careful about how they conduct research and decide how to present findings given the risks of negative consequences such as the inability to apply for future research funding, or potential arrest and imprisonment of themselves or even their families. Xu helps provide context for the present state of academic scholarship in China by referring to its history prohibiting the development of social sciences, which has stifled not only critical scholarship but also adequate training in research and methods. Similar to Adorjan, Xu reflects on his positionality as both an insider and outsider during the course of conducting research, referring to both his prior experience as a police officer and criminology student as well as his experiences conducting research in Hong Kong and the University of Macau, both Special Administrative Regions of China. He writes about the impact that 'Guanxi', a Chinese form of social connection, played in negotiating access to police for interviews. The chapter raises ethical issues and questions generalizable to researchers broadly, and also shows how such issues take on locally shaped forms and processes.

The final part of this book highlights emerging areas in which ethical issues are being explored. The part begins with Justin Piché, Kevin Walby and Craig Minogue's analysis of the ethical issues arising from participation in carceral tours. These tours, which continue in many regions as part of university-based student excursions rationalized on pedagogical and research-based grounds, are problematized for both their staged and sensational nature. Not only do these tours provide limited if not distorted insights for students and others, but they also engender a 'zoo-like' quality that degrades prisoners. Indeed, here the chapter benefits from the telling experiences of one of the authors, Craig Minogue, who has been imprisoned since 1986, and highlights the humiliating and dehumanizing experiences of carceral tours he draws from his prisoner ethnography. Piché and his colleagues strike a clear argument for not conducting carceral tours. However, the chapter also addresses how other professors have reacted to this call, with some ceasing to provide tours for criminal justice and criminology students, others continuing tours but aiming to engage prisoners and staff in a more ethical manner, and a third camp that continues to defend the pedagogical value of such tours. The chapter proceeds by underscoring how carceral tours tend to operate through a denial of their (unintended) consequences, with proponents deploying 'techniques of neutralization' to defend and praise tours. Furthermore, ethical problems arise in relation to carceral tours during which prisoners are observed without their consent and voluntary participation, and especially when such tours widen the net of social control and disciplinary practices. Piché and his colleagues demonstrate that the pedagogical ends such tours may offer clearly do not justify the means through which they are conducted. They also provide compelling arguments critiquing the notion that carceral tours can be conducted ethically *if* one is 'careful'. As they contend, "carceral tour proponents fail to acknowledge that the power relations *inherent* in prisons are reproduced through these excursions" (p. 181). The chapter concludes by going beyond these critiques with suggestions for potential alternatives to carceral tours, including greater use of prisoner ethnography by academics, helping to make visible prisoner experiences of incarceration, as well as increased collaborations with prisoners in research and academic mentorship. Alternative opportunities for students are also explored.

The following chapter, by James Martin, offers one of the first sociological and criminological examinations of online 'cryptomarkets' – anonymous online marketplaces where a range of licit and illicit substances and 'services' may be purchased, particularly illicit drugs. While Martin offers an overview of the dynamics of cryptomarkets, his focus here remains on the unique ethical dilemmas facing online cryptomarket researchers, including the limits to institutional ethics review, the various harms that may result from such research and issues that arise within law enforcement collaborations. These issues are discussed with a view to the international War on Drugs. The chapter highlights a lack of consensus regarding appropriate online research methods and applied ethical practices. Researchers require a certain level of technical proficiency, for instance, to even access the 'dark net' via The Onion Router – a sophisticated web browser enabling encrypted and anonymized transmissions of information. Even when access is obtained, the vast array of data available still leave open what questions the data may be used to answer. Criminologists conducting cryptomarkets research and institutional ethics review boards alike may find interpreting the Hippocratic oath of doing no harm difficult given the ambiguous and shifting terrain of cryptomarkets, the direct and indirect harms produced, and questions of 'whose side' academics are on. Martin argues that even where ethics approval is obtained, new scholars should be careful to engage in an ongoing and self-critical, reflexive assessment of their research online and its potential impacts. The chapter proceeds to delineate between direct and indirect harms potentially produced by this research, involving inappropriate research practices or promoting and/or legitimizing harmful ideologies, social movements, and so on, respectively. The chapter concludes by considering both advantages and benefits of scholarly cooperation with law enforcement agencies, as well as potential unintended consequences that may result from such collaborations. As Martin provocatively notes, while perhaps counter-intuitive, cryptomarkets may be acting to ameliorate some of the dangers associated with illicit drugs, both to individual users and regarding broader systemic violence at the level of international criminal networks.

Taken as a whole, our contributors all emphasize the significance of developing an ongoing and dynamic view of ethics in practice whose horizons of impact extend well beyond individuals involved in particular projects. Perhaps more questions are raised than answered in the pages that follow. This is our goal; indeed, we hope that the issues and questions raised by our contributors provoke further reflection and discussion.

References

Bachman, R & Russell, S 2014, *The Practice of Research in Criminology and Criminal Justice*, Thousand Oaks, CA, Sage.

Champion, D 2006, *Research Methods for Criminal Justice and Criminology*, Upper Saddle River, NJ, Pearson/Prentice Hall.

Hagan, F 2014, *Research Methods in Criminal Justice and Criminology* (9th ed), Boston, MA, Pearson.

Holt, T 2012, 'Exploring strategies for qualitative criminological and criminal justice inquiry using on-line data', in *Advancing Qualitative Methods in Criminology and Criminal Justice*, ed H Copes, London, Routledge, pp. 79–100.

Israel, M 2004, *Ethics and the Governance of Criminological Research in Australia*, Sydney, New South Wales Bureau of Crime Statistics and Research with assistance from the Regulatory Institutions Network at the Australian National University.

King, R & Emma, W 2008, *Doing Research on Crime and Justice* (2nd ed), Oxford, Oxford University Press.

Neuman, WL & Wiegand, B 2000, *Criminal Justice Research Methods: Qualitative and Quantitative Approaches*, Needham Heights, MA, Allyn and Bacon.

Noaks, L and Wincup, E 2004, *Criminological Research: Understanding Qualitative Methods*, London, Sage.

Tsing, A 2005, *Friction: An Ethnography of Global Connection*, Princeton, NJ, Princeton University Press.

Weber, M 1968, *Economy and Society: An Outline of Interpretive Sociology*, New York, Bedminster Press.

Institutional arrangements and positionality

PART I

Institutional management
and positionality

1

ETHICS CREEP*

Governing social science research in the name of ethics

Kevin Haggerty

The institutionalized production of knowledge never proceeds unencumbered. As philosopher Michel Foucault suggested, knowledge is produced by multiple forms of constraint. The social sciences[1] are currently witnessing the emergence of a host of new fetters on our knowledge production endeavors. Research involving First Nations communities, for example, now routinely requires that findings be vetted by a Band Council before publication. Criminology, the subfield that I am most familiar with, has seen the increased use of remarkably specific research contracts. Police agencies that previously granted scholars comparatively easy access now require contracts containing ominous provisions stipulating that the police approve any research findings before they are communicated. Such developments constrain scholarly research and, in so doing, structure what truths can be spoken and by whom.

We can add to these constraints the comparatively new development of research ethics protocols. Such regulations have existed for several years in the medical sciences and have increasingly been institutionalized in the social sciences. In Canada, the country I focus on for this analysis, the *Tri-Council Policy Statement: Ethical Conduct for Research Involving Humans* (hereafter the *Policy*), established in 1998, requires that all university research involving human subjects be approved by a Research Ethics Board (REB).[2]

Concerns about the ethical quality of research are characteristic of a society where anxieties about the unintended consequences of science and technology are increasingly common (Beck 1992). Where modernity manifests a general trust in the ability of science to resolve our most pressing problems, we have become attuned to the truth that science itself poses risks and that these risks can no longer be explained away as temporary aberrations in the march of progress. While the natural and medical sciences have been singled out for producing some of our most colossal risks, such as nuclear energy and genetic engineering, the social sciences are now also recognized as a risk-producing endeavor. Research ethics protocols are a formal attempt to manage such risks.

As a regulatory system, however, the research ethics process now poses dangers to the ability to conduct university based research. This article documents four such risks in relation to: 1) the scope of research ethics protocols, 2) the notion of "harm" employed by REBs, 3) the place of informed consent in research ethics, and, finally, 4) the presumption of anonymity as a means of mitigating the risks of research. These topics are singled out because of the way in which ambiguous terms such as "harm," "consent," and even "research" have been interpreted. Such ambiguity is not unique to the operation of REBs, as all new legal regimes employ broad and unspecific concepts, the meanings of which only solidify over time as they are applied to different cases. We have now reached the point in the evolution of the Canadian research ethics infrastructure that the meaning of such terms is crystallizing into a more regular and predictable form. Part of this has involved an ethical "creep" whereby REBs have unintentionally expanded their mandate to include a host of groups and practices that were undoubtedly not anticipated in the original research ethics formulations. After detailing some of the specifics of this creep, I conclude by suggesting some reasons for its occurrence. Over time, I fear that the REB structure will follow the pattern of most bureaucracies and continue to expand, formalizing procedures in ways that increasingly complicate, hamper, or censor certain forms of nontraditional, qualitative, or critical social scientific research.

This article draws primarily from my four years' experience as a member of the University of Alberta's Faculty of Arts, Science and Law Research Ethics Board. Serving on the REB for one of Canada's top social science research universities I have reviewed hundreds of research ethics proposals from the departments of Sociology, Political Science, Law, Anthropology, Psychology, Music, English, and Linguistics. Undoubtedly, our REB has its own idiosyncrasies, but formal and informal discussions with faculty, members of other REBs, and officials working for the Tri-Council suggest that our board operates much like the other social science REBs across Canada and deals with comparable issues.

While I focus on the Canadian system, aspects of my analysis are germane to developments in the United States where comparable Institutional Review Boards (IRBs) have existed since 1981. The American boards are concerned with similar issues relating to harm, consent, and anonymity that I address below. The analysis also serves as a cautionary tale for those countries which are currently contemplating establishing their own formal research ethics bureaucracy.

Despite the critical tone of this article, I support the concept of ethical research. That said, supporting research ethics in the abstract displays all of the moral fortitude of unconditionally voicing support for motherhood. As with all regulatory matters, the devil is in the details, and as I demonstrate, some of the details about the regulation of research in the name of ethics should give us pause.

Ethics creep

The ethical status of research was historically governed through a combination of discipline-specific codes of conduct and the professional standing of research scientists. The training that academics received in research methods, ethics, and, most importantly, their practical experience in conducting research were previously presumed to offer sufficient protections against unethical behavior. That system has now been supplanted and effectively replaced by a formal process of bureaucratic oversight. This marks a move away from a system based on an assumption of professional competence and responsibility to one based on institutionalized distrust, where researchers are presumed to require an additional level of oversight to ensure that they act ethically.

By introducing a bureaucratic system to manage the risks of academic research, universities have also assumed many of the characteristic deficiencies of regulatory bureaucracies. For the purposes of this analysis the most important of these attributes is the tendency for bureaucracies to expand, assuming new responsibilities while refining and intensifying their regulatory structure. The sociological interest in processes of bureaucratic expansion can be traced to Max Weber's arguments (1978) on bureaucracy and rationality. One of the iron rules of bureaucracy identified in the literature involves a proclivity towards rule breeding and proliferation (Galanter 1992; Zhou 1993). Evidence of this process is apparent in the *Tri-Council Policy Statement*, which now runs to a full ninety pages including procedures, clarifications, and appendices.

The concept of "creep" has acquired a degree of sociological purchase in recent years as a means of denoting processes of unintended transformation and expansion of systems. The most familiar of these uses is the notion of "mission creep," used to characterize how governmental initiatives, typically military engagements, tend to assume new and unanticipated agendas. Gary Marx employs the expression "surveillance creep" to designate the processes whereby surveillance practices gradually assume novel uses. Recently, Martin Innes (2001) has expanded on that usage to suggest a more general process of "control creep" whereby social control mechanisms tend to expand and penetrate different social arenas. In all of these uses the concept of "creep" accentuates the types of unanticipated expansion that I am drawing attention to in relation to research ethics protocols. "Ethics creep" involves a dual process whereby the regulatory structure of the ethics bureaucracy is expanding outward, colonizing new groups, practices, and institutions, while at the same time intensifying the regulation of practices deemed to fall within its official ambit.

Demonstrating ethics creep requires scrutiny of the decisions of regulatory bodies. In the case of REBs, however, this scrutiny is made extremely difficult by how these boards are structured. While REBs communicate their decisions and recommendations to individual applicants, they do not publicize these decisions. Moreover, each REB is the final arbiter for research issues within its domain. There is no appeal to a higher authority such as an "ethics Supreme Court." As such, there are no public documents for analysts to scrutinize in order to discern the authoritative positions on research ethics matters. These structural factors make it very difficult for outsiders to gain an appreciation of tendencies in how the rules governing ethics are being interpreted and applied in practice. Fortunately, I have been able to surmount this methodological problem by virtue of being able to draw from my four years of experience as a member of my faculty's REB. In this capacity I have acquired a privileged insider's view of the content of such decisions, their rationale and cumulative direction. The examples and anecdotes that I present here are derived from a theoretical sampling of cases that have been dealt with by our REB. While this sampling of cases is not representative in a strict statistical sense, I believe that it accurately represents some of the more troubling trends in the operation of these boards.

To accentuate the direction and extent of this ethical creep, I compare research ethics protocols in the academy with what is permissible in journalism (print, televised, radio, and Internet). This comparison is not intended to suggest that journalism serve as a standard to which academics should necessarily aspire, but rather as a benchmark against which we can demonstrate the degree to which ethical concerns in the university have crept into a host of new and problematic domains. It allows us to push the logic of ethics regulation, accentuating its ironies, contradictions, and dangers.

Some might argue that journalists and academics are involved in different enterprises. Academics tend to draw broader conclusions from their findings than do journalists. Academics also manipulate quantitative data using more sophisticated statistical tools and situate their findings in different discourses than do journalists. That said, the broad methodologies used by members of both institutions – how they produce their facts – are often hard to distinguish. Both social scientists and journalists conduct interviews, videotape people and events, undertake forms of participant observation, and, in recent years, have increasingly scrutinized online discussion groups. Media outlets also produce a host of quantitative knowledge through their own in-house research units or contracts with private research firms. Newspaper and magazine surveys of university students are prominent examples of such media generated statistical studies. Television broadcasters routinely conduct opinion polls, and web surveys are now an omnipresent attribute of the media. Journalists have produced an impressive volume of research on pressing social issues. A small sampling would include James Dubro's *Mob Rule: Inside the Canadian Mafia*, Victor Malarek's *Merchants of Misery: Inside Canada's Illegal Drug Scene*, and Jeffery Robinson's *The Laundrymen: Inside the World's Third Largest Business*.

Another ostensible important difference between academics and journalists concerns the commercial nature of journalism. Given that the knowledge produced by journalists can be crucial in shaping public opinion, influencing elections, and motivating social action campaigns, and that commercial interests can bias knowledge production, it would logically follow that journalistic knowledge production should receive considerable ethical scrutiny. Instead, journalists are comparatively free from the types of ethical scrutiny to which academics are now subjected. There is a heightened concern in the academy about the ethical implications of forms of knowledge production that, when performed by journalists, raise few, if any, ethical concerns. Ultimately, this raises the provocative question of whether university ethical protocols are making it easier to produce certain forms of knowledge as a journalist rather than as a university affiliated researcher.

Scope of research ethics protocols

The *Tri-Council Policy* aims to strike a balance between the potential harms and benefits of research. Every Canadian university must have a Research Ethics Board (and often more than one) to evaluate whether researchers have attained this balance. Before research commences, researchers must submit an application to their respective REB outlining the specifics of their methodology, any potential harms that it might produce, and the procedures they have established to alleviate these harms. To date, REBs have focused on analyzing prospective accounts of what a researcher says she will be doing. The actual conduct of research is not monitored, although there has been some discussion that such policing might occur in the future.

Ethics approval must be granted before federal research funds are released, and researchers who fail to comply with ethical protocols can be disciplined or fired by their respective universities. While not all research must undergo ethical vetting, the scope of these provisions is already quite extensive. If a researcher is in any way connected with a Canadian university and is conducting research involving human subjects then that research must receive ethics clearance, irrespective of whether or not the research is funded. Research that does not involve human subjects need not undergo ethical vetting. As such, archival research or secondary data analysis is excluded from research ethics scrutiny. On its face this seems entirely reasonable. Closer examination reveals that the REBs are working with rather expansive definitions of both "researcher" and "research."

Researchers

Research ethics protocols apply to full-time academics and graduate students. They also apply to a host of other individuals who have more tangential university affiliations.

Perhaps most surprisingly, professors and students who conduct private research entirely on a contractual or consultative basis, using no university resources, must have such research approved. The implications of this logic are potentially quite profound. If a journalist is enrolled in university courses, for example, she would apparently have to submit an ethics application each time she wanted to interview someone. Given that a) such a student is affiliated with the university and b) interviews are a form of research, the student's journalistic "research" would not seem to be exempt. As the University of Alberta does not have a school of journalism I am unaware of any test case for such a scenario, but the implications of any such determination for freedom of the press should be self-evident.

Retired professors who want to maintain their emeritus status must submit their research for ethical approval. Visiting professors or sessional instructors who are conducting research while at their host university must also submit their research for ethical assessment. The same is true of ongoing research that has received ethics approval from another university and collaborative research conducted with a researcher from another institution. Such projects must receive approval from the REB of each university with which the different researchers are affiliated, and ongoing research must cease until it receives ethics approval from the institution with which a faculty member or student is currently affiliated – no matter how temporary that affiliation might be.

Another interesting paradox that seems to be emerging is that research conducted by professionals who are not university affiliated falls outside of the Tri- Council mandate. As I stress throughout this article, this is true for "research" conducted by the media, but it is also true for a host of other institutions. Most large organizations now have sections dedicated to producing various in-house studies, none of which undergo ethical vetting. This is not to say that any of this research is unethical, but simply that it need not be examined by an REB. Continuing the process of ethics creep, however, a study by the Centre of Governance found that individuals on the Tri-Council oversight committees envisage "broadening the policy to include other groups in government and in the private sector" (quoted in Kellner 2002, p. 29). In some contexts this expansion is already occurring, such as when a private or quasi-private research institute situated on a university campus contracts with governmental or private sector agencies. Such research must now conform to the Tri-Council guidelines, effectively extending the reach of the *Policy* into a host of non-university institutions.

Research

A comparable expansive process is apparent in the types of activities that REBs have deemed to be "research." Beyond a core set of unambiguous research practices are a host of more tangential and ambiguous knowledge generating activities that have been deemed to be research requiring ethics approval.

Various on-campus surveys about, for example, library patron satisfaction, campus newspaper readership, or computer services usage must now undergo REB vetting. The same is true for administrative studies conducted by the university such as exit surveys of graduates. None of these studies are part of an academic research program, nor are they envisioned as a means to advance scholarship. However, since they involve encounters with human subjects in a university setting, they fall under the ambit of the Tri-Council guidelines.

In-class student research must also be approved. Students routinely want to quote a parent or friend of the family who, by virtue of their occupation or biography, has insights into particular social issues. They are inevitably surprised to learn that such discussions, in the context of writing a term paper, constitute a form of research and as such must receive ethics approval and conform to ethics protocols. Needless to say, most students are reticent to submit such a proposal, and simply choose to concentrate entirely on textual resources. Hence, I fear that one unintended consequence of this inclusive definition of "research" is that it stifles the initiative of some of our most enthusiastic students.

Instructors who want their students to engage in rudimentary knowledge generating exercises can submit a research ethics proposal on behalf of the entire class. This goes a considerable distance towards streamlining this component of the ethical review process. Every student, however, must conduct the same research (same topic, same type of subjects, same questions), and any departure from the protocol requires the instructor or student to submit a separate application. Ultimately, this all means that students cannot undertake simple knowledge generating activities without ethics approval. A case came before our REB of a student in a methodology class who, as a means to improve her interview skills, wanted to interview her father about his recent vacation. That such activities are deemed to be research and not simple dinnertime conversation starkly reveals the contextual nature and expansive dynamic of ethical standards.

This is also apparent if we consider the "entertainment" section of the weekend newspaper. A staple feature of such publications is the interviews with authors, producers, and actors who are queried about their methods, motivation, or the symbolism of their works. Such inquiries are unremarkable when undertaken by a journalist. When the exact same interview is conducted by a professor of humanities or cultural studies, the researcher should start planning weeks or perhaps months in advance, as this "research" must receive ethics approval, and might have to seek exemption from the ethical presumption that research subjects will remain anonymous, as I discuss further.[3]

Hence, the types of people deemed to be "researchers" and the activities that fall under the heading of "research" already extend well beyond what is reasonable or practicable. The research ethics bureaucracy is in the process of colonizing other practices, institutions, and individuals, imposing its rules and conceptions of harm on very different institutional contexts. This is a troubling development given the broad ways in which REBs have interpreted the potential "harms" of research.

The risks of producing harm

Harm

The Tri-Council guidelines suggest that research should not be conducted if it "might cause serious or lasting harm to a participant." This standard is intended to be flexible, allowing REBs to evaluate the unique risks and benefits of the proposed research. In the eventuality that a research project poses a greater risk than what a person might encounter in his/her daily life, these risks must be managed by the researcher or the research cannot be conducted. On its face, this appears unremarkable, but again interpretive questions arise as to what denotes serious harm and the real likelihood of such harm ever materializing.

The harms that are apt to result from social scientific research are rarely of the same magnitude as those produced by research in the medical sciences, which have placed the lives of unwitting research subjects at risk by infecting them with dysentery and malaria and using them as guinea pigs for LSD research (Beecher 1966). Nonetheless, there are a number of prominent instances where social scientists have engaged in research practices that many now see as unethical (see, generally, Fadan and Beauchamp 1986). Three cases in particular have become inescapable referents in any discussion of research ethics in the social sciences. These are Stanley Milgram's (1974) research on obedience, Philip Zimbardo's (1973) prison experiments, and the research conducted by Laud Humphreys (1970) for his book *Tearoom Trade*. Each study raises important questions about informed consent, deception, and manipulation of subjects, all of which REBs continue to grapple with. Arguably, the most famous of these cases involved research conducted by Stanley Milgram into the process of obedience to authority. His basic study involved an "experimenter" overseeing an experiment where two research participants are informed that they are involved in a study of the effects of punishment on memory retention. One participant served as the "learner" and the other as the "teacher." The learner was taken into a different room out of sight, but within hearing distance, of the teacher, and hooked up to electrodes. The teacher was to ask the learner a series of questions. Each time a question was answered incorrectly he was to administer a shock. The electrical voltage of these shocks was ostensibly increased with each incorrect answer. As the voltage increased, the learner started to grunt, object, demand to be released, scream, and, as the shocks reached the most extreme level, became ominously silent. All of this was overseen by the experimenter. Unbeknownst to the teacher, however, both the learner and the experimenter were confederates, and the true research was being conducted on the teacher. Milgram was really investigating the degree to which the teacher would conform to the demands of authority, as represented by the experimenter and experimental setting. Milgram's results were startling. Approximately 60 percent of research subjects punished the learner through the most extreme level of shocks. Critics, however, condemned the research for psychologically harming the research subjects, using deception, and disregarding the use of informed consent. Concerns about harm were also raised in response to Philip Zimbardo's (1973) research on the social psychological response to incarceration. He recruited male college students to participate in an experiment in institutional behavior. Participants were randomly assigned the role of "guard" or "inmate." These roles were played out in a mock prison created in the basement of a laboratory at Stanford University. The experiment ran only for six days. It was prematurely terminated because the guards had begun to systematically abuse the inmates through ridicule, verbal abuse, and other forms of harsh treatment, at one point even turning a fire extinguisher on them. Critics objected that these research participants had not been informed of the risk of psychological stress, physical discomfort, and humiliation to which they were ultimately subjected.

Another prominent case that raised concerns about ethical research practices in the social sciences involved research conducted by Laud Humphreys. Motivated by a concern for how gay men had been negatively stereotyped by the authorities, Humphreys' research investigated homosexual sex performed in public restrooms, a practice known as "tearoom sex." To try and understand the personal motivations for such behavior Humphreys conducted both direct observational studies and follow-up interviews, misrepresenting himself in both instances. He first posed as a "lookout" for the authorities while others engaged in public sex. Later, he secretly followed some participants, recording their license plates and subsequently appearing at these men's homes posing as a health service interviewer in order to solicit information about their personal affairs. His research prompted heated debate about deception, informed consent, and the invasion of privacy.

Notwithstanding the now iconic status of these early examples, the harms that social science REBs routinely try to mitigate are generally of a considerably lower magnitude. Social science REBs tend to be concerned with the prospect that research might damage a research participant's reputation, finances, or relationships or upset, offend, or traumatize a research participant. The range of potential research related harms envisioned by REBs at times seems to be limited only by the imagination of different reviewers. Any change in a research participant's condition or disruption of their routine can be conceived of as a potential harm. Concerns about research risk extend into consideration of such things as the possibility that a research participant might be embarrassed by personal questions or that they might experience disruption in their family routine or a loss of respect by others. Research that might traumatize research participants can include questioning individuals who have experienced distressing events or who have been victimized in any number of ways. The ethical concern is that such research might rekindle disturbing memories, producing a form of re-victimization. Individual REB members differ on how they evaluate the seriousness of the harms associated with upsetting or traumatizing a research participant in this way, and whether these risks are any greater in the research setting than in daily life. Questions persist about where the line separating minimal from greater than minimal harm will be drawn in practice.

Contemplating the prospects that research might result in trauma places REB members in the tricky position of predicting the types of psychological relationship different individuals will have to the same experiences. Unlike some of the more objective physical harms that can be produced by the medical sciences, trauma is notoriously subjective (McNally 2003). How traumatic or stressful research subjects are apt to find the same experience can vary markedly. From the point of view of REBs, the difficulty with contemplating such subjective harms is that it introduces an expansionist dynamic into the regulatory structure. Given that it is possible to anticipate that a vast array of research *might* be stressful or upsetting to *someone*, researchers can be required to establish protocols to manage a host of highly speculative harms.

A classic example of research that would now probably be seen as posing a risk of re-victimization is presented in Kai Erikson's award-winning book

Everything In Its Path (1976), which studied the West Virginia community of Buffalo Creek after a flood destroyed the town and killed 125 people. Erikson conducted face-to-face interviews with a number of survivors, and asked others to complete a survey on their recollections of the flood. Few would suggest that Erikson's research was unethical, and it appears that many participants welcomed the opportunity to discuss the tragedy. That said, if his study were submitted to an REB today, certain aspects of the research would probably have to be managed differently, while still other components might not be allowed at all. Both the survey and face-to-face interviews would likely require measures to mitigate the prospect that a research subject would have an adverse reaction. This usually involves having trained counselors on hand or readily available during the interview. The prospect of such adverse reactions would likely mean that Erikson's paper-and-pencil survey would not be allowed as originally formulated, as having individuals complete such a survey alone in their homes would not permit the researcher to monitor them for adverse reactions.[4] While some commend this greater sensitivity to the prospect of re-traumatization, it comes at a cost of new administrative qualifications and protocols for academic researchers. Tellingly, such protocols are not required if the identical research is carried out by journalists. It is a cornerstone of both investigative journalism and "action news" to interview people about all manner of potentially traumatic events, often immediately after they have occurred. None of these inquiries undergo ethical vetting and it seems only minimally relevant that such practices might pose a remote risk of traumatizing some interviewees.

This is not to suggest that academics should embrace the distasteful spectacle of journalists thrusting microphones into the faces of grieving parents. Instead, I am emphasizing the academy's introduction of impediments in the name of ethics to scholarly research that would pose no ethical concerns if it were done by representatives of another institution. If Kai Erikson wanted to reproduce his study today, he would face fewer bureaucratic hurdles if he were to do so as a journalist.

Risk

After REB members have contemplated the types of harms that a research project might pose, they must then decide on the likelihood of these harms actually occurring. In practice both considerations are done simultaneously, but approaching them as two distinct moments allows us to accentuate a second level of subjective decision-making relating to the assessment of harms. Specifically, how likely must an eventuality be before a researcher must initiate protocols to mitigate that risk? Does any harmful research related eventuality imagined by REB members need to be addressed, or is there a threshold beyond which eventualities are so vanishingly remote that they do not have to be seriously considered?

The Tri-Council guidelines dictate that "research participants must not be subjected to unnecessary risks of harm." An unspecified level of harm is allowable, if it is proportional and justified, and if it is not, the research should not be conducted. However, this language of "unnecessary risks" is actually quite misleading, as Research Ethics Boards are generally not dealing with risks at all. Risk has a precise meaning, most commonly associated with actuarial science where statistics about previous events are used to analyze the likelihood of future untoward potentialities. Risk involves "trying to turn uncertainties into probabilities" (Douglas 1986, p. 19). While there is disagreement over how statistical regulatory knowledges must be in order for a governmental project to be deemed a form of "risk management," at a minimum it entails some consideration of empirical evidence about the likelihood of untoward events (Sunstein 2002).

In contrast, what distinguishes efforts to manage the risks of social scientific research is that they involve almost no consideration of empirical evidence of risk. As such, the REBs are not working within an actuarial framework and generally do not know the empirical likelihood of the potential untoward outcomes that they try to regulate. For example, in 2003 our REB evaluated a research proposal that entailed interviewing romantic couples. Part of the research would have involved having each couple sit together and answer questions about what they liked and disliked about their relationship. We decided that such questioning posed more than a minimum risk because there was the prospect that such an interview might harm the relationship, as individuals might be prompted to reflect critically on their relationship and perhaps even decide to end the relationship as a result.[5] Such a scenario is certainly imaginable, but how likely is it that relationships would be damaged or destroyed due to such interviews? The answer is that we simply do not know. Nor is this lack of concrete predictive information an aberration. Such an empirical void is the norm with most such decisions, a situation that reveals that pronouncements about the "risk" of research projects are more akin to a subjective imagining of potential scenarios unconstrained by empirical evidence. As such, they have a tendency towards a form of decision-making that in another context I have deemed "precautionary" (Haggerty 2003), characterized by an attempt to respond to subjectively assessed worst-case scenarios rather than empirical consideration of what is likely or probable.

If REB members can imagine that an untoward eventuality *might* occur, then they can ask a researcher to manage that scenario. Given that the members of these boards are bright, motivated, well-intentioned, and highly skilled at dealing with hypothetical scenarios, they seem to have no difficulty envisioning any number of potentialities that should be managed through increasingly onerous regulations. At the recent Advances in Qualitative Methods conference I listened intently as several members of the research ethics community advocated a two-day "cooling off" period between when a researcher approaches a potential research participant and when the person actually agrees to participate. The proposal was based on the suggestion that the simple presence of a researcher can subtly pressure people into participating in a study, thereby undermining the voluntary nature of their consent. This cooling off period was proposed as a "good idea" for all research, but was advanced with no evidence to suggest that this was indeed a real problem. While

I suspect that a cooling off period *might* be an appropriate protocol for a very narrow set of research activities posing dramatic risks of physical harm, it makes little sense for the vast majority of social scientific research. The danger with this and comparable proposals is that such well-intentioned but onerous regulations are justified on the basis of hypothetical worst-case scenarios and then normalized across a vast range of research.

This is not to say that the harms imagined by REBs are fictional, but that decisions about future potentialities are much more subjective and *ad hoc* than one might have concluded from the discourse of "risk" used in the *Policy*. The danger is that with little to constrain imaginings of possible harms, researchers are being asked to mitigate a host of potentialities precisely because we do not know how likely or unlikely they might be.

Informed consent

Contemporary concerns about research ethics would undoubtedly be quite different were it not for the almost incomprehensible cruelties of a group of German physicians in Nazi Germany. Drawing their "research subjects" from the concentration camps, these physicians subjected Jews and Gypsies to "experiments" that included immersing them in freezing water, and injecting them with poison, diseases, and even gasoline – in an effort to learn how the body responds to such extreme manipulations (Annas and Grodin 1992). Twenty Nazi doctors were ultimately indicted for their actions, and appeared before the Nuremberg War Crimes Tribunal in 1946. This tribunal condemned the sheer barbarity of these experiments and repeatedly emphasized that the experiments were conducted without the consent of the participants. In an effort to establish the basic principles that must be adhered to in conducting research on human subjects the tribunal drafted the famous Nuremberg Code. The requirement that researchers must secure the consent of research subjects, and that this consent must be voluntary, competent, informed, and comprehending is the very first item on that code.

The informed consent requirement has been embraced by various regulatory bodies that oversee medical and scientific research. In recent years this has been extended to the social sciences (Fadan and Beauchamp 1986; Wax 1980). In Canada, the explicit expectation of the Tri-Council is that participants will sign a release form demonstrating that they have read and understand a summary of the research and any risks that it might entail. In some contexts, oral consent will suffice, such as when the use of legalistic forms is culturally inappropriate or when conducting telephone surveys. In either case, consent must be voluntary, and participants must be aware that they are free to withdraw from the research at any time without facing any repercussions.

The movement of informed consent provisions from the medical sciences to the social sciences has proved to be a point of contention. At least three downsides to this protocol can be identified. The first is that when used in the context of eth-nographies, participant observation, or exploratory interviews, consent forms seem alien, unduly formal, and occasionally unworkable (van den Hoonaard 2001, 2002). Consent forms can unnecessarily color interview or ethnographic situations, trans-forming encounters that are routinely more informal and exploratory into unneces-sarily official and legalistic exchanges. These apprehensions are particularly germane to research on large groups of people. The Tri-Council guidelines stipulate that participant observation research can be conducted on political rallies, demonstra-tions, and public meetings since "it can be expected that the participants are seeking public visibility," but this does not seem to extend to the day-to-day observation of behavior in the public or quasi-public realm. Van den Hoonaard (2002, p. 11) recounts how an ethics committee at his university informed a graduate student that she should look away when her participant observation research brought her into contact with individuals who had not explicitly consented to being studied. Comparable difficulties were encountered by Steadman Rice in his research on co-dependency groups when he sought to acquire the consent of all individuals attending such meetings. He routinely had to leave the session each time a member arrived so that the group could vote on whether he could remain. This became so onerous that he ultimately had to abandon this component of the research entirely (Steadman Rice 1996, p. 224).

Our REB struggled with a research proposal that involved videotaping Ukrainian New Year celebrations because of the impracticality of acquiring informed consent from everyone that might appear on tape. We ultimately decided that the researcher should concentrate on filming the main participants in the festivities who had pro-vided explicit consent. It should be stressed that this celebration was a community event that would have undoubtedly included a host of individuals videotaping and photographing whatever and whomever they pleased for their own personal use; such actions obviously do not raise legal or ethical issues.

The second drawback of the standard expectation that researchers will secure formal written consent is that it seems to preclude or seriously complicate forms of scholarly endeavor that otherwise seem entirely unproblematic. So, for example, some of the proposals that my REB has refused, or returned for revision, because they did not contain informed consent provisions include a proposal to conduct a discourse analysis of Internet chat room conversations, a proposal to analyze private conversations overheard in public places, and yet another proposal that would have studied video recordings of people interacting in public places.

How informed consent provisions will shape Internet research is a particularly pressing concern. Discussions are currently underway in the global research com-munity about what ethical protocols should govern Web based research. Opinions on this issue can be roughly divided into two camps. On the one hand are those individuals who equate Web postings with public pronouncements, comparable to letters to the editor, and as such amenable to academic analysis without the necessity of ethical review (Kitchin 2002). Others, however, accentuate how some Internet users operate with an assumption of privacy and confidentiality. These individuals are more inclined to suggest that Internet research should undergo ethics review and adhere to the *Policy*, raising difficult questions about the practicalities of acquiring informed consent. While this matter is far from resolved, if the latter view becomes dominant the academy risks becoming the only social institution that cannot routinely quote and analyze information posted on what will likely become the dominant social communication system.

Informed consent provisions have also made it increasingly difficult (although not impossible) to conduct research that employs deception. Concerns about the use of deception in research have a long history, most famously articulated by Kai Erikson (1967) in his reaction to the development of methodologies where researchers deliberately misrepresent their identity in order to enter otherwise inaccessible social situations. Erikson proposed that such research was unethical on several grounds, including the facts that it undermined the responsibilities a researcher owed to his/her subjects and that it could damage the reputation of the field of sociology. His position has not gone unchallenged, and there is now a voluminous literature on the ethics and pragmatic necessities of deception in social scientific research (see Korn 1997). The general trend, however, has been toward restricting the use of deception in research because of the practical difficulties or impossibilities of securing informed consent.

While some applaud this development, it is now apparent that "deception" can be shaded in many different ways. Advocates of banning deception in the research process tend to accentuate the most onerous and unpalatable forms of deception imaginable in a research context. This includes use of elaborate sets and confederates designed to make research participants falsely believe that they are ill or in mortal danger. However, prohibiting deception is akin to outlawing lying, something that at first blush might seem wonderful until it becomes apparent that lying and deceit lubricate daily life while serving large and small legitimate institutional purposes (Bok 1978). The concept of "deceit" encompasses a massive range of behaviors, the majority of which are rather innocuous. Our REB, for example, rejected a proposal to measure the participation rates of research subjects when different styles of informed consent forms were used. Given that the research participants could not be informed about the true aims of the research this constituted a form of deception, and was consequently rejected by our board.[6] In the United States, sociologist Richard Leo faced allegations that his research on police interrogation practices was unethical because in his encounters with the police he adopted a more professional and conservative persona than he did in his daily life. These modifications included dressing formally and cutting his hair (Allen 1997). These are clearly not the types of extreme manipulations envisioned by people opposed to deception in research, but are nonetheless encompassed by a blanket prohibition on deception. Whatever one's opinions about the restrictions on deception in research, we should not underestimate the loss that this development has entailed for scholarship; between 1965 and 1985 approximately one-half of all social psychology articles published in the United States involved some form of deception (Korn 1997, p. 2). Most of that research, some of which has produced significant and lasting insights, would not be permitted today as it could not provide opportunities for informed consent.

Finally, the presumption that research participants will provide informed consent augments and reinforces the difficulties in conducting critical scholarship. The requirement to be "up front" about the focus of your research can simply preclude valuable forms of critical inquiry. Researchers, for example, who wanted to accompany and interview police officers at work in order to learn about police racism (or corruption, sexism, excessive use of force, etc.) would likely see their research grind to a halt at the first sign of a consent form informing officers of the research topic. The same is true for a host of other critical scholarship that might seek to investigate high-profile, contentious issues involving powerful people or agencies.

Returning to our comparison between the academy and journalism, the issue of informed consent again accentuates the marked differences in the regulation of identical behavior when undertaken by representatives of these two institutions. Journalists generally do not acquire formal written consent to interview people. As anyone who accepts calls from the media knows, one is simply asked a series of questions, and some of the answers are apt to appear in the newspaper the following day. The mere act of talking with a journalist, whether one is a professor or a waitress, is a self-evident demonstration that one is willing to be interviewed and must self-evaluate any risks that might entail.

Research strategies that are increasingly problematic in the academy because they pose difficulties for acquiring informed consent are common and indispensable journalistic practices. Journalists routinely film or photograph people interacting in public places, none of which is ethically dubious. Or, more accurately, journalists have the discretion and professional standing to judge for themselves whether these might pose an ethical risk. Journalists also regularly refer to Internet chat room discussions and have long reported on overheard private conversations. Where deception is now severely restricted in the academy, it has become a routine practice in all manner of television game shows and assorted *Candid Camera* types of reality programming. Deception is also a staple of policing, where the public is regularly deceived through elaborate hoaxes and outright lies in the furtherance of criminal justice agendas (Marx 1988). Deception undertaken by scholars to advance knowledge and address larger social problems is generally prohibited on ethical grounds. When it is done in the name of entertainment or policing, deception is allowed and occasionally applauded.

Anonymity

The final measure to be discussed is the presumption of anonymity. Following the *Policy*, researchers are now expected to protect the identity of their research participants. There are, however, some important qualifications to this rule. If researchers learn of instances of child abuse they must report it. Likewise, if researchers encounter other instances of criminal behavior they can be legally compelled to reveal their sources.

While academics have only rarely been asked to reveal their sources, because research is not a statutorily protected form of communication researchers can be faced with difficult decisions about whether they are willing to go to jail rather than reveal their sources. This dilemma faced Russel Ogden, a Canadian M.A. student in criminology at Simon Fraser University. As part of his research, which had received ethics approval, Ogden attended the suicide and euthanasia of persons with AIDS. In 1994 Ogden was subpoenaed to testify before the Vancouver Coroner in a case involving the death of an "unknown female." When he refused to identify his research participants he was threatened with a charge of contempt (Palys and Lowman 2000). Although Ogden was ultimately able to convince the judge to treat his communications with research participants as privileged, Simon Fraser University offered almost no support for his case, forcing him to sue the university to recover his legal costs. An even more extreme example involved the American case of Rik Scarce, who was incarcerated for 159 days in 1993 for contempt of court because he refused to surrender his research notes on the radical environmental movement (Scarce 1994).

While journalists also have procedures to ensure the anonymity of confidential sources, there is a marked difference in the operating assumptions of the two institutions. Journalists generally expect that the people they interview or film will be identified by name unless they specifically indicate that they would like to remain anonymous. For the Tri-Council, the starting assumption is that all research participants will remain anonymous unless they provide explicit permission to be identified.

This difference can have interesting and occasionally bizarre consequences. Consider, for example, the case of a journalist and an academic who both want to interview a prominent author, for example Margaret Atwood. Neither the journalist nor Ms. Atwood would presume that her identity would be suppressed. However, if the academic were to conduct the *exact same* interview, she could not identify Ms. Atwood by name without acquiring her explicit written approval. Prior to the interview the researcher would have to submit a proposal to the REB that included a justification as to why the normal protocols prescribing anonymity should be waived. Our REB recently reviewed a file where a researcher in the humanities wanted to interview a prominent poet and consequently had to undergo precisely such a process.

The effects of the presumption of anonymity extend beyond increasing the bureaucratic hurdles that academics must surmount. It can also mean that academic knowledge may be less robust when compared to journalistic accounts. Evidence of this can be seen in relation to the topic at hand. Consider the fact that one consequence of establishing formal ethical guidelines could be that some academics will simply ignore or consciously subvert such protocols. Several scholars I have interviewed for a research project on how ethics procedures are being received in the academy have indicated that they have "made up" interview questions to satisfy the REB demand to provide exactly what interviewees would be asked. Others noted that the real-life practicalities of conducting research have led them to abandon the formal consent forms once the research commences. Such practices are corroborated by Christopher Shea (2000) in an article written for the academic magazine *Lingua Franca*. He reports that award-winning sociologists Paul Rabinow and Mitchel Dunier did not receive ethics approval for their studies. In that article Howard Becker, arguably the most famous sociologist of his generation, claimed that should the ethics people come knocking, he would simply say that his ethnographic studies are a form of performance art.

For the issue at hand, the important point about these examples of avoidance and subversion of the research ethics process is that Christopher Shea's journalistic account can identify these individuals by name. In contrast, my interview based research on the academic response to research ethics, because it conforms to research ethics protocols, can only speak broadly of "prominent sociologists" because of the presumption of anonymity and the fear that revealing their identities might jeopardize their careers. This suggests that academic claims can inadvertently lose their political weight and critical edge because of ethics requirements. It is often vitally important to know *who* these prominent individuals are. Their actions and opinions matter because they are known sociologists, union leaders, or KKK members, and not just nameless members of a larger social grouping. Academic accounts that must avoid identifying such individuals are comparatively less robust and critical than the forms of investigative journalism that can and does "name names."

Conclusion

In this article I have sought to demonstrate the process of ethics creep occurring in the operation of research ethics protocols in Canadian universities. I now briefly consider some reasons why this creep may be occurring and accentuate the danger it poses.

The differences between the ethical protocols established for journalists and those for social scientific researchers accentuate several interesting attributes about their respective institutions, and about formalized ethical protocols more generally. The first point is one I have accentuated throughout this article: the ethical standards of one institution can serve as a benchmark to evaluate the regulatory framework in a different institution. In this case, journalism serves as a telling yardstick that accentuates the increasingly restrictive and expansive nature of the ethical governance of academic research. Such a situation reaffirms the sociological truism that deviance and normality, or, in this case, ethical and unethical conduct, are contextual and institutionally specific.

The reason for the different ethical standards used by journalists and social scientists appears to relate to how these institutions have historically imagined their relationships with their informants or research subjects. Social scientists have often studied poor and marginalized individuals. As such, they have positioned themselves as the authorized "knowers" about assorted dispossessed and marginal groups. The epistemological and political difficulties of speaking for other groups, combined with an awareness of the marginal status of such research participants, has fostered a tendency to view all research participants as vulnerable, lacking power, and needing protection. In contrast, journalists often interview and question individuals drawn from more powerful segments of society. Rather than speaking for such individuals, these accounts tend to employ the journalist's characteristic point/counterpoint style of narrative, where interviewees are (ostensibly) allowed to present their own views. As such, journalists work on the assumption that interviewees are capable of speaking in their own voice, and only rarely require special protection. This distinction is obviously more true in the institutional imaginary than in practice, but it helps explain why the social sciences have been more willing to embrace an image of their research participants as being more vulnerable and fragile than a journalist's sources – even when these sources may be the exact same individuals.

One of the paradoxes of the formal research ethics systems is that there is often a distinct but unquestioned rupture between following the rules and conducting ethical research. If, following Bauman (1993), ethical relationships are characterized by an ongoing interrogation of the types of responsibilities that we might owe to others, and which cannot be reduced to a simple exercise in rule-following, it becomes apparent that the application of many of the existing rules bears little relationship to ethical conduct whatsoever. We have reached the point where breaking many of the rules imposed by REBs would not in fact result in unethical conduct – if ethics is conceived of as anything beyond simple rule-following.

This becomes apparent if we consider the hypothetical, but not atypical, case of a researcher who wants to interview teenagers about their music preferences as part of a study on gender identity. The Tri-Council rules are clear that because these "research participants" are minors the researcher cannot interview them without acquiring parental consent. While the motivations for this rule are above reproach, applying it in this instance is a form of rule fetishization that needlessly hampers research. At times this rule has impeded the development of potentially important insights into otherwise inaccessible behaviors. An American IRB effectively foreclosed Wax's (1980, p. 280) research into teenage glue sniffing because he did not have provisions for securing parental consent – an impracticality given the nature of the topic being studied. Enforcing this rule for such research bears little relationship to the aim of protecting research subjects from harm. This is increasingly true for the application of any number of research ethics rules.

The fetishization of rules can reduce ethical systems to a form of conformist rule-following. Researchers risk being seen as acting unethically when they fail to submit an application to the REB or obtain a signed consent form, whether or not there was ever the slightest prospect of anyone being harmed by virtue of such research. When following the rules hampers research but seems disconnected from any prospect of producing harm, researchers conform not because they accept the moral authority and ethical insights of the REB structure, but because their reputations and careers can be damaged should they fail to do so. The authority of the ethics structure risks becoming more coercive than moral.

A paradox of such a system is that it can itself become an instrument of unethical behavior. An incident from our REB provides a telling caution. A faculty member had recently been hired on the condition that he complete his Ph.D. dissertation within a set period of time. He learned about the research ethics process during his faculty orientation, and realized that research he conducted several years ago in France as the basis for his dissertation did not receive ethics clearance and probably should have been submitted to an REB. The research involved audio-recording choral conducting practices and then analyzing the recordings. When he submitted an application to see if he could acquire retroactive ethical approval he was informed that such approval could not be granted because, following the *Policy*, ethics approval must be secured before research commences. Consequently, he faced the prospect of being forced to abandon the data he had collected, which would likely have resulted in his failing to earn his Ph.D. and forfeiting his academic position. After weeks of anxious discussions with the highest levels of our research ethics bureaucracy he ultimately received something akin to retroactive approval for his research. However, this result was not preordained and occurred only after much hand-wringing and debate.

The interesting point about this case is that I believe it would have been fundamentally unethical if this individual had failed his dissertation and potentially lost his career as a result of the strict application of formalistic regulations to an undertaking that posed no prospect of producing harm. Writing in a more polemical vein, Howard (1994) has accentuated how comparable rule fetishization by a range of regulatory bodies in the United States routinely produces decisions that are patently unjust, unethical, and divorced from common sense. That REBs will occasionally feel compelled to render such decisions in an attempt to appear consistent or to avoid violating the formal guidelines appears to be one of the inherent risks in the move to a more bureaucratic system for governing research.

Academics opposed to the ethics review process have singled out university lawyers as the main culprits responsible for these new restrictions (Adler and Adler 2002). There is a perception that university administrators are motivated by a fear of lawsuits to embrace research ethics. However, even if we accept this, it merely explains how the ethics system was originally structured and does not address why the REBs have tended to interpret these regulations in such a way as to expand and intensify the regulatory structure.[7]

One explanation for these developments is the open-ended nature of the *Policy*'s formal guidelines. Few of the central concepts set out in the *Policy*, including those of "research," "researcher," or "harm," have clear referents that unproblematically direct how the regulations should be applied in different situations. Instead, they are empty signifiers, capable of being interpreted in a multitude of ways, and occasionally serving as sites of contestation. Accentuating such open-endedness, however, only draws attention to the unavoidable fact that there is an interpretive process involved in deciding how to apply vague legalistic concepts to specific situations. It does not help explain the cumulative direction that such interpretations appear to have taken. To explain that process, I believe that we must address the dynamics of the REBs themselves.

The culture of REBs is cautious and conservative, inclined to take a "just in case" approach to managing the dangers posed by research projects. This is probably both inevitable and desirable for a body charged with evaluating whether research poses risks to research participants. Hence, there is a tendency for REB members to perceive eventualities that others might see as innocuous as being sufficiently risky to necessitate some precautionary measures. With few constraints on the types of harms that can be imagined, a process is set in motion that has the potential to introduce ever more regulations to manage potentially undesirable eventualities, the true likelihood of which is routinely unknown.

This tendency is augmented by the fact that the dynamic that seems to drive the ethics boards is a form of legal consistency. While the Tri-Council guidelines accentuate the need for flexibility, the Boards seem to be concerned with a desire for something akin to formal equality, where like cases are treated alike. Rather than treat each case as a unique undertaking, they tend to look for parallels and commonalities across different research programs. This is similar to the use of legal precedent, but much less formalized. The cumulative effect is an expansionist logic as ethics protocols creep into a host of new domains because of board members' desire for consistency. The unarticulated logic is that it is better to require all researchers in situations that might be seen as roughly comparable to operate in a similar fashion, rather than risk the perception of inconsistency or bias.

The various rules that I have accentuated in this analysis are open to reform, and I hope that some of the more contentious policies will be modified in the coming years. However, my suspicion is that the systematic creep of the ethical structure will continue its expansionist dynamic and the bureaucracy will become larger, more formal, and more rigid. Signs of this are already on the horizon. Discussions are now underway to require REBs to be accredited, adding another layer of permanent bureaucratic oversight onto the REBs themselves to ensure that they are properly constituted and that the Ph.D. qualified researchers who staff these boards are properly trained.

An unfortunate consequence of these developments will likely be that researchers will choose to employ certain types of unproblematic and often predictable research methodologies rather than deal with the uncertainty and delays associated with qualitative, ethnographic, or critical scholarship which do not fit easily into the existing research ethics template. The more ethical roadblocks are installed for innovative and critical research, the more we risk homogenizing inquiry and narrowing vision, as scholars start to follow what they perceive to be the path of least institutional resistance.

None of this would be a problem and would, in fact, be commendable if the REBs clearly served as a bulwark against a tide of unethical research. However, I have seen no evidence that this is the case. The vast majority of the proposals that come across our desks are so innocuous that they shade into the mundane or trivial. Not even the most adamant supporter of research ethics would have anticipated that the Tri-Council bureaucracy would necessitate regular meetings, where six or more Ph.D. qualified academics scrutinize senior scholars' proposals to study overheard conversations, or students' requests to interview friends. It is now time to seriously reconsider whose interests are served by such measures and what is being lost as a result.

Acknowledgements

Many individuals have contributed to the development of this article. I would like to thank Herb Northcott, Serra Tinic, Matthew Yeager, Ted Palys, Aaron Doyle, and the anonymous reviewers of *Qualitative Sociology* for their helpful comments on earlier drafts. I would also like to thank the members of the Arts, Science and Law Research Ethics Board at the University of Alberta for the often fascinating discussions that helped to stimulate my thoughts on this topic.

Notes

* Reproduced with permission from Kevin Haggerty and Springer Science+Business Media. Originally published in *Qualitative Sociology*, vol. 27, no. 4, 2004, pp. 391–414.
1 I refer to "social sciences" for the sake of convenience. The provisions discussed in this article apply to all research activities involving human subjects, including the humanities and law.
2 These regulations can be found at: www.pre.ethics.gc.ca/english/policystatement/policystatement.cfm.
3 There are provisions in the guidelines dealing with public figures such as authors that would seem to provide some leeway in interviewing such individuals. However, the actual text of the regulations suggests that these interviews are exempt only if the interviewee is speaking about information that is already publicly available. Hence, if the interviewee might stray in any way from what is already available in public (which would be the point of all interviews, to hopefully learn something new), then the interview must receive ethics approval.
4 One reviewer suggested that as Erikson's research was undertaken in his capacity as a consultant to a legal firm it would not have to pass IRB muster. In fact, as I stated in the section "Scope of research ethics protocols," in Canada university affiliated academics must vet their private, contractual, consultative research with the university Research Ethics Board.
5 Tellingly, no one (myself included) raised the prospect that if the research participants were in a bad relationship, the fact that the research might prompt the couple to end it might constitute a net benefit.
6 An additional reason this proposal was rejected was that the REB felt that consent forms should be treated as being akin to sacrosanct. As such, they should not be manipulated, even in order to test which is the most effective.
7 The deliberations of our REB have rarely included the legal implications of our decisions for the university or the board. Instead, we have tended to concentrate on questions of precedent – how we have handled comparable cases in the past.

References

Adler, PA & Adler, P 2002, 'Do university lawyers and the police define research values?', in *Walking the Tightrope: Ethical Issues for Qualitative Researchers*, ed WC van den Hoonaard, Toronto, University of Toronto Press, pp. 34–42.

Allen, C 1997, 'Spies like us: When sociologists deceive their subjects', *Lingua Franca*, vol. 7, pp. 31–39.

Annas, G & Grodin, M (eds) 1992, *The Nazi Doctors and the Nuremburg Code: Human Rights in human experimentation*, New York, Oxford University Press.

Bauman, Z 1993, *Postmodern Ethics*, Oxford, Blackwell.

Beck, U 1992, *Risk Society: Towards a New Modernity*, London, Sage.

Beecher, HE 1966, 'Ethics and clinical research', *New England Journal of Medicine*, vol. 274, no. 24, pp. 1354–1360.

Bok, S 1978, *Lying: Moral Choice in Public and Private Life*, New York, Vintage.

Douglas, M 1986, *Risk Acceptability According to the Social Sciences*, London, Routledge and Kegan Paul.

Erikson, KT 1967, 'A comment on disguised observation in sociology', *Social Problems*, vol. 14, no. 4, pp. 366–373.

Erikson, KT 1976, *Everything in its Path: Destruction of Community in the Buffalo Creek Flood*, New York, Simon & Schuster.

Fadan, R & Beauchamp, T 1986, *A History and Theory of informed consent*, New York, Oxford University Press.

Galanter, M 1992, 'Law abounding: Legalisation around the North Atlantic', *Modern Law Review*, vol. 55, no. 1, pp. 1–24.

Haggerty, KD 2003, 'From risk to precaution: The rationalities of personal crime prevention', in *Risk and morality*, eds RV Ericson & A Doyle, Toronto, University of Toronto Press, pp. 193–214.

Hoonaard, van den W 2001, 'Is research-ethics review a moral panic?' *Canadian Review of Sociology and Anthropology*, vol. 38, no. 1, pp. 19–36.

Hoonaard, van den W (ed) 2002, *Walking the Tightrope: Ethical Issues for Qualitative Researchers*, Toronto, University of Toronto Press.

Howard, PK 1994, *The Death of Common Sense: How Law is Suffocating America*, New York, Random House.

Humphreys, L 1970, *Tearoom Trade: Impersonal Sex in Public Places*, Chicago, Aldine.

Innes, M 2001, 'Control creep', *Sociological Research Online*, vol. 6, no. 3. www.socresonline. org.uk/6/3/innes.html.

Kellner, F 2002, 'Coping with guidelines from the Tri-Council', in *Walking the Tightrope: Ethical Issues for Qualitative Researchers*, ed W.C van den Hoonaard, Toronto, University of Toronto Press, pp. 26–33.

Kitchin, HA 2002, 'The Tri-Council on cyberspace: Insights, oversights and extrapolations', in *Walking the Tightrope: Ethical Issues for Qualitative Researchers*, ed WC van den Hoonaard, Toronto, University of Toronto Press, pp. 160–174.

Korn, JH 1997, *Illusions of Reality: A History of Deception in Social Psychology*, New York, SUNY.

Marx, GT 1988, *Undercover: Police Surveillance in America*, Berkeley, University of California Press.

McNally, RJ 2003, *Remembering Trauma*, Cambridge, Harvard University Press.

Milgram, S 1974, *Obedience to Authority*, New York, Harper & Row.

Palys, T & Lowman, J 2000, 'Ethical and legal strategies for protecting confidential research information', *Canadian Journal of Law and Society*, vol. 15, pp. 39–80.

Scarce, R 1994, '(No) trial (but) tribulations: When courts and ethnography conflict', *Journal of Contemporary Ethnography*, vol. 23, pp. 123–149.

Shea, C 2000, 'Don't talk to the humans: The crackdown on social science research', *Lingua Franca*, vol. 10, pp. 26–34.

Steadman Rice, J 1996, 'Appendix A: Methodology', in *A Disease of One's Own: Psychotherapy, Addiction, and the Emergence of Co-dependency*, ed J Steadman Rice, New Brunswick, Transaction, pp. 219–228.

Sunstein, C 2002, *Risk and Reason*, Cambridge, Cambridge University Press.

Wax, ML 1980, 'Paradoxes of "consent" to the practice of fieldwork', *Social Problems*, vol. 27, no. 3, pp. 272–283.

Weber, M 1978, *Economy and Society*, Berkeley, University of California Press.

Zhou, X 1993, 'The dynamics of organizational rules', *American Journal of Sociology*, vol. 98, no. 5, pp. 1134–1136.

Zimbardo, PG 1973, 'On the ethics of intervention in human psychological research: With special reference to the Stanford Prison experiment', *Cognition*, vol. 2, no. 2, pp. 243–256.

2

THE ETHICAL IMAGINATION

Reflections on conducting research in Hong Kong

Michael Adorjan

Introduction

In this chapter I offer a reflection on my experiences conducting criminological research in Hong Kong, a Special Administrative Region of mainland China. I begin by detailing my position as an 'outsider' arriving in Hong Kong and the associated challenges I faced starting up new qualitative research. I draw from recent approaches to positionality in research which problematizes a static dichotomization of insider–outsider taxonomy, suggesting how these concepts must be treated as fluid and dynamic over the course of research, especially as ethical issues are encountered.

I reflect on my research during several phases: initial planning, data collection and research dissemination. Ethical issues related to initial planning center on how to capture the complex and varied lived experiences of Cantonese-speaking Hong Kong citizens given my naivety and outsider-status as an English-speaking white male. I discuss how the research team was assembled to face this challenge, how letters of information and consent forms were formulated, and the process of institutional ethics review. Ethical issues during the data collection stage relate to the planning and conducting of 30 focus groups with a cross-section of Hong Kong citizens, representing various regions of Hong Kong (including Hong Kong island, Kowloon, the northern New Territories, and outlying islands). I reflect on issues arising from focus group research design in general and conducting focus groups in Hong Kong in particular. Here too 'insider–outsider' issues came to be very important in steering the direction of the project, especially in relation to how participant experiences related to wider (media and political) discourses of crime and policing in Hong Kong. Finally, ethical challenges encountered during research dissemination are related, perhaps ironically, to my position as an 'external-insider' presenting results to 'outsiders'. The particular challenges here relate to communicating findings to publics whose impressions of post-colonial Hong Kong are often influenced by popular culture and international media coverage (the latter which, relatively recently, centered on issues of social order through the 'Umbrella Movement' clashes between protestors and the Hong Kong Police Force).

Drawing from this case study, I develop the notion of an 'ethical imagination' to underscore the impact of ongoing and situated decisions in the field and the importance of considering the potential long-term effects of these decisions for the researcher, participants and various publics, including other researchers and criminal justice institutions, in a particular project.

An outsider: arriving as the stranger

I am an English-speaking white male born and raised in Canada – a post-colonial nation. I completed my Ph.D. in sociology in 2009 at McMaster University in Canada. I had some experience traveling outside of Canada, but not in Asia and had never lived abroad for an extended period. After receiving the position at the University of Hong Kong, set to commence January 2010, I was asked several curious questions by friends, academic colleagues, and family such as if I would be able to lecture in English, if I would have any constraints placed on my research, and if I would be able to write freely, especially if what I wrote was, in any way, critical of 'China'. Even before arriving, however, I had an awareness that Hong Kong was different in many respects to mainland China; for example it retained press freedoms and the rule of law, and indeed, I was *required* to teach all my courses at the University of Hong Kong in English (surely not a problem as I spoke only a few words in Cantonese).

Despite 'reading up' on Hong Kong and my arms' length familiarization before travel, living in Hong Kong certainly instilled in me a sense of anomie and culture shock. I read the English language news, discussed Hong Kong's history and present situation with colleagues, and tried to immerse myself in everyday life (especially the food!). I was not only anxious about how I would adapt to living in Hong Kong, but also acutely conscious of how I would approach research as an outsider. I saw every advantage in being a stranger in the Schutzean tradition (see also Fraser 2013, p. 252). The essay, titled *The Stranger*, where Alfred Schutz (1976) writes about "the typical situation in which a stranger finds himself … attempt[ing] to interpret the cultural pattern of a social group which he approaches and to orient himself within it" (p. 91) resonated with me in my new home. Schutz writes:

> the sociologist (as sociologist, not as a man among fellow-men which he remains in his private life) is the *disinterested* scientific onlooker of the social world. He is disinterested in that he intentionally refrains from participating in the network of plans, means-and-ends relations, motives and changes, hopes and fears, which the actor within the social world uses for interpreting his experiences of it. (p. 92, emphasis added)

Schutz argues that the 'stranger', being an outsider, is enabled to make observations regarding events and situations which insiders may take for granted as common sense or 'truth': "He becomes essentially the man who has to place in question nearly everything that seems to be unquestionable to the members of the approached group" (Schutz 1964, cited in Hellawell 2006, p. 486). Simmel once made similar remarks, suggesting that the stranger has a measure of freedom granting the outsider "a particular kind of objectivity not usually granted to the insider" (ibid).

While at the time of first arriving in Hong Kong I had a rather romanticized notion of the advantages of being 'the stranger', I was aware of problems of representation and how my outsider status would shape both research questions and how I would proceed with conducting research (e.g. shaping the questions ... journals). Shaping the questions I ask, the presumptions informing those questions, the way I presented findings at conferences and through publications, especially in international journals. Edward Said (1994 [1978]) has long identified the problem of orientalism, referring to a mode of representation and domination, projected from the 'West' onto the 'East', which reifies essentialist narratives of 'we' versus 'the Other'. Cain (2000, p. 239) insightfully comments that orientalism

> involves the discursive constitution of an often romanticized but also wayward and unknowing 'other' which, because of these besetting albeit (to liberals) endearing characteristics, requires the guidance and advice of the 'us' to find and/or accept its proper place in the world.

Criminologists seeking to develop comparative research programs have argued that criminological theories developed in the Anglo-Global North may not necessarily map onto regions outside the occident (Aas 2012; Cain 2000; Sheptycki 2008). Differing political economies, cultural factors, and institutional arrangements suggest different points of social assemblage requiring empirical study. Chen's (2010, p. 212) work on *Asia as Method* responds to these issues, through Asian societies becoming "each other's points of reference, so that understanding of the self may be transformed, and subjectivity rebuilt" in order to cultivate "alternate horizons and perspectives". From Chen's perspective, Hong Kong-based scholars who grew up and continue to live in Hong Kong are best able to appreciate social context, the lived experience of Hong Kong residents and the "local historical currents" (2010, p. 214) which foreign scholars may not appreciate or may misinterpret.

Chen's arguments are certainly valuable and should inspire research in South East Asia that seeks to produce scholarship on its own terms – including theory and methods not beholden to the 'Western gaze'. Nevertheless, this approach did not help provide me with epistemological insights for developing my own research. More relevant were post-colonial critiques of sociological scholarship that reproduces orientalist assumptions (e.g. Bhambra 2007; McLennan 2003). Weber and Marx were themselves criticized for their presumptions of an Asiatic mode of production, which was placed in contrast to the (enlightened) progress of Western materialism (Zeitlin 2001). Likewise, post-colonial critiques have been levied against prior characterizations of the 'insider–outsider problem' in anthropological and sociological research. Merton's (1972, p. 11) classic definition of the problem refers to "the problem of patterned differentials among social groups and strata in access to certain types of knowledge". Yet especially when conducting research outside of one's culture and nation, it is crucial to problematize the notion that one's status as 'the stranger' offers an objective vantage point producing 'better knowledge' *for* 'the Other' (indeed, this model seems geared to the unidirectional dissemination of research and knowledge from western regions to 'benefit' policies and practices in other regions). This issue has long been recognized by anthropologists, who have argued that

> the assumptions fostered by the objective approach coincide with those engendered by the colonial relationship. Further, they blind the anthropologist, like the colonizer, to the validity of other than a single view of reality. (Lewis 1973, cited in Hellawell 2006, p. 485)

Indeed, 'insider–outsider' is a "bipolar construction", which

> sets up a false separation that neglects the interactive processes through which 'insiderness' and 'outsiderness' are constructed. 'Outsiderness' and 'insiderness' are not fixed or static positions, rather they are ever-shifting and permeable social locations that are differentially experienced and expressed by community members. … These negotiations simultaneously are embedded in local processes that reposition gender, class, and racial-ethnic relations among other socially constructed distinctions. (Naples 1996, p. 84)

Naples' prescient observations here (see also Merriam et al. 2001) resonated with my experiences in Hong Kong – clearly I was identifiable as an outsider to the Hong Kong citizens participating in my research. Yet whether my status as male, as an academic from a privileged class, as white, or someone who did not speak Cantonese mattered shifted across the various groups we interviewed. My *positionality* in relation to my research team and participants became methodologically and ethically relevant to consider. At the time, I tried my best to navigate issues related to positionality and ethics, though no doubt my *explicit* consideration of positionality is still emerging today, facilitated by the writing of this chapter.

Some have aimed to enrich the typology associated with being an insider or outsider in research. Banks offers four positions:

> The *indigenous-insider* … "who endorses the unique values, perspectives, behaviors, beliefs, and knowledge of his or her indigenous community" and "who can speak with authority about it." … The *indigenous-outsider*, [who] "has experienced high levels of cultural assimilation into an outsider or oppositional culture" but remains connected with his or her indigenous

community. ... The *external-insider*, [who] both rejects much of his or her indigenous community and endorses those of another culture to become an "'adopted' insider." Finally, the *external-outsider*, [who] is "socialized within a community different from the one in which he or she is doing research". (Banks 1998, pp. 7–8, cited in Merriam et al. 2001, p. 412)

This typology, as a heuristic device, is useful, though perhaps overplays the requirement to reject one's community one way or another in order to take on a certain status and role. I do not see this process as a zero-sum game. These categories should themselves be examined as shifting and fluid roles that one takes on when facing particular methodological and ethical issues encountered in the field. As such, in the following sections, I explicate in more detail the various experiences and issues encountered which required continuous adjustment along the insider–outsider continuum. In Hong Kong I soon felt less like an external-outsider and more like an external or 'adopted' insider. This positionality was accepted by some research participants and not others, resulting in informed methodological adjustments.

Researching perceptions of crime and police: project formulation

Issues of positionality and insider–outsider dynamics could easily have paralyzed me, and were initially backgrounded as I familiarized myself with Hong Kong and developed a research agenda. My graduate research in social constructionism influenced my appreciation of being agnostic to the objective status of conditions and social problems (such as youth crime) (see Gubrium & Holstein 2011; Spector & Kitsuse 1977). I became attuned to complexity and ambiguity in debates over social problems (Adorjan 2011a), and the ways qualitative research can unpack these complexities. I became interested in pursuing comparative research based on my dissertation, which examined the social construction of youth crime in Canada (Adorjan 2009). I brought this agnosticism with me to Hong Kong while learning and teaching about crime and criminal justice in an eclectic yet synergistic department, with many colleagues conducting qualitative research in anthropology, sociology, and criminology.

My lack of prior knowledge of Hong Kong's history or present socio-political circumstances made it difficult to grasp current perceptions of police or fear of crime beyond media headlines that often took polarized positions in relation to, for instance, events such as protests against governmental initiatives and the policing of those events. Some reports, for instance, criticized the Hong Kong Police Force for excessive use of force against protestors, and questioned their political neutrality and impartiality in maintaining law and order. Some media sources, such as the populist and 'watchdog' *Apple Daily* (especially through its multimedia presence online), are overtly critical of the government and consistently depict governmental officials, especially the Chief Executive, as pawns of the Communist Party of China.[1]

In relation to the often polarized media discourses, a primary ethical question for me became how to conduct research into citizen perceptions of crime and police without exaggerating antagonism towards government and police nor voices that feed into hegemonic narratives of order and criminal justice success. I began by drawing from my prior research examining youth crime within a social constructionist framework (Adorjan 2009, 2011a, 2011b). Social constructionism seeks to examine the processes through which social problems are formulated, contested, accepted as 'social facts', and institutionalized (Spector & Kitsuse 1977). Significantly, social constructionists are agnostic to the objective status of social problems, placing emphasis instead on member understandings, situated within their 'mundane ontology' (i.e. everyday understandings through lived experience) (see Gubrium & Holstein 2011).

Beyond official police reported crime statistics and government-sponsored representative surveys regarding crime victimization, I found a lack of research on fear of crime and perceptions of policing, especially from a qualitative, interpretivist framework (outside of isolated dissertations). Quantitative surveys of representative samples of the population regarding crime and policing are essential, yet often service an administrative criminology I sought to push beyond. I thus considered it important to research Hong Kong citizen perceptions and experiences of crime, and fear of crime, alongside perceptions of police, and trust in police, through focus group discussions. Recognizing early on that such a project would be exceedingly difficult and frankly unethical to conduct alone, considering my 'external-outsider' status in those early days, it was imperative that I brought on a co-investigator fluent in Cantonese and familiar with Hong Kong (i.e. an insider certainly). I applied to the Research Grants Council of Hong Kong for funding for this project alongside co-investigator Maggy Lee from my department. As a junior scholar aiming to manage my first (not so) large-scale research project, I benefitted from collaborating with an experienced criminological researcher who could also guide the formulation of research questions, participant recruitment, translation of Cantonese transcripts, and data analysis and dissemination.

Although the research proposal could have potentially touched upon potentially sensitive areas, such as policing and crime, the process of applying for the grant and undergoing subsequent ethical review once the grant was awarded was rather uneventful. The topic and methodology were not of concern given that the Research Grants Council of Hong Kong stipulates that "all applications for research funding are professionally assessed by local and overseas experts ... based on the academic quality of research proposals. The type of research is not one of the determinants" (www.ugc.edu.hk/eng/ugc/faq/q305.htm). Further, I remain unaware of concerns over 'ethics creep' in Hong Kong (see Haggerty, this volume). Based on my experiences with this project as well as three others since, institutional ethics review at the University of Hong Kong is primarily concerned with rather predictable issues of participant confidentiality and informed consent. Indeed, the Human Research Ethics Committee receives frequent applications from criminologists, sociologists, and anthropologists in the department of sociology that propose to conduct ethnographic or interview-based research. It is this "methodological cosmopolitanism" (Fraser 2013, p. 258) that the department of sociology is known for and which helps maintain a 'Hong Kong School' of criminology that is informed by critical and interpretivist approaches.

The feedback received from the ethics review process emphasized the importance of having all letters of information and consent forms written in both English and Chinese. Although we expected some of our participants to be fluent in spoken English as well as reading and writing, providing Chinese language translations for informed consent was essential to clearly communicate project goals, processes, and the assurances of confidentiality. The consent forms also addressed an ethical issue inherent in acquiring informed consent in focus group research. Unlike one-to-one interviews, where securing formal consent from participants and conveying assurances of confidentiality are relatively straightforward, the group context of focus groups requires further consideration of *external* and *internal* confidentiality. External confidentiality (i.e. ensuring anonymous use of discussion transcripts by the researchers) is insufficient given the group contexts where members, by virtue of being exposed to each other, may reveal confidential details to other group members during the course of interacting. Consent forms thus made additional reference to internal confidentiality, and participants signing the form agreed to respect the privacy and confidentiality of all group members present.

Nonetheless, ethics 'on paper' does not necessarily prepare researchers for issues encountered in the field. In my case the ethical issues that arose during data collection related to my external-outsider status. As much as I was already feeling like an emerging external-insider, what mattered here was how research participants viewed me and my research team.

Researching perceptions of crime and police: in the field

Focus groups generate knowledge through dynamic group interactions that extend beyond attitudes and opinions (Morgan 1997, p. 20). Often employed by scholars researching sensitive populations, focus groups elicit "a level of frankness which is seldom achieved by using survey questionnaires" (p. 3). While moderators are trained to keep discussions on track, the advantage of focus groups is that discussions progress in directions controlled by participants more than moderators (Madriz 1997, p. 164), and as such garner a "certain ecological validity" illuminating participants' lived experiences (Stewart et al. 2007, p. 39). I placed value in the potential for focus group discussions to enable participants to express themselves in their own words – albeit in English or Cantonese – during their reflections on crime and policing in Hong Kong. While we recruited some participants through local non-governmental organizations (e.g. community centres), we also decided not to involve the Hong Kong Police Force nor other criminal justice institutions. Instead, we targeted a broad cross-section of the population, from Hong Kong island to the northern New Territories, populated urban centres and rural outlying islands.

In total, 30 focus groups were held with 156 participants. Groups ranged from three to eight members, with an average of five members per group (see Morgan 1997, pp. 34, 42; Twinn 1998, p. 657). A broad cross-section of Hong Kong citizens was included, ranging from those living in private and public housing, middle-class communities, and 'satellite' towns in areas near the Hong Kong–mainland China border. Sixty-four per cent of participants were female; 50% were aged 16–29 and 42% aged 30–59, with a small number of retired persons; 50% of the sample were living in private housing, 38% in public housing, and 12% in subsidized housing. Overall, our goal was to hold focus group discussions with a wide range of participants that may reveal patterns according to gender, class and age, but also indicate consistent themes across all respondents.

Each participant consistently, as established in the ethics application, received $HK200 (about US$25) *before* group discussions began. Withholding honorariums until the groups were finished, we felt, was too coercive and not in the spirit of respecting the decision of participants to attend the group. Nevertheless, some participants seemed more eager to take the money and ask the research assistant when they could leave. Participants in these cases were reminded they had every right to leave at any time, yet fortunately all stayed for the duration of the discussions. $HK200 may well be a decent amount of cash for a discussion lasting about an hour, especially for our younger groups, as well as those more socioeconomically marginalized (a couple of groups were held with persons living in 'subdivided' units).[2] However, given the range of participants in our sample, including professionals with relatively high household incomes, the honorarium may not be as much of an incentive for participation. It would be interesting to consider how this issue could have been addressed retrospectively. Should a higher honorarium be set to help persuade persons with higher incomes to participate, and then should that honorarium be applied uniformly for all other participants? Would a 'tiered' honorarium model be ethical, where the honorarium amount is adjusted based on personal income? Perhaps not, but the issue provides another example of how ethics 'on paper' may not anticipate challenges in the field.

We aimed to keep groups relatively homogeneous along age, gender, and class (i.e. those living in public versus private housing) lines. Focus group researchers have found such uniformity important when having group discussions centred on 'crime talk', helping to ensure participants will be interacting with others they will not likely perceive as threatening (see also Madriz 1997, 2000; Morgan 1997, p. 36). This advice takes on a particular angle in Hong Kong. Having more heterogeneous groups could lead some participants to be more reticent for fear of losing 'face', loosely involving prestige, honor, and reputation (Bond & Hwang 1986). In group situations, face relates to the positive image members project and the social acceptance they seek from other members (Hallahan et al. 1997). Keeping groups either wholly male or female when discussing fear of crime (including sexual assault) is thus prudent. On the other hand, since many of our groups consisted of members familiar with each other (e.g. groups of housewives, adolescent friends), the research assistant sometimes had difficulty keeping groups focused. Thus, by keeping groups relatively homogeneous, we may have avoided generic issues related to conducting focus groups and interactional dynamics affected by Hong Kong cultural practices (i.e. 'face').

Regularly scheduled meetings between myself, my co-investigator, and senior research assistant were held over the course of the project to debrief research findings and make methodological adjustments, where necessary. These debriefing sessions illuminated that our focus groups, which lasted on average one and a half hours and were held at locations on or in close proximity to members' own 'turf', helped participants feel comfortable and facilitated open and dynamic discussions (Madriz 1997, p. 3). Venues included community centres, churches, private club houses and residences, university campuses, local schools, places of work, non-governmental organization offices, and food courts. Some outdoor venues did pose technical challenges, for example difficulties capturing participant voices due to wind or other background noises associated with urban life. At times the conditions were noisy, very hot and humid and bore the persistent distraction of mosquitos. The research team, however, made a conscious effort to attend venues at times and locations most convenient to the group (which included ... venues) to convey to participants that their views mattered, and that we respected wherever they felt most comfortable interacting (see Scoggins 2014, p. 395). This did however mean that the research team had to attend groups, often arranged on short notice, later at night. Our debriefing sessions also revealed that perhaps the single best facilitator of dialogue was a venue where participants could freely smoke cigarettes. Groups held in locations where participants could not smoke were not unproductive, but members seemed much more relaxed and dialogue freely flowed in groups where they could smoke (e.g. public spaces or private residences).

The decision to permit groups to be held in public spaces was also based on the fact that this research project was not asking participants to reflect on personal victimization experiences *per se*. Some participants did recall stories of crime victimization, but these were mostly experiences with 'minor' cases of theft, pickpocketing, and being scammed. This dynamic was revealed in some of the early pilot groups we held and helped justify the decision to continue to hold groups in public spaces.

I planned on being present for most focus group discussions, with my senior research assistant trained to facilitate the discussion and explain the informed consent procedures before proceeding. My co-investigator, Maggy Lee, also attended some of the groups, and I felt that having academics present would help instil confidence in participants. Lee's presence as arguably an external-insider (external in relation to our participants given her status as a tenured professor and respected researcher) and my status as an external-outsider led to differing responses among some respondents. How I was being perceived by groups was revealed during the debriefing sessions. In one I was informed that some groups early on expressed reservations over whether there would be any 'gwai lo' (foreigner) research assistants or investigators (for the opposite dynamic, see Merriam et al. 2001, p. 410). I did not feel this reservation directly but am certain this view was not held by the majority of participants, especially in the two groups I attended which were held in

English. I was, in those groups, more of an external-insider than external-outsider based on our shared language fluency. Learning of the potential unease of members regarding my presence, I opted to more carefully manage my presence at group discussions. I would often introduce myself at the beginning of groups, speak a few words of thanks in my broken Cantonese (aiming to project an external-insider status), but then leave the group in the hands of my senior research assistant and/ or my co-investigator. During a debriefing meeting my senior research assistant reported that this "made it real" to groups. I believe what she meant was that I did not impose my 'power' (the 'gaze' of a foreign academic) on groups, and reinforced through my actions the guarantee of confidentiality and free expression that groups were offered. I also felt that, while an initial greeting projected a symbolic legitimacy to the project, it was important to physically remove myself from groups when discussions were in Cantonese. I could return and thank participants formally, in Cantonese, after the discussion finished and ask them – through the facilitators – whether they had any questions or concerns about the research. Thus positioning myself strategically (i.e. temporally, ergonomically, and linguistically) while focus groups were conducted was a process imbued with ethical dimensions and implications for whether participants felt comfortable expressing themselves freely.

Careful positioning, ultimately, was geared toward facilitating group participants of their views and experiences of crime and police without inhibition or self-censor. The goal of the research, after all, was to push beyond narrow and dichotomous characterizations of fear of crime and trust in police. Indeed, for the majority of the 30 groups we conducted in total, most participants were quite positive about the Hong Kong Police Force, and expressed strong feelings of personal safety living in Hong Kong. Some concerns, however, across groups did emerge regarding social order and crime in areas of Hong Kong resembling mainland China (see Lee & Adorjan forthcoming), and with the police role in policing public order events. For instance we unpacked two currents of perceptions related to the police from this research: confidence in their ability to combat crime (e.g. celerity of response, ability to apprehend criminals) *alongside* concerns over police powers during 'stop and search' questioning and handling protests. Our research findings reveal *multi-faceted experiences and ambiguities* not readily apparent through the existing surveys conducted through administrative criminological tenets and goals. Dichotomous variables (i.e. safe, not safe; trust, distrust) or even Likert-scale gradations fail to capture hermeneutic nuances that suggest the complex ways in which citizens experience crime and social order in Hong Kong, as well as respond to ongoing tensions.

We did encounter some groups through referrals that were more decidedly antagonistic towards the police, for instance through a local politician who was active in supporting actions against the government. The groups coordinated through this politician's office seemed politically motivated to participate, while another group consisting of mothers in a public housing estate who all had children who had been involved with the police, seemed to participate solely to 'vent' their feelings regarding these negative experiences. From these groups, held early on in the project, we learned to avoid referrals that may lead to groups whose views would be influenced heavily by political factors. That said, these groups do present new questions related to how future findings are to be presented. Would such groups be excised completely from the analysis based on their 'tainted' nature? I would argue excluding responses from these groups based on positivistic measures of validity are not only misguided when conducting interpretivist research on 'crime talk', but also unethical: they silence the voices of important sectors of a society. At the same time, the way such voices are highlighted in research and presentations also bears important ethical implications.

Although translation and transcription started while focus groups were still being conducted, as with any qualitative research project, the general issue of losing much of the quality of focus group conversation through written transcripts (e.g. participant body language and mood) remains a factor. Further, I had to wait for audio recordings to be translated and transcribed before being able to truly access my data. This situated me very much as an external-outsider during this phase of the research, despite regular meetings where I was debriefed on findings. Nonetheless, we soon had a good system in place for ensuring that the difficult process of translation would not dilute or distort the original meaning and intention of participants' lived experiences. One research assistant was tasked with producing Chinese language transcriptions – not translations – of the original audio recordings to allow my co-investigator and a second research assistant to compare the audio with the written text: particularly necessary (and challenging) for colloquial Chinese phrases and passages that may have multiple meanings. Correct meanings were assessed based on the context of the conversation. Despite unavoidable imperfections, the second research assistant would then translate the Chinese language written text to English, and this was again vetted by the senior research assistant and co-investigator. Sending audio recordings to professional translators would not have sufficed, thus I was fortunate to have a team I could trust (see Merriam et al. 2001, p. 415), familiar with criminological theory as well as methodological and epistemological issues related to research in Hong Kong. It was their internal-insider status that helped produce, as accurately as possible, rich and nuanced findings that were neither ideologically nor politically angled. In this phase the ethical stance for me as an external-outsider was to stand apart and trust in my internal-insider research team. Indeed, the significance of having an internal-insider collaborative team for this process cannot be underestimated. Frankly, my external-outsider status was frustrating at times, and I felt rather helpless in my reliance upon my research team.

With the research now complete (e.g. Lee & Adorjan forthcoming), new challenges are emerging when presenting findings at international conferences that capture the ambiguities and complexities of participant voices, particularly in North America or the United Kingdom. Some challenge stems from the need to situate the post-colonial context of Hong Kong, while explicating study design, methods, and key qualitative findings in the short time allocated to speak. Further, largely academic audiences may bring with them pre-conceived notions of the 'global South'. It would be too easy (and unethical) to present a particularly 'pithy' quote sampled from a group highly antagonistic to the police or the government and let this emotionally resonate with hegemonic assumptions regarding Hong Kong or the South East Asian 'periphery'. The dissenting voices must be contextualized within the larger framework of our findings, which tells a story of strong confidence in the Hong Kong Police Force and strong feelings of safety and security living in Hong Kong. Yet audiences digesting international news may, for instance, have received images of the recent 'Yellow Umbrella' protests, which featured news coverage both critical of police actions in their efforts managing protests as well as sympathetic to the position of police in maintaining social order during protest events (see Agence France-Press 2014; McKirdy 2014).

How this project's findings are conveyed in conference talks or international journals matters – not only so participants are 'given a voice' (see Carlen, this volume, p. 61), but also for future research in Hong Kong, and for scholars currently situated in Hong Kong who may desire to follow up on this project in collaboration with the police or other criminal justice practitioners. This cognizance of potential broader impact and affect is a component of what I dub an ethical imagination.

Fostering an ethical imagination during criminological research

Maintaining a reflexive attitude towards research which informs ethical issues as they emerge is invaluable. In the words of Helen Callaway, drawing from anthropology (1992, p. 33, quoted in Hertz 1996, p. 5):

> Often condemned as apolitical, reflexivity, on the contrary can be seen as opening the way to a more radical consciousness of self in facing the political dimensions of fieldwork and constructing knowledge. Other factors intersecting with gender – such as nationality, race, ethnicity, class, and age – also affect the anthropologist's field interactions and textual strategies. Reflexivity becomes a continuing mode of self-analysis and political awareness.

Hertz (1996) leverages Callaway's insightful comment to argue that it is imperative for researchers to locate their selves within power hierarchies of gender, race, class, and citizenship. This introspective process, she argues, leads to greater awareness of all phases of research design and implementation, including what questions are asked and, perhaps more significantly, which are ignored – always in the processes of writing up findings "to produce less distorted accounts of the social world" (p. 5). Yet, too often a rather unsociological vision of the researcher akin to other creative endeavors exists – that of a scholar wrestling with reflexivity and ethical dilemmas by him or herself (cf. Collins 1998; Montuori & Purser 1995). Even where research involves only one primary investigator there are invariably many who contribute advice that becomes incorporated into the methodological design and theoretical framework, on through final published results. Individual research success is socially mediated; this is quickly evident when reviewing acknowledgements to those who helped review sole authored publications, often outside the formal peer review process. In this volume the value of collaborative work between criminologists and criminal justice practitioners (e.g. police) is underscored, highlighting how ethical issues may arise and be addressed more effectively as a collective working towards mutually identified goals. In my own research on 'crime talk' in Hong Kong, while not a collaboration with police, I experienced how invaluable collaborative input is in identifying methodological and ethical challenges in the field – often well outside the anticipations of initial formal ethical review.

Rose (1985, p. 77, quoted in Dwyer & Buckle 2009, p. 55), forcefully writes, "There is no neutrality. There is only greater or less awareness of one's biases. And if you do not appreciate the force of what you're leaving out, you are not fully in command of what you're doing." Qualitative researchers are "uniquely equipped" to break away from the orthodoxy of dichotomies in their research (Dwyer & Buckle 2009, p. 62), which includes discovering the situated standpoints of people's lived experiences (often with all their inherent contradictions and ambiguities). It also requires breaking away from dichotomous readings of researcher positionality as insider or outsider, alongside the often orientalist assumptions of outsider objectivity and superior knowledge. Coming from a post-colonial nation, Canada, to another post-colonial society, Hong Kong, I am not ultimately certain that I was, or am, 'in command' vis-à-vis greater awareness of blind spots and what I am 'leaving out' in my approach to research and writing. It is too easy to suggest that I am simply an outsider who, over the course of my four years in Hong Kong, became bestowed with insider knowledge that has led to the prize of better knowledge; this is rather atomistic and, moreover, teleological. I would like to think I gave it a good shot, and writing this chapter itself has helped me reflect on the dynamic process through which the insider–outsider continua is experienced. Rather than just being an out-sider I felt variously positioned as external-outsider (most strongly while helplessly awaiting translation of group interviews), and internal-outsider (e.g. when disseminating research results). As an internal-outsider, after spending four years in Hong Kong and learning through this project as well as countless micro-experiences and encounters interacting with people, I felt I had a better grasp of local exigencies than many of the publics I presented to at international conferences. Sociologists are, if anything, experts at understanding and illuminating social context. Here, the challenge remained not only the generic one regarding how to convey multifaceted results of qualitative research, but also how to convey results in a way that does not reinforce stereotypes and media discourses as they relate to images of crime and policing in Hong Kong, especially the policing of protests.

My experiences have helped foster what I would dub an ethical imagination. C.W. Mills' (1959) original, inspiring concept examines how the personal troubles experienced by individuals are inextricably related to public issues. This sociological insight can be applied beyond the analysis of social problems, to include here eth-ical dilemmas faced by the individual. My insider–outsider positionality was based on constantly morphing projections from research participants, which generated the need to shift how I presented myself to various groups. Ethical concerns were thus simultaneously relatively generic, like those often encountered by qualitative researchers in the field, yet took on particular 'glocal' flavours (cf. Bauman 1998) based on the specific standpoints of the research team and participants – and later publics during dissemination events.

Unanticipated ethical issues were raised when certain groups, either politically affiliated or affected by their contact with police, would discuss policing in Hong Kong in more broadly antagonistic terms. Ethical issues familiar to qualitative researchers emerged from these groups; yet does that suggest they are 'tainted' samples that should not be included? I felt it important to include their voices among others who were either more overtly positive about the police or had mixed views (e.g. positive regarding police ability to fight crime yet variously sympathetic to assessments of the policing of public order events). Additional challenges were tied to the presentation of research findings where my status as an external-outsider or internal-outsider shifted to an external-insider as I did so. Presenting hermeneutically attuned qualitative data is always difficult under the usual time constraints, though situating findings from Hong Kong brings specific challenges. For instance, some audience members, no doubt influenced by media coverage, hold preconceptions regarding the crime situation in Hong Kong and/or the Hong Kong Police Force.

An ethical imagination regarding the various consequences of how research findings are presented and written up is explicitly attuned to the broad reception of findings and how they may impact future participants, researchers, and collaborations with criminal justice organizations. If I chose not to approach this project collaboratively I may not have become sensitized to the complex ways in which Hong Kong citizens experience crime and crime control. My findings may well have offered conclusions conveniently in line with media depictions unsympathetic to the police. Such findings, presented internationally and published in international journals, may have acted to undercut future access among criminologists based in Hong Kong to collaborations with the police – albeit unintentionally. I do not mean to suggest that a researcher with an active ethical imagination and reflexive approach to research is able to anticipate all potential contingencies and unintended consequences. The ethical imagination instills, most broadly, a wide empathy for those we conduct research with, and for.

Acknowledgements

The research project discussed in this chapter, 'Fear of crime and trust in crime control in Hong Kong' (January 2012–December 2014), was funded by the Research Grants Council of Hong Kong under HKU 740211H. I wish to thank my co-investigator, Maggy Lee, and Ms. Garlum Lau and the research assistants for their invaluable collaboration and work on this project. Deep thank you also to Maggy Lee, Alistair Fraser, and Rose Ricciardelli for their prescient and rapid comments on earlier versions of this chapter. I am solely responsible for any errors and omissions that remain.

Notes

1 One *Apple Daily* journalist, interviewed for a dissertation research project, was asked whether *Apple Daily* has any particular political stance. His response: "Not to flatter the Communist Party of China may be regarded as our stance" (Chan 2002, p. 235).
2 The problem of cubicle homes is an ongoing problem reflecting the widening gap between rich and poor in Hong Kong. See Ngo, 10 March 2014: www.scmp.com/news/hong-kong/article/1444585/plight-hong-kongs-cage-home-dwellers-worse-now-25-years-ago.

References

Aas, K 2012, '"The Earth is one but the world is not": Criminological theory and its geopolitical divisions', *Theoretical Criminology*, vol. 16, no. 1, pp. 5–20.

Adorjan, M 2009, 'Discord and ambiguity within youth crime and justice debates', Doctor of Philosophy thesis, McMaster University, Hamilton.

Adorjan, M 2011a, 'Emotions contests and reflexivity in the news: Examining discourse on youth crime in Canada', *Journal of Contemporary Ethnography*, vol. 40, no. 2, pp. 168–198.

Adorjan, M 2011b, 'The lens of victim contests and youth crime stat wars', *Symbolic Interaction*, vol. 34, no. 4, pp. 552–573.

Adorjan, M 2013, 'Igniting constructionist imaginations: Social constructionism's absence and potential contribution to public sociology', *American Sociologist*, vol. 44, no. 1, pp. 1–22.

Agence France-Press 2014, 'Hong Kong protests: A "blue ribbon" backlash in support of city's police force', *Straits Times*, 4 October. www.straitstimes.com/news/asia/east-asia/story/hong-kong-protests-blue-ribbon-backlash-support-citys-police-force-2014100.

Banks, J. A 1998 'The lives and values of researchers: Implications for educating citizens in a multicultural society. *Educational Researcher*, vol. 27, pp. 4–17.

Bauman, Z 1998, 'On globalization: Or globalization for some, localization for others', *Thesis Eleven*, vol. 54, no. 1, pp. 37–49.

Bhambra, GK 2007, *Rethinking Modernity: Postcolonialism and the Sociological Imagination*, Basingstoke, Palgrave Macmillan.

Bond, MH & Hwang, K 1986, 'The social psychology of Chinese People', in *The Psychology of the Chinese people*, ed MH Bond, New York, Oxford University Press, pp. 213–266.

Cain, M 2000, 'Orientalism, occidentalism and the sociology of crime', *British Journal of Criminology*, vol. 40, no. 2, pp. 239–260.

Chan, HJ 2002, 'Making news: A cultural study of the text, production and political implication of *Apple Daily* and *Ming Pao*', Master of Philosophy thesis, University of Hong Kong, Hong Kong.

Chen, K 2010, *Asia as Method: Toward Deimperialization*, London, Duke University Press.

Collins, R 1998, *The Sociology of Philosophies: A global theory of intellectual change*, Cambridge, Belknap Press of Harvard University Press.

Dwyer, S & Buckle, J 2009, 'The space between: On being an insider-outsider in qualitative research', *International Journal of Qualitative Methods*, vol. 8, no. 1, pp. 54–63.

Fraser, A 2013, 'Ethnography at the periphery: Redrawing the borders of criminology's world-map', *Theoretical Criminology*, vol. 17, no. 2, pp. 251–260.

Gubrium, J & Holstein, J 2011, '"Don't argue with the members"', *American Sociologist*, vol. 43, no. 1, pp. 85–98.

Hallahan, M, Lee, F, & Herzog, T 1997, 'It is not just whether you win or lose, it's also how you play the game: A naturalistic, cross-cultural examination of the positivity bias', *Journal of Cross-Cultural Psychology*, vol. 28, no. 6, pp. 768–778.

Hellawell, D 2006, 'Inside-out: Analysis of the insider–outsider concept as a heuristic device to develop reflexivity in students doing qualitative research', *Teaching in Higher Education*, vol. 11, no. 4, pp. 483–494.

Hertz, R 1996, 'Introduction: Ethics, reflexivity and voice', *Qualitative Sociology*, vol. 19, no. 1, pp. 3–9.

Lee, M & Adorjan, M Forthcoming, 'Fear of crime', in *Understanding Criminal Justice in Hong Kong* (2nd ed), eds WH Chui & TW Lo, London, Willan.

Madriz, E 1997, *Nothing Bad Happens to Good Girls: Fear of Crime in Women's Lives*, Berkeley, University of California Press.

Madriz, E 2000, 'Focus groups in feminist research', in *Handbook of Qualitative Research* (2nd ed), eds N Denzin & Y Lincoln, Thousand Oaks, CA, Sage, pp. 835–850.

McKirdy, E 2014, 'The end of trust? Hong Kong sees police force in a new light', *CNN*, 16 October. http://edition.cnn.com/2014/10/07/world/asia/hong-kong-police-public-trust/.

McLennan, G 2003, 'Sociology, Eurocentrism and postcolonial theory', *European Journal of Social Theory*, vol. 6, no. 1, pp. 69–86.

Merriam, S, Johnson-Bailey, J, Lee, M, Kee, Y, Ntseane, G, & Muhamad, M 2001, 'Power and positionality: Negotiating insider/outsider status within and across cultures', *International Journal of Lifelong Education*, vol. 20, no. 5, pp. 405–416.

Merton, R 1972, 'Insiders and outsiders: A chapter in the sociology of knowledge', *American Journal of Sociology*, vol. 78, no. 1, pp. 9–47.

Mills, CW 1959, *The Sociological Imagination*, Harmondsworth, Penguin.

Montuori, A & Purser, R 1995, 'Deconstructing the lone genius myth: Toward a contextual view of creativity', *Journal of Humanistic Psychology*, vol. 35, no. 3, pp. 69–112.

Morgan, D 1997, *Focus Groups as Qualitative Research* (2nd ed), Thousand Oaks, CA, Sage.

Naples, N 1996, 'A feminist revisiting of the insider/outsider debate: The "outsider phenomenon" in rural Iowa', *Qualitative Sociology*, vol. 19, no. 1, pp. 83–106.

Said, E 1994 [1978], *Orientalism*, New York, Vintage Books.

Schutz, A 1976, *The Stranger: Collected Papers II*, The Hague, Netherlands, Springer.

Scoggins, S 2014, 'Navigating fieldwork as an outsider: Observations from interviewing police officers in China', *PS: Political Science & Politics*, vol. 47, no. 2, pp. 394–397.

Sheptycki, J 2008, 'Transnationalisation, orientalism and crime', *Asian Journal of Criminology*, vol. 3, no. 1, pp. 13–35.

Spector, M & Kitsuse, J 1977, *Constructing Social Problems*, Menlo Park, CA, Cummings Publishing Company.

Stewart, D, Shamdasani, P, & Rook, D 2007, *Focus Groups: Theory and Practice* (2nd ed), London, Sage.

Twinn, S 1998, 'An analysis of the effectiveness of focus groups as a method of qualitative data collection with Chinese populations in nursing research', *Journal of Advanced Nursing*, vol. 28, no. 3, pp. 654–661.

Zeitlin, I 2001, *Ideology and the Development of Sociological Theory* (7th ed), Upper Saddle River, NJ, Prentice Hall.

3

ETHICS, POLITICS AND THE LIMITS OF KNOWLEDGE

Pat Carlen

> *Humour and anger are always the most important ingredients for a good piece of academic work. ... Methodology is rather over-rated in present-day criminology.* (Jock Young, cited in Van Swaaningen 2014)

I began my academic career by doing a PhD without ever putting forward a formal proposal. When I graduated in the early 1970s, funding for a PhD was forthcoming from the national research council via the University of London and after about three months of reading social theory, jurisprudence, industrial sociology and criminology I decided that studying the proceedings in some London magistrates' courts would allow me to pursue my ongoing interest in all four subjects. Accordingly, I sat in the public gallery of one or other of the magistrates' courts every day for over a year. Occasionally, I attended a postgraduate seminar at the university; whenever I wrote anything my supervisor read and commented on it; and I had some very stimulating friends among the other graduate students. Gradually, I negotiated informal permission to conduct taped interviews with magistrates, probation officers, police officers, solicitors, social workers and, sometimes, defendants. When the court was not sitting, I hung around. None of us graduates discussed ethics, though social theory and politics were high on the agenda.

I was also reading an immense amount of general sociology, including qualitative social research methods books. From the latter I learned how I was supposed to be conducting the project. I seemed to be failing on every front. Formal research access was lacking. I had approached the relevant government department in London, but it had not replied, and this was not surprising given the vagueness of my request. The project's ethical dimensions had never been discussed with anyone and there was no institutional requirement to have the research vetted by an ethics committee. As a result of what I had learned about conventional sociological research practice during my undergraduate methods course, I had assured all interviewees that what they told me would be kept confidential and that any quotations from them would be published anonymously. But at no point had any of the interviewees been told the purpose of the research – how could they have been? I did not know myself – except that I was 'trying to find out what happens in the magistrates' courts'. Nor had I explained to them how I would use the tape recordings of our conversations. A recording schedule had not been designed for the interviews; instead, an ever-changing list of questions was jotted down before each new interview. And, although I had been advised that it was customary to do a 'literature review' at the commencement of study for a doctorate, I had not managed even to plan one because I could not decide how to make any sense at all of what I was observing in the courts. I had read Glaser and Strauss' (1967) *The Discovery of Grounded Theory*; the problem for me was that 'the grounds' that attracted my interest seemed to be continually shifting. Which literature was I supposed to be reviewing? (Later, I did pen a brief discussion of varieties of rule-usage, drawing mainly on the works of philosophers such as Searle (1971) and Rawls (1955) – but not until I had decided that that was what 'magistrates' justice' (Carlen 1976; 2009, pp. 45–61) was going to be about.) My note-taking in court was as rudimentary as the rest of my 'methodology'.

The only 'ethical' thoughts in my head in those early days of court-watching were first and foremost the feeling that I was fraudulently going through the motions of 'doing a PhD'; second, that I would try to ensure that nobody was harmed either by my conduct of the project or by any resultant publications; and, third, that having received a publicly-funded grant, I would try to earn it by quickly submitting a thesis and then getting it published as soon as possible. I have at least held to those last two principles ever since (though whether with the intended effect I cannot know). Gradually, however, the daily parade of inequality and poverty which I was witnessing in and around Central London's lower courts ignited within me an anger which fuelled not only the courts research, but all my social investigation for the next 40 years. It was not a textbook introduction to social inquiry. Nor was it one that I would particularly recommend. But I learned a lot; and by the time I had finished the courts project, my rather minimalist approach to research methods and ethics had been forever supplemented by a passion for the politics of social knowledge and social research. From then on I found it difficult to separate ethics from epistemology and to separate both from politics. As a result, even now, when I have not been doing any field research for several years, I find it problematic whenever I attempt to categorise research issues, to map the boundaries between ethics and power, between ethics and knowledge and between ethics and politics. And I still feel confused by my own continuing confusion about how best to respond as a sociologist ethically, theoretically and emotionally to social situations constituted by disparate cultural knowledges; to identities shaped by different experiences of class, race and gender; and to discourses imbued with diverse (and often alien) ideologies, objectives and imagery.

The remainder of this chapter is divided into five sections, the first four of which each addresses a differently shaped context within which ethical principles can be very differently defined and have variable saliency according to the differentially interlocking interests, politics and human emotions situationally involved. The actual research dilemmas described have all been selected to illustrate the argument put forward in the fifth and concluding section: that, save for some few over-arching minimalist ethical principles – such as 'do no harm' – the spirit of which are usually incorporated into professional ethical codes, it is impossible to tease out in advance a hierarchy of ethical and other principles which ought to be, might be or will be situationally operative during the conduct of qualitative empirical research. For qualitative social research involving deconstruction and reconstruction of social meanings via interviews, participant observation and ethnography is necessarily undertaken by human research tools, the ethical propriety of whose research behaviour and subsequent theoretical analyses is likely to be as much empowered and limited by their interests, emotions, politics and theoretical prowess as by their ethical principles. This being the case, it is concluded that institutional ethics committees should be confined to playing advisory and watchdog roles in the assessment of the ethical dimensions of research project proposals. They should advise researchers where they feel that the proposed research methods blatantly breach a professional ethics code; and they should require authors of texts ready for publication to give undertakings that their reports, articles or books do not knowingly contain anything that is likely to harm research respondents or subjects. For this is social, not medical, research. Loss of life or limb is not usually at stake. What is most at stake is the reputation and confidentiality of people who have trustingly unburdened themselves to a researcher. And in my experience, the main concerns of respondents are that they will not be identified or identifiable in any published work (though some insist that they want to be named!); and that the researcher will always protect their anonymity and never reveal to anyone anything that she knows about them solely as a result of their participation in the project. A researcher respecting these respondent concerns is unlikely to do much harm to any research participant. And even though in participant observation research the risk of harm via emotional entanglements between researcher and research participants is much higher than in other types of research, it is equally unamenable to governance either in advance or at a distance by bureaucratic ethics committees (see Clarke et al. 2015 for a detailed discussion about emotions in research).

Other ethical issues, those, for instance, relating not to human subjects but to the integrity of the data interpretation and analyses, are much more difficult to define and disentangle as some of the illustrative research examples constituting the bulk of this chapter suggest. Given the situated interrelationships between power, knowledge and politics, however, the main conclusion is that it is impossible for ethics committees to micro-manage research processes in advance of the unpredictable outcomes of situated research relationships and negotiated meanings. When they do so attempt, it is usually not on ethical grounds but to avoid some (probably imaginary) reputational or financial risk to the researcher's university.

Ethics and power: competing definitions of research ethics

This section seeks to illustrate this chapter's fundamental argument: that operative research principles cannot be legislated for in advance, nor according to any codes or conventions. Operative definitions of research ethics are often shaped as much by the pragmatism of the powerful as by the morality of the researcher.

The term 'professional ethics' when applied to social research refers to rules of behaviour to be followed by researchers. The formal reference point, in many countries, has traditionally, and until relatively recently, been the ethical code of a researcher's professional association. Social science professional associations lay down ethical codes about the rights and protections of research subjects and the protocols for data collection and interpretation (American Sociological Association 1999; British Society of Criminology 2006). Primarily governing the formal relations between researcher and researched, researcher and research team and researcher and funder, the codes tend to be couched in highly generalisable language and at first sight appear easy to interpret; for example, the meaning of an injunction to promise protection of a research subject's anonymity is usually considered to be straightforward (even if the researcher, nonetheless, later decides that circumstances have developed in which breaking the promised anonymity is justified by a higher moral obligation, or some respondents insist that they want their names to be published). It is also usually taken for granted that all academic social research practitioners will be bound by law, common conventions of trustworthiness and truth-telling and professional commitments to disinterested (i.e. non-self-seeking) knowledge production. Beyond that, social researchers are also informally bound to observe acceptable forms of social interaction, such as common politeness and consideration towards others. If they fail to do so they will not get very far in their investigations. Most researchers do not find it difficult to keep their word to interviewees or other research subjects concerning confidentiality and anonymity, though exceptions to the rule are known to have occurred when professional malpractice or serious criminal activity have been either observed or detected; or when researchers are obliged to disclose either their sources or knowledge to a higher authority such as a court of law.

Prior to the advent of local university ethics committees, it was assumed that when issues of interpretation arose in a particular research situation researchers would resolve them by application of the spirit of their professional association's ethics code to the situation as they understood it and according to their specific research expertise and local knowledge. Where the issue proved to be too complex to be resolved by the researcher alone, he/she was expected to go back to the professional association and seek further advice. Numerous textbooks also addressed the complex relationship problems likely to arise between researchers and researched, within the research team and between research team and funding body. The implicit understanding was that the professional nourishing of an ethical research culture would be sufficient either to prevent or to minimise any harm to the research participants or any damage to the funding organisation. The reality was usually somewhat different,

especially for social researchers engaged in qualitative research where the relationships between researcher and researched are frequently not formalised (and, indeed,
are not capable of formalisation) at the beginning of the research and thereafter may
change more than once, and in a variety of ways. William Foote Whyte was one of
the first to confess in the appendix to the second edition of *Street Corner Society* how
one of his informants became unsettled for life as a result of being involved as a key
informant in Whyte's (1943) research into a Chicago street gang.

Examples of the complexity of developing research relationships have, nonetheless, usually only been discussed in terms of researchers' responsibility for the
well-being of their research subjects, their research team and the integrity of interpretation of the findings according to a professionally approved and declared methodology and a professional (or, nowadays, institutional) ethics code. This is not surprising. Ethics are not universals, professional codes cover only the most general and
obvious of ethical dilemmas in research and, with the public funding and marketisation of university research, academics in the UK and elsewhere have long since
lost formal control over the ethical organisation of their research, either in terms of
how research subjects are treated or in terms of how results are interpreted (Carlen
& Phoenix forthcoming). Nowadays it is usually a university ethics committee that
has the final say as to whether or not a research proposal is ethically acceptable. Yet,
ultimately, individuals (including individual researchers) are expected to make their
own ethical decisions; or, are forced to make them whenever they come up against
situations not covered by known and approved principles of ethical research. It is
time therefore that more thought be given to the question of whose ethics or whose
definitions of ethics are actually paramount in research assessments and processes.
Take the following example of how one funder and one researcher differed over the
definition of ethics.

About 25 years ago, I made an application to a public research funding body
for money to finance a project investigating (amongst other things) the experiences of poverty suffered by women who were serving, or who had recently
served, a prison sentence (Carlen 1988). In the section on the application form
enquiring about ethical issues that might arise from the research, I argued that
it would be unethical to interview poverty-stricken women for two hours (at
least) without making them proper financial remuneration. I acknowledged that
some people might argue that paying ex-prisoners was in fact unethical, insofar
as it could be seen as rewarding people for crime. Against that possible argument, I contended that unemployed ex-prisoners contributing to the research
should be seen as doing work and paid for their time just as other workers are
and that they should not be denied the opportunity to earn a legitimate fee;
after all, the professional criminal justice workers who participated in the same
research were all to be interviewed during working hours with permission of
their employers and without loss of pay. In the financial costing of the research,
therefore, I applied for funding to pay the interviewees £10.00 per hour, i.e. a
maximum of £20.00 per interview. I made the application under the section on

the grant form headed 'ethical issues'. The full research grant, including the fees for interviewees, was awarded without comment. Fourteen years later I made a similar application to the same grant-awarding organisation for a project again involving interviews with women ex-prisoners and, as previously, a case for paying the women was made under the heading 'ethical issues'. The result was very different. Again, the research proposal was successful in obtaining overall funding for the project, but money to pay the ex-prisoners was withheld. I had made the same supporting argument as in the previous application but this time the case had been rejected as not being an ethical issue. As the amount of money involved was relatively small and as I had other funds which I was able to disburse for research purposes as I pleased, I did not initially challenge the decision. However, something occurred which led me to change my mind.

Three weeks after I had learned that money for paying the respondents was not to be forthcoming, I was dining with a colleague who was doing research funded by the same public body. He was interviewing corporate criminals and described how he interviewed them over meals in good restaurants and then sent them home by taxi. 'That must be expensive,' I said. 'Where do you get the money to do that?' 'It's part of the grant,' he replied. 'It's the only way I could get them to talk. It's what they're used to. They wouldn't spend an evening talking to me without some inducement.' Next day I telephoned the contact officer at the grant-awarding body, and asked how come the funder would pay for interviews with corporate criminals but not with ex-prisoners. Having consulted and compared the two research applications, he called me back with the following explanation:

> You applied for the interview money under the wrong heading. The Committee didn't consider payment of interviewees to be an ethical issue, but a methodological issue. Your colleague argued his case on methodological grounds; that his proposed informants would not consent to be interviewed without reward. He was, therefore, awarded money to entertain them at an appropriate level. If you had applied for payment for interviewees on the methodological grounds that they would not consent to be interviewed without payment you would most probably have been more successful.

But, in fact, it would not have been ethical for me to argue for the interviewee fees on methodological grounds because, as a result of my experience and knowledge of the interviewees, I also knew that they would do the interviews for nothing. So! On that occasion researcher and funding bureaucrats had a difference of opinion over ethics. And, maybe, it is not surprising that the funder's definition should win out over the researcher's – the stereotypical example of 'he who pays the piper calls the tune' – as the old adage says. Be that as it may, since that time, about 11 years ago, questions of ethics in social research have become much more complex and this change has coincided with the increasing marketisation of university research.

Ethics and the marketisation of research

In this section it is argued that the increasing marketisation of university research raises questions about the ethical propriety of designing criminology research projects more to meet market demand and/or to promote a university's corporate image than to engage in the fundamental theoretical research essential to a discipline's vitality.

Universities have always encouraged their researchers to gain research funding via patronage, the sale of their products and by entering bidding competitions. They have also traditionally provided a space where theoretical innovation can be experimented with and imaginative 'hunches' pursued. In recent years, however, a number of countries have introduced assessment exercises for universities with grading criteria which inhibit researchers from developing small-scale, ethnographic or library-based theoretical research projects (see Wacquant 2002). For these last-mentioned types of research neither demand large-scale financial backing nor are they likely, in the short-term, to have immediate, quantifiable results (Brown, with Carasso 2013; Mathiesen 2013; Nussbaum 2010). As a result, university managers are unimpressed by research which first of all fails in pure market terms by not adding significantly to university coffers; and then, second, also fails to enhance a university's corporate image by easily quantifiable results attracting high media exposure. These market considerations now raise ethical questions for researchers at every stage of the research. They can affect: the choice of topic and method; the claims that are made in funding applications; the 'permissible' findings' (see Hope 2004); the decision as to where and when to publish; and the decision of university, school or departmental ethics committees as to the authorisation (or not) of a research proposal (Winlow & Hall 2013).

The fundamental ethical issue in all the instances described above is that, under most codes of ethics, criminologists are enjoined (in the words of the British Society of Criminology 2006) "to identify and seek to ameliorate factors which restrict the development of their professional competence and integrity". Under marketisation, the ethical issue then arises because there is an essential conflict between a professional ethic ostensibly committed to disinterestedness in pursuit of new knowledge and a market ethic committed to making as much money from its research product as possible. And even if professional ethic and market ethic can co-exist in parallel (though sometimes culturally opposed) worlds, ethical issues can still arise for individual researchers as they prioritise different ethical principles: for instance, should they risk their jobs (and their families' financial security) by sticking their heads above the parapets and refusing to bid for money from unethical corporations, or to investigate crime issues in projects obviously designed to provide 'policy-led' evidence? Should senior academics advise early-career researchers to choose their research solely according to a topic's capacity to contribute new knowledge in the research area? Or should they advise them to focus on 'bringing in' to the university as much external research funding as they can – regardless of any reservations they might have about the research topic or the scientific importance of the problem to be investigated or the integrity of the methods to be used? Giving the latter advice would certainly be in contradiction of a professional code of ethics, but the former advice, if followed in such a way that it led to a refusal to bid for applied research funding, might jeopardise a younger colleague's promotion prospects. However, the issue might well then be resolved by recipients of conflicting advice of this kind invoking a totally different and personal ethical principle: that their prime ethical obligation is to the institution that pays them and that therefore they should act according to their institution's research agenda rather than their own. Of course, and as we have already seen, once researchers begin negotiating with outside bodies about research funding they may find that the ethical principles of the funding body are operating with an altogether different logic again – to a bureaucratic pragmatism which, while allowing the disbursement of funds to appear logical, economically sound and judiciously consistent, in fact encourages violation of researchers' own ethical principles as shaped by their professional culture and ethical code. Once researchers are forced by context, market and pragmatism to abandon the professional ethical code and engage in a situational ethics, they soon find that ethical choices are both discursively limitless and situationally limited. They are limitless because there is always an alternative hierarchy of principles according to which they can attempt justification of their decisions (to themselves and/or to others); they are limited because researchers are usually located within a set of power relations over which they have little control.

Ethics and knowledge: competence and researcher/ respondent limitations

This section seeks to illustrate the argument that unstructured qualitative social research and analysis is limited by the varying competences of both researcher and respondent in recalling, defining and analysing information. Recall, definitions and analysis are existentially honed by the researcher's and respondent's self-identities, emotions and politics. Accordingly, researchers and respondents alike prioritise some types of knowledge over others and then are variously competent in their abilities to order and interpret it. One ethical issue for researchers relates to the degree to which they can enable respondents to give informed consent to the uses to which interview (and other) data will be put.

> Methodologically, researchers often hold one aspect (*either* race or gender) constant, so that their comparisons are more manageable. However, intersectionality research requires more than simply performing separate analyses by race and gender and using traditional theories to interpret the results. (Simien 2007, p. 271, emphasis in original)
>
> Not surprisingly, all of the women asked me what I intended to do with the taped interviews. … In reassuring them that all quotations … would be made pseudonymously, I was also able to explain that no individual oral history would be used in full … I would be trying to ascertain what each individual's career had in common with the 38 others … and attempt to describe and explain the

> variety of effects these shared social factors had had on their criminal careers. A majority of the women seemed very interested in how I was going to make sense of their stories, though Muriel (unknowingly) spoke for many of them when she said, I did things for different reasons … I mean at different times when I look back I come up with a different thing each time. It all contradicts itself … It depends what sort of mood I'm in. (Carlen 1988, p. 176)

In 1986 and 1987 I interviewed 39 women about their criminal careers. Using a version of control theory as the theoretical perspective framing both our discussions and their analysis I was especially interested in trying to locate the moments when the women had felt that they had 'absolutely nothing to lose (and maybe something to gain) by engaging in criminal activity' (ibid, p. 11). As it happened, ten of the women interviewed in prison had either one or two ethnic minority British parents. Although, as a sociologist, I was very aware of the complex interrelationships between class, gender and ethnicity in identity formation and life chances, I believed then (and I think I still believe now, Simien 2007, quoted above, not withstanding) that it is impossible to locate the phenomenological relationships between all three in order to go on to explain systemicities of experience between people sharing some social structural and cultural components (such as class, gender, ethnicity), but in the different combination that renders each unique (Carlen 1988, p. 72). When I came to analyse the transcripts, therefore, I decided that as the common factor for all the women was gender, and as they were all in poverty, I would inform the analysis by two concepts only: class and gender. However, as all of the black women also mentioned that they had experienced racism in one form or another I tried to accommodate that in the analysis as well. I told all the interviewees I would only be using their words selectively to illustrate an argument I expected to make about how poor women were especially vulnerable to crime, criminalisation and imprisonment (though I did not use those words).

I do not think that subsequently there was any significant departure from the declared logic of analysis that is summarised in the second quotation introducing this section (p. 176). I chose quotations to illustrate the women's experiences as they chose to describe and interpret them … except when it came to considering the black women's comments on black men. It was not because they said their partners were extremely violent that I had a problem – white women said the same – and I knew from other sources that both black and white women in the UK experience levels of domestic violence far greater than are ever reported and/or prosecuted. The problem for me came when black women argued that black men in general treated their women worse than white men treated theirs. They argued that it was part of their culture, and, again, I had also heard that from other sources. According to my analytic principles, if several women perceived something to be the case I had to explain it. But, although I noted the black women's opinion that black men are more violent towards women than are white men, I did not know how to deal with it and omitted any reference to such views. I feared that if I repeated comments that made comparisons between white men and black men that favoured white men I would be accused of racism against black men. Choosing to leave out such comments, therefore, was a 'save my own skin' decision, and not related to any questions of ethics or theory at all. I was aware of the possible ethical issues but, when choosing what to write, I pushed questions of ethics to the back of my mind. So, for nearly 30 years I have been unable to decide whether this was a failure of ethics or theory. I have now decided it was a failure of ethics, not because I lacked the knowledge to explain the women's perceptions and therefore left out reference to them – I had given no undertaking to give an intersectional analysis and would have felt perfectly justified in leaving out questions of ethnicity on the grounds that I was giving a class and gender analysis only. Nor did I feel that I had any duty to 'give the women a voice' (see Carlen 1992); each of the women I have ever interviewed has been perfectly capable of speaking for herself. No. The reason my analytic decision was unethical was because it was not based on any theoretical perspective or methodological or ethical principle at all – I just decided, 'I do not want to go there'. It was also a decision based upon an appraisal of the politics of my immediate research situation (as discussed in the next section of this chapter).

Yet even without the specific situational complication of intersectional analysis (of which I was acutely aware at the times of interview and analysis), how much trouble did I really take (or could any qualitative theoretical researcher effectively have taken) to get the women's informed consent as to how their interviews would be used? This is one difference between social and medical research. When patients are about to undergo medical procedures physicians can at least provide the best information they have about the nature and likely outcomes of treatment. But until I read and reread the interview transcripts I did not even know myself exactly what themes the book would ultimately be addressing. How many of the women I interviewed would have consented to their comments being in a book that had a scurrilous photo of Margaret Thatcher on the cover? The problem was the old one of neither the respondents nor I knowing what we did not know and not knowing what each other did not know either (see Lyman & Scott 1970)! Ultimately, the stories and the Story that was told in *Women, Crime and Poverty* (Carlen 1988) were a product of selection by the women and me; and we did it according to our diverse and different memories and our diverse and different competences in selecting the narrative elements conducive to realising the different stories we – each and all of us! – wanted to tell. I was conscious at the time of having a duty to make the theoretical perspectives informing the analyses as explicit as I could. And at the same time I was also committed to retelling the women's own understandings of their narratives – even if I made it clear that my own understanding was different. But all the time, I was also aware that ultimately the stories would be shaped by my own theoretical competence; and, in the instance described above, a desire to avoid controversy about an ideological issue I felt unable to handle. I make no apology for the theoretical commitment; nor for a political commitment to exposing the relationships between poverty, gender and crime. But I was uneasy then, and think it wrong now, that I omitted to address what was an important issue for some of the women, and that I knowingly did so to suit my own convenience.

Ethics and politics: whose ethics? whose politics?

By discussing two examples of researcher decision making, this section tries to illustrate the argument that researchers are constantly confronted with issues of political strategy, resolution of which may or may not be informed or straightforwardly resolved by application of ethical principles. In the first example the author explains how she came to prioritise personal convenience over ethical principle. The second illustration considers an example, taken from recently published research, where, although the researcher gave first priority to honouring the anonymity principle promised in the access agreement, this decision was subsequently challenged as not being in the best interests of the research subjects.

At the time when I was involved in interviewing for the 39 women in crime and poverty project, I was also very much involved in working with the UK Women in Prison (WIP) campaigning group for the abolition of women's imprisonment. As a result, I was constantly in discussions with other campaigning groups and one was a black ex-prisoner group which was very much against white women doing research involving ethnic minority women. Many of the women being interviewed for the current project had been interviewed by me on previous occasions. And because I had also been working and campaigning with them, we already knew each other well. But I still needed to interview some women in prison and, as there were disproportionate numbers of ethnic minority women in prison, ten of the women I interviewed in prison were from ethnic minorities. I was pleased that they were properly represented in the project and spent some time arguing with some of my campaigning colleagues about the rights and wrongs of including ethnic minority women in a project that was not designed to do a three-pronged (intersectional) analysis involving race as well as class and gender, and which would involve black women being interviewed by a white woman. I realised that the situation was not ideal but justified it to myself and others with the argument that the project was about women, poverty and criminalisation; a substantial number of ethnic minority women were in prison and in poverty and therefore it would be discriminatory to leave them out of the sample. I knew of course that my life experience had been very different to theirs but thought that, as a woman who had come from a very poor home myself, I could empathise on at least two dimensions of experience. And so it seemed in the interviews – we appeared to get on well and to chat with a mutual understanding of the issues we were discussing. But when it came to analysing the transcripts, I realised that references to their identities as black or other ethnic minority women framed much of the respondents' talk about their experiences in the criminal justice system and their histories of domestic violence. The former I could incorporate into the analyses; the latter, because they involved what I saw as the perpetration of an image of black men which fed into a currently widespread white stereotyping of all black men as violent, I did not know how to deal with. I guessed that however I dealt with the subject of black male violence against women, I would be subject to a lot of hassle that would detract from the book's main purpose – explicating the relationships between gender, poverty and criminalisation. So I left it out. It was one absence amongst many in the text, but it was one of which I was very much aware at the time and about which, since that time, I sometimes feel guilty and sometimes still feel I can justify by reference to the chosen theoretical strategy of restricting analysis to the relationships between gender, poverty and criminalisation.

The second example is taken from Jill McCorkel's (2013) *Breaking Women: Women, Race and the New Politics of Imprisonment*, which tells of an ethnographic study of East State Women's Correctional Institution (a pseudonym) where the focus is on an anti-drugs programme, pseudonymised in the book as Project Habilitate Women (hereafter PHW). The tale told of PHW is a saga of verbal abuse, disrespect, mental torture and the attempted brainwashing of poor black women. Not surprising, then, that one reaction to such a report is to want to know the real name of the company responsible for so cruel a regime. Indeed, in reviewing the book, Meda Chesney-Lind (2014), for instance, argued that. although McCorkel defends her use of pseudonyms, 'this … protects the corporate entity whose troubling behaviour she documents … it seems important that one names names' (p. 128). I disagree. Although I can think of situations where, in the interests of justice, a researcher might feel ethically obliged to break her confidentiality or anonymity agreements, I cannot see what would have been gained in this case. It is unlikely that McCorkel's naming of 'the Company' would have had any effect other than making it more difficult for future researchers to gain access to prisons to do this type of research (Carlen 2014, pp. 32–35).

Here, we have several ethical principles at war with each other. Whereas Chesney-Lind's stance is based upon the ethical principle that institutional cruelty should be exposed, stopped and the perpetrators brought to account (a whole lot of assumptions about the likely effects of exposure of corporate wrongdoing there!), McCorkel's decision is based upon an ethical commitment to honouring her promise of anonymity to the corporation that allowed her access to the prison. But the authorial justification for the decision is also tempered by a pragmatism, which I share: that once researchers begin to renege on their promises of anonymity to research gatekeepers, they can say goodbye to any hopes of access, either for themselves or others, in the future. Nonetheless, the clinching rationales for decisions like this are not transferable trans-situationally, and ongoing questions of how to rank competing ethical and political principles are integral to qualitative social research. That is why one specific feature of university research marketisation, the ethics committee, is such an inappropriate tool for the governance of research ethics. Critics of ethics committees frequently make the point that neither the application of a medical model of ethics nor the invocation of an insurance risk model is wholly appropriate to social research. But … the criteria being applied may be based neither on a medical model of ethics nor on a second guessing of insurance risk. As universities move more and more towards competing solely as businesses, some of their personnel appear to embrace the business ethos at the same time as losing all sight of what type of business they are supposed to be in. Engaging in the micro-management of ethical research practice and lacking experience of both business and empirical social research, academics-turned-managers too often base their ethics committee decisions on a multiple lay ignorance: of the varied contexts of field research; of how insurance risk is actually computed; and of what medical ethics involve (for a more benign and conciliatory view of ethics committees, see Israel & Hay 2012).

Conclusion

When I began my PhD in 1971, I truly believed that I would always adhere to the moral principle, 'Do no harm to anyone involved in a research project.' I subsequently tried to act in ways calculated to fulfil that intention. But, although researchers may know about certain instances of harm, they can never know for certain whether the conduct of their research project ever caused harm or not. For instance, I knowingly witnessed illegal or dangerous behaviour on several occasions; did I therefore collude in it? Did such collusion encourage the deviant behaviour that was resulting in the frequent imprisonment of some of my respondents?

Should I have complained when I saw some prison staff verbally tormenting or abusing women prisoners? I did not complain – and I rationalised my silence on the grounds that I was also interviewing prison staff and should treat all interview respondents equally. But maybe I should have prioritised another principle – that of defending the powerless against the powerful – over the research principle of treating all respondents equally. The research access would have been terminated there and then, of course – or would it? I did not take the risk and I did not find out. In terms of Howard Becker's question, 'Whose side are we on?' it seems that, like other researchers who prioritise the long-term completion of a research project over a short-term situational dilemma, I was on my own side (Becker 1967; Gouldner 1968).

So, back to the decades-old debate between Howard Becker (1967) and Alvin Gouldner (1968), Whose side are we on? and the sad reflection that, for most of the time, I was on my own side. There are, however, exemplary instances of academics who have returned a research grant rather than risk the integrity of the proposed project by acquiescing in unpalatable access conditions. In the UK, for instance, in the 1970s, Stan Cohen and Laurie Taylor famously returned a prestigious grant rather than accept the prison authorities' ruling that prison officers should be present at all prisoner interviews (Cohen & Taylor 1977). I cannot help wondering how such an ethical stance, resulting in the loss of a large grant, would be seen by the marketing managers in today's universities.

In retrospect, I wish I had had the opportunity for more discussion of the situatedness of research ethics when I was a graduate student and especially with experienced qualitative researchers who had already suffered all the ambiguities of research situations where moral dilemmas are not just about how to treat people but also about how to respect their meanings, their memories and their emotions. Once I was doing professional research I was totally committed to the ethics codes of my professional criminology and sociology associations. But I was also fully aware that these enunciated principles to which I had to adhere as best I could while juggling all the mix of research principles operative both in situ and ex post facto. I cannot help thinking that I would not have been assisted by any present-day ethics committee composed of academics whose ethics allow them to attempt micro-management of research in topics and methods of which, sometimes, they have had no experience; who frequently show little understanding of the nature of an ethical issue as opposed to a potential corporate image or insurance risk; and who too often can appear to have a rather meagre grasp of the complexity of moral reasoning in either the academy or the social world beyond its ken.

Of course social scientists should adhere to an ethics code. Of course researchers should maintain an ethical approach at all stages of a project. But it is easier said than done. It is well-nigh impossible for either a researcher or an ethics committee to tease out in advance the situational ethics which either are, or should be, operative in observational, participant-observational or ethnographic research. For the same reason, it seems to me that the much-vaunted exhortation that researchers be reflexive about their work cannot mean much more than, 'Think about what you are doing all the time, and especially about the moral dimensions'. On the one hand, the empirical world does not stand still; and nor does our position within it. On the other hand, imaginative qualitative researchers are likely to define and redefine the research for as long as it takes; and then again when the empirical data is being analysed. However ethically vigilant we try to be, we can never know for sure what we are doing. Ethics, after all, are nothing more than principles for the guidance of behaviour. They are ethically desirable inputs to the governance of research, but they cannot guarantee ethically desirable outcomes. The operative relationships between ethics, politics and knowledge are in constant flux and it is impossible to recapture – even in discourse – the effective but unknowable mix of conditions that temporally fashions the research stories we tell, our own ethical histories and other people's socio-biographies.

Acknowledgements

I thank Jo Phoenix for bringing many articles on intersectionality to my attention and Jacqueline Tombs and the editors of this volume for their very pertinent and engaged comments on the issues discussed here.

References

American Sociological Association 1999 [2008], *Code of Ethics and Policies and Procedures of the ASA Committee on Professional Ethics*. www.asanet.org/images/asa/docs/pdf/Codeof Ethics.pdf.

Beck, U 1992, *Risk Society: Towards a New Modernity*, London, Sage.

Becker, H 1967, 'Whose side are we on?' *Social Problems*, vol. 14, no. 3, pp. 239–247.

British Society of Criminology 2006, *Code of Ethics for Researchers in the Field of Criminology*. http://britsoccrim.org/.

Brown, R, with Carasso, H 2013, *Everything for Sale? The Marketisation of UK Higher Education*, London, Routledge.

Carlen, P 1976, *Magistrates' Justice*, Oxford, Martin Robertson.

Carlen, P 1985, *Women, Crime and Poverty*, Buckingham, Open University Press.

Carlen, P 1992, 'Criminal women and criminal justice' in *Issues in Realist Criminology*, eds R Matthews & J Young, London, Sage, pp. 51–69.

Carlen, P 2010, *A Criminological Imagination: Essays on Justice, Punishment and Discourse*, Farnham, Ashgate.

Carlen, P 2014, 'Review of Jill McCorkel *Breaking Women: Gender, Race and the New Politics of Imprisonment*', *British Journal of Criminology*, vol. 54, no. 6, pp. 1232–1235.

Chesney-Lind, M 2014, 'Review of Jill McCorkel, *Breaking Women: Gender, Race and the New Politics of Imprisonment*', *Punishment & Society,* vol. 16, no. 1, pp. 126.

Clarke, C, Broussine, M, & Watts L 2015, *Researching with Feeling: The Emotional Aspects of Social and Organisational Research*, London, Routledge.

Cohen, S & Taylor, L 1977, 'Talking about prison blues', in *Doing Sociological Research*, eds C Bell & H Newby, London, George Allen and Unwin, pp. 67–86.

Glaser, B & Strauss, A 1967, *The Discovery of Grounded Theory: Strategies for Qualitative Research*, Chicago, IL, Aldine.

Gouldner, A 1968, 'The sociologist as partisan: Sociology and the welfare state', *American Sociologist*, vol. 3, no. 2, pp. 103–116.

Hope, T 2004, 'Pretend it works: Evidence and governance in the evaluation of the burglary initiative', *Criminology and Criminal Justice*, vol. 4, no. 3, pp. 287–308.

Israel, M & Hay, I 2012, 'Research ethics in criminology', in *Criminological Research Methods*, eds D Gadd, S Karstedt, & S Messner, London, Sage, pp. 500–514.

Lyman, S & Scott, M 1970, *A Sociology of the Absurd*, New York, Appleton Century Crofts.

Martin, B 2011, 'ERA: adverse consequences', *Australian Universities Review*, vol. 53, no. 2, pp. 99–102. www.bmartin.cc/pubs/11aur2.pdf.

Mathiesen, T 2013, *Towards a Surveillant Society: The Rise of Surveillant Systems in Europe*, Hook, Waterside Press.

McCorkel, J 2013, *Breaking Women: Gender, Race and the New Politics of Imprisonment*, New York, New York University Press.

McGettigan, A 2013, *Great University Gamble: Money, Markets and the Future of Higher Education*, London, Pluto.

Nussbaum, M 2010, *Not for Profit: Why Democracy Needs the Humanities*, Princeton, NJ, Princeton University Press.

Rawls, J 1955, 'Two concepts of rules', *The Philosophical Review*, vol. 64, no. 1, pp. 3–32.

Searle, J 1971, *The Philosophy of Language*, Oxford, Oxford University Press.

Simien, E 2007, 'Doing intersectionality research: From conceptual issues to practical examples', *Politics and Gender*, vol. 3, no. 2, pp. 264–271.

Swaaningen, R van 2014, 'In memoriam: Jock Young', *Punishment & Society*, vol. 16, no. 3, pp. 353–359.

Wacquant, L 2002, 'The curious eclipse of prison ethnography in the age of mass incarceration', *Ethnography*, vol. 3, no. 4, pp. 371–397.

Whyte, WF 1943, *Street Corner Society* (esp. Appendix), Chicago, IL, University of Chicago Press.

PART II

Trust and research with vulnerable populations

4

A HISTORY OF COERCIVE PRACTICES

The abuse of consent in research involving prisoners and prisons in the United States

Mark Israel

Introduction

You have to feel for Philip Zimbardo. His Stanford-based experiment into the effects of the prison setting was abandoned after six days when the students assigned as 'guards' subjected students assigned as 'prisoners' to physical and psychological abuse and many student-prisoners started to behave in pathological ways. Zimbardo has spent a considerable part of his subsequent career exploring why things went so badly wrong (Zimbardo 2007; Zimbardo et al. 1999). Yet, the study is regularly trotted out together with Milgram's (1974) and Humphreys' (1970) as one of an unholy trinity of classical cases of unethical research that occurred without the free and informed consent of research participants in the social sciences, and that are routinely deployed as justification for our current systems of research ethics review in the social sciences (Sieber & Tolich 2013). Of course, Zimbardo's prison was not a real prison and yet the mistreatment of students at Stanford University receives more prominence among social scientists than a long history of abuse of real prisoners in the name of scientific research.

The abuse of prisoners within research programs has not simply stemmed from a lack of consent. It reflects power relations between prisoners, prison officers and prison authorities, and a relationship between the state, biomedical researchers and pharmaceutical companies that has done little to protect the interests of prisoners. It seems strange that a critical criminology that takes state crime and corporate crime seriously has invested little effort in analyzing the exploitation of prisoners by medical researchers. What makes it all the more surprising is that it is precisely this history of abuse of prisoners by non-criminologists that has justified limiting the access of criminologists to prisons for research purposes.

In this chapter, I explore how the concept of consent has been constructed within research, how requirements to obtain consent have been systematically evaded within prison-based research in the US, and how responses to scandal have led to the overprotection of institutions at the expense of prisoners' ability to exercise autonomy, access justice, and benefit from the research process. Sadly, this chapter also demonstrates the apparent irrelevance of criminologists to the ongoing regulation of research ethics in American prisons.

Constructing consent

The principle of consent rests on the basis that participants in research are entitled to know what they are getting themselves into. In most circumstances, researchers need to provide potential participants with information about the purpose, methods, demands, risks, inconveniences, discomforts, and possible outcomes of the research, including whether and how the research results might be disseminated.

Research participants may not know what is expected of them during this consent process and, consequently, researchers may need to explain the nature of informed consent in an environment conducive to genuine discussion. In some cases, this may take considerable time and effort on the part of researchers and research participants, as both struggle to deal with complex risks, uncertainties, and problems of cultural and linguistic divides. In other cases, it may be sufficient to provide potential participants with a list of their entitlements and a range of possible information that they can choose to request from the researchers.

Standard approaches to consent often require participants to have high levels of literacy and linguistic ability. While some people may have the competence to make independent decisions about involvement in a research project, this competence can be masked if written information is unclear or constructed without sensitivity. Written consent forms can be difficult to follow and may not be helpful in guiding queries. This may not always be the fault of the researcher. Some scholars, from a range of disciplines and countries, have complained that university, government, and corporate gatekeepers have required changes to consent forms that make forms more convoluted and less easily understood by participants (Federman et al. 2002; Gunsalus et al. 2005; Israel 2004).

In most circumstances, researchers have to be careful to ensure they negotiate consent from all relevant people, for all relevant matters and, possibly, at all relevant times. However, many criminologists find themselves in situations where obtaining consent from one group might be impracticable or endanger either the researcher or other research participants. Participants' consent might also be restricted to specific issues and times. Several researchers have argued that consent should not be limited to a formalized show, tell and sign consenting ceremony located at the beginning of the research project. Rather, it should be dynamic and continuous as the researchers' and participants' understanding of the study evolves or circumstances change. This point has been made particularly forcefully by anthropologists (El Dorado Task Force 2002). However, criminologists have also been vocal in their criticisms of what Grounds and Jamieson (2003) termed "the 'data raid' model of consent whereby consent is obtained from participants only at the beginning" (p. 353).

In the context of biomedical research, Faden and Beauchamp (1986) depicted informed consent as a kind of autonomous action, an act committed intentionally, with understanding and without controlling influences resulting either from coercion or manipulation by others or from psychiatric disorders. However, researchers may find it difficult to assess whether potential participants do have freedom of action. This problem of assessing participants' freedom of action arises repeatedly when engaging in research on staff in institutions that maintain strong hierarchical command structures. Lower-ranking members of the institution might either resent the presence of researchers or question their intentions. For example, some social scientists have found prison staff need to be reassured that researchers are not being planted by management to spy on subordinates in correctional institutions (Owen 1998). Mark Fleisher's (1989) study of a federal penitentiary in California was approved by the warden, but Fleisher was required to start working in the institution without explaining himself to the majority of staffers: "Warden Christensen wanted it that way, so that's the way it was" (p. 93).

Not surprisingly, the issues are starker in relation to prisoners. There are graphic examples where, despite the best efforts of the researcher, the ability to negotiate consent with prisoners appears to have been shaped by the coercive nature of prisons. However, consent can also be compromised by more subtle forms of manipulation such as manipulating information, changing available options, offering rewards, or threatening punishment (Faden & Beauchamp 1986). For example, Quina et al. (2007) interviewed incarcerated women in Rhode Island, noting "subtle pressures to participate, or not to participate, from peers, COs, and staff" (p. 133). They also witnessed supervising correctional officers barking not-so-subtle orders at female prisoners, instructing them to participate in the research, and were aware that women who resisted requests to be involved might face "negative repercussions" (ibid). Research that offers improved clothing, housing conditions or health services to prisoners living in overcrowded, inhumane and unhealthy conditions might also compromise consent. The matter of payment in cash is particularly sensitive as researchers may find it difficult to identify a level of payment for prisoners that lies between exploitation and undue inducement and, indeed, many parts of the prison system in the US have rejected *any* compensation of prisoners for research (Smoyer et al. 2009; Wyman 2000–2001).

While the concept of consent is explored in the biomedical literature, the matters of concern often relate to the process of obtaining free and informed consent, and seem to evade two critical questions that ought to concern criminology: how has the failure to obtain consent been linked to the broader exploitation and abuse of prisoners and, in the face of corporate and state violence and continuing moves by those bodies to escape scrutiny, under what circumstances might it be appropriate not to obtain consent from all participants?

The abuse of informed consent in prison-based research

For much of the last century, civilian or military prisoners have been used as research subjects. Not 'participants', 'subjects' – despite the preference of many contemporary codes for participants (Gontcharev 2013) and the implication of agency. Many prisoners in these studies were deprived of real choices. In some cases, they did not consent to the research. In other cases, their capacity to offer informed consent can be questioned. For example, during the Japanese occupation of Manchuria, Unit 731 of the Japanese military ran biological warfare experiments on thousands of Soviet and Chinese prisoners initially outside Harbin and then at Ping Fan. The unit probably also operated in Beijing, Shanghai, Guangdong, and Singapore (Moreno 2000). A Japanese investigator, Yuki Tanaka (1996), alleged that almost 1,500 American, Australian, British, and New Zealand prisoners of war were inoculated with typhoid, cholera, and dysentery and forced to drink various pathogens, though these claims remain unverified (Moreno 2000). Tanaka also reported experimentation on Australian prisoners of war held at Ambon in Indonesia and at Rabaul in Papua New Guinea. While the US failed to prosecute members of Unit 731, 12 members were executed by the Soviet Union following a war crimes trial at Khabarovsk in 1949.

Between 1943 and 1945, a series of protests and petitions from prisoners held in German concentration camps alerted the Allies to the fact that German medical personnel had engaged in a broad range of human experiments varying from crude wounding to sophisticated comparative vaccine trials (Annas & Grodin 1992). In 1945, physicians who had been held as prisoners in Auschwitz launched an appeal that the doctors responsible for such experimentation should be brought to trial. Evidence to support these claims was collected during the Allied advance into Germany that year. Leo Alexander, a neurologist working for the Allied Combined Intelligence Operations, documented medical experiments at Dachau (Berger 1990; Shevell 1996, 1998). In a memorandum written to guide the prosecution of 23 German doctors in 1946–47 (the Nuremberg Medical Trial), Alexander wrote:

> Our evidence was that they [prisoners] were picked at random, that none of them was asked whether he was willing, that none of them signed any written agreement ... a concentration camp was certainly no setting for anything voluntary. (1946, cited in Weindling 2001, p. 61)

During the trial, defense counsel argued that German doctors had simply engaged in practices similar to those followed by their American counterparts (Harkness 1996a, 1996b). As one example, they pointed to the death in 1906 of 13 prisoners awaiting execution in Manila, then under US civil administration. The prisoners had died during a cholera experiment conducted by a leading American specialist in tropical medicine.

While there were several other cases of dubious human experimentation in American-run prisons before the Second World War, they appear to have been "uncommon medical oddities of dubious worth" (Hornblum 1997, p. 1438). However, during the war the use of American prisoners in research became routine. Justified by the needs of the military, state and federal prisoners were recruited for a series of dangerous experiments. Some of these studies continued after 1945.

Immediately after the war, researchers funded by the United States Public Health Service deliberately infected human subjects in Guatemala with sexually transmitted diseases (Presidential Commission for the Study of Bioethical Issues 2011). The research started at Haute Terre in the US but, facing restrictions on experiments within the US, went on to target highly vulnerable subjects in a low-income country. The subjects in Guatemala included 219 prisoners. The Presidential Commission for the Study of Bioethical Issues, appointed by President Obama, found no evidence to suggest the prisoners understood they were taking part in an experiment let alone that they consented to their involvement. Indeed, there was evidence that the experimentation occurred after active deceit by the researchers and despite some prisoners' objections. As a result, the Commission concluded that the experiments "involved gross violations of ethics as judged against both the standards of today and the researchers' own understanding of applicable contemporaneous practices" (Guttman & Wagner 2011, p. v).

After the war, the pharmaceutical industry replaced the military as the major client of researchers experimenting on prisoners in the US (Jonsen et al. 1977). By 1972, the Food and Drug Administration estimated that over 90 percent of investigational drugs were initially tested on prisoners (quoted in Advisory Committee on Human Radiation Experiments 1996). This use of prisoners in clinical research was an unusual one for a Western democracy. There is evidence that in the 1960s and 1970s Canadian prisoners in Manitoba, Quebec, and Ontario were involved in non-therapeutic drug trials as well as tests of shampoo and cigarettes (Osborne 2006). However, such drug and other non-therapeutic research on prisoners was prohibited or heavily restricted in France and Germany and seems not to have taken place in the UK. In contrast, Hornblum (1997, 1998) concluded that Nuremberg marked the beginning of a utilitarian approach to human experimentation on prisoners in the US, "a quarter century of unrestrained use of prison inmates as cheap and available raw material" (Hornblum 1997, p. 1440). In the words of the Advisory Committee on Human Radiation Experiments, "it is difficult to overemphasize just how common the practice became in the United States during the postwar years" (1996, p. 273).

Some of the most flagrant examples of abuse of prisoners in the US resulted in legal action by civil liberties organizations. In the absence of other meaningful forms of oversight, judicial intervention became the most significant way of holding American correctional systems to account (Morgan & Bronstein 1985). For instance, Dr Austin Stough reportedly earned $1 million per annum from drug companies as a result of his research on prisoners in Oklahoma, Arkansas, and Alabama. Several prisoners contracted viral hepatitis and some died as a result of Stough's drug tests and blood plasma projects (Rugaber 1969). The federal district judge responsible for trying the case against Stough described Alabama's health and research program as "shocking" and "barbarous" (*Newman v Alabama* 349 F. Supp. 278 1972). Between 1963 and 1973, 171 prisoners in the states of Oregon and Washington were subjected to testicular irradiation by two researchers funded by the American Atomic Energy Commission. Although participation in the study appears to have resulted in an increased risk of cancer of less than four-hundredths of 1 percent, in 1970 a review committee run by the Department of Institutions in Washington State recommended the research be closed down because the work appeared to be inconsistent with standards of freedom of choice and consent established in the Nuremburg Code. The Committee believed money paid to prisoners as a result of their participation and their expectation that they would receive privileges could constitute undue inducements (reported in Advisory Committee on Human Radiation Experiments 1996).

Investigation of these studies formed part of a wider examination of human radiation experiments by the Advisory Committee on Human Radiation Experiments (ibid), which reported to President Clinton. On the basis of an examination of consent forms and testimony from participants and researchers, the Advisory Committee established that participants:

> were adequately informed about the possibility of skin burns; sometimes informed, but perhaps inadequately, about the possibility of pain; informed about the possibility of bleeding only from 1970 on; and never informed of the possibility of orchitis [testicular inflammation] ... the evidence suggests that many if not most of the subjects might not have appreciated that some small risk of testicular cancer was involved. It is also not clear that all subjects understood that there could be significant pain associated with the biopsies and possible long-term effects. (p. 426)

The Advisory Committee found that irradiation experiments had also been conducted on prisoners in seven other parts of the US.

Prisoners' ability to consent has been attacked on two grounds. Opponents of experimentation in the US in the 1970s claimed, first, that prisoners were rarely fully informed (Wells et al. 1975; see also Meyer 1976; Miller 1970, cited in Jonsen et al. 1977) and, second, that prisoners could not be said to be acting voluntarily. Even if prisoners were not to be judged incompetent on grounds of mental disorders, intellectual disabilities or drug and alcohol dependence and had not succumbed to institutionalization, other problems might have existed. Many experimenters offered financial and non-financial inducements to prisoners to encourage them to volunteer. Although considerably above what they might have received for other work within the prison, research wages for prisoners remained well below payments to volunteers outside prison. Mitford (1972, 1973) pointed out that even low wages were important to a prisoner denied decent conditions and "reduced to bartering his body for cigarettes and candy money" (1972, p. 72). And, even low wages might place prisoners involved in research programs at an advantage over those who were not. Disturbingly, it seems that many prisoners also expected their involvement in research to be taken into account during parole hearings even though there was no official acceptance of such practice. Jacobs and Wright (2006) argued that, while the intention of the researcher might be immaterial,

> No matter how much they are assured otherwise, incarcerated offenders often associate researchers with prison staff and other criminal justice functionaries who can provide benefits or mete out punishment. (p. 10)

Criticism of this period of prison experimentation was largely structured around prisoners' vulnerability, the lack of consent, and the consequent harm they experienced. Prisoners did not freely consent to the risks or, if they did, they were inadequately informed. They were vulnerable and they were taken advantage of by researchers. As a result, responses were framed as an issue of research ethics requiring the protection of prisoners.

In 1978, the American federal government banned medical research on federal prisoners, following a damning report from the Department of Health, Education, and Welfare (1976). By then, only a few American states still allowed such research. By 1980, only 15 percent of all drug testing was carried out in prisons, using facilities in Michigan and Montana. Regulations disseminated in 1981 by the Food and Drug Administration imposed such stringent provisions on the use of prisoners that they constituted a de facto ban on non-therapeutic experimentation on prisoners. Unfortunately, this also meant that prisoners were denied access to some new drug therapies that might have improved their condition (Verdun-Jones et al. 1998).

Ten years later, Federal Department of Health and Human Services (DHHS) regulations issued in 1991 allowed research to be conducted on prisoners if the study involved minimal risk and no more than inconvenience to prisoners who participated and concerned the study of possible causes, effects, and processes of incarceration and criminal behavior, the study of prisons as institutional structures, or of prisoners as incarcerated subjects. Research on conditions affecting prisoners as a class or institutional practices required the approval of the Secretary of the Department and the posting of a notice in the *Federal Register*.

In 2003 the Office for Human Research Protections (OHRP), a division of the DHHS, published a *Guideline on the Involvement of Prisoners in Research*. This became part of Title 45 of the Code of Federal Regulations, and continued to allow an Institutional Research Board (IRB) to review and allow research on prisoners if the Board included as a voting member either a prisoner or a prisoner representative – someone knowledgeable about and experienced in working with such groups. While supportive of such a move, Mobley et al. (2007) were concerned that giving prisoners a voice might have symbolic rather than practical significance without clear mechanisms for incorporating that voice into the decision-making processes.

The Guideline also provided additional safeguards for the protection of prisoners as they "may be under constraints because of their incarceration which could affect their ability to make a truly voluntary and uncoerced decision whether or not to participate as subjects in research" (45 CFR 46.302). These safeguards included additional regulation of risks and potential benefits, including an assurance parole boards would not take the participation (or refusal to participate) of any prisoner in research into account when reaching decisions concerning parole. In addition, the Guideline required that information be presented to prisoners in language they could understand. In the past, some researchers had included complex language in their informed consent document and in 2000 the OHRP had criticized forms used by the University of Miami (Reiter 2009) and the University of Texas Medical Branch (UTMB). In the latter case, the OHRP found several examples of forms that overstated potential benefits to participants, understated reasonably foreseeable risks, and attempted to release the investigator and the institution from liability for negligence. The OHRP suspended federally-supported research projects at UTMB that were not eligible for expedited review and recommended that the institution use independent consent monitors to observe and audit the consent process for prisoners (Carome 2000).

Following these incidents, the OHRP commissioned the Institute of Medicine to review the ethics of conducting research on prisoners. While clearly weighted toward ethical considerations associated with biomedical research, the resulting report (Committee on Ethical Considerations for Revisions to DHHS Regulations for Protection of Prisoners Involved in Research 2006) should be seen as a significant document. It recognized the lengthy history of the abuse of prisoners within research, the difficulties of securing consent within the prison context, the patchy nature of oversight of research within prisons, the value of allowing some research within prisons, and the dangers of reducing the ethics of prison-based research to the issue of consent.

The report also provided an overview of the impact of regulations that governed research in prisons. DHHS regulations had restricted the use of prisoners in research to particular categories. However, these regulations only applied in some circumstances, as most federal departments and agencies had not adopted the additional protections for prisoners (Subpart C of the Common Rule). As a result, the majority of research within prisons in the US was not subject to review by an IRB and, while internal research boards established by departments of corrections might have played a similar role to IRBs, they rarely included prisoner representatives. The report also noted that departments of corrections in different states had reached very different decisions about the research they might allow. Only a few allowed therapeutic interventions by external investigators, effectively ending research by pharmaceutical companies. Most states permitted the use of administrative data, and social and behavioral studies involving minimal risk if of a non-therapeutic nature. However, the response to other forms of research varied between jurisdictions.

Drawing on a limited empirical base, the Institute of Medicine's Committee specifically addressed the difficulties of obtaining consent within correctional institutions, accepting that researchers should pay attention to "ameliorating basic power and knowledge differentials, which may undermine information sharing, understanding, and voluntariness" (2006, p. 118). Like the OHRP, it considered the value of using independent advocates for research participants within the consent process.

Finally, it recommended that voluntary and informed consent be obtained from participants in all research involving prisoners (Recommendation 6.1):

> There is no question that, within correctional settings, it is more difficult to provide integrity to the process of informed consent, but this does not remove the obligation. If it is determined that voluntary informed consent is not obtainable, then a research proposal should not go forward. (ibid, p. 148)

The Committee's recommendations were seen as controversial and not acted upon. The Committee argued that there was a danger of reducing research ethics to matters of informed consent and, wary of paternalism, instead maintained that prison-based research might be better served by use of risk–benefit analysis, an analysis favored in most European countries (Council of Europe 2005), albeit not in the form advocated by the Committee. It also explored the value of a notion of justice that engaged with the just distribution of both risks and benefits, and had regard for the relationship between research, policy, and service provision. Within the constraints allowed by a principlist approach to research ethics (Israel 2015, see below), the work of the Committee could be seen as progressive. It is surprising therefore that, to the extent that the Committee paid any attention to criminology, its analysis was reliant on the administrative criminology undertaken within government departments. As a result, the report contains no coherent assessment of the body of critical research on prisons. Only occasionally do we see a glimpse of the work of critical scholars – Jeffrey Ian Ross appears in the report (2005, p. 65), but not specifically as a critical criminologist. Rather, he is identified as a member of the Prisoner Advocates Liaison Group and later also as a former analyst with the Department of Justice.

Understanding the abuse

In the face of abuse of prisoners, it was entirely appropriate that federal authorities stepped in to regulate research on prisoners in the US. It took them far too long to act, but clearly the protection of prisoners is a worthy goal. And, in this more punitive time, initiatives that do so should be welcomed, however cautiously.

However, there have been limits to the federal intervention. The DHHS regulations were only binding on research supported by the DHHS and research within the Central Intelligence Agency and the Social Security Administration – the two agencies that had chosen to extend the regulations to non-DHHS funded work on prisoners. Of course, it now appears that the CIA's director had discretion to "approve, modify, or disapprove all proposals pertaining to human subject research" and that the Agency may have manipulated its definition of human experimentation to enable torture of detainees (Ackerman 2015). The 2003 Guideline was also binding on those state prison systems that adopted the Guideline. Where regulations were adopted, there have been many examples of breaches. Reiter (2009) reviewed the 778 OHRP non-compliance determination letters available online between

2000 and 2008. She found that there were at least three determinations per year involving research on prisoners, and in some years more than a dozen.

Beyond the reach of the Guidelines, prison research was subjected to varying, overlapping, and sometimes inconsistent regulations. So, research funded and conducted by private contractors might well fall outside its scope, as might research in probation and work-release programs, and drug-treatment facilities. The Institute of Medicine's report called for a national approach covering a broader definition of the term 'prisoner' that might extend to these settings but, like the rest of its recommendations, was not implemented.

There were also conceptual limitations in the approach taken by the Institute of Medicine. Most cross-disciplinary national and international codes and guidelines on research ethics are based on principlism (Israel 2015). The approach to ethics advocated by principlism rests on the idea that our conduct should be based on widely accepted principles. Sometimes these principles conflict with each other, in which case we ought to use our moral judgement and intuition to decide what we should do. While originally conceived as a general approach to ethics, principlism was applied to research ethics in the 1970s by American bioethicists Tom Beauchamp and James Childress. The approach offers a relatively simple way of addressing ethics and is based on prima facie principles of respect for autonomy, beneficence, non-maleficence, and justice.

Unfortunately, principlism is not always sympathetic to the agendas and methodologies of critical scholarship. Despite the claims of its advocates that principlism provides a straightforward framework for problem-solving that is "neutral between competing religious, cultural, and philosophical theories, [and that] can be shared by everyone regardless of their background" (Gillon 1994, p. 188), it has been criticized variously for its lack of foundational theory; Western-dominated methodology; failure to capture common morality adequately; capacity to obstruct substantive ethical inquiry and contemplation, and its individualistic bias (Evans 2000; Walker 2009; Wolpe 1998).

The problem for criminologists is that what research ethics guidelines might deem correct may well run directly counter to what researchers from particular disciplines regard as the right thing to do. Contemporary codes such as the Common Rule in the US, and those statements, codes and guidelines that draw from it, often overgeneralize positions derived from biomedical research ethics (Israel 2015). In doing so, they may overprotect individuals and organizations that may not need, want or warrant protection and underprotect the most vulnerable (Schneider 2015). They also reify an impoverished conception of justice. For Martyn Hammersley (2013), principlism might undercut attempts to tackle broader ethical issues and we always need to consider "who is setting principles on behalf of whom, with what authority, and with what potential effects" (2013, p. 3). In short, for critical, feminist and postmodernist criminologists, principlism poses similar challenges to those we face from positivist versions of criminology.

The Institute of Medicine report revealed awareness that exploitation of prisoners had structural causes "that create special vulnerabilities in prison populations"

(2006, p. 115), "including conditions of social and economic deprivation and the possibility or even likelihood of manipulation or corruption on the part of prison authorities and prisoners in positions of privilege" (p. 116). Sadly, it failed to engage with those parts of criminology that might help understand this; nevertheless it did look to analogous examples for strategies for responding to structural problems. For example, the report called for ways to ameliorate "basic power and knowledge differentials, which may undermine information sharing, understanding, and voluntariness" (p. 118), recommending the use of study-specific, independent, "prison research study advocates", local to the research sites. Advocates would monitor compliance with the approved protocol and other regulatory requirements, monitor adverse events and the consent process, provide a way for responding to questions from staff and prisoners, and assess the degree to which privacy and confidentiality were being protected. The role of the prison research study advocate was modeled on patient advocates used within clinical trials and also drew on the prison visitors established under the European Convention for the Prevention of Torture and Inhuman or Degrading Treatment or Punishment.

In the end the recommendations, like much of principlist-derived research ethics, reduced the problem to the level of the researcher–subject relationship and glossed over power relationships associated with the relationship between the research participant and the wider society. The Institute of Medicine report did call for research into ways of improving corrections, facilitating the successful re-entry of prisoners into society and reducing recidivism (Recommendation 5.4). However, it failed to address the control correctional services have exerted over research agendas – defining problems worthy of study; determining who gains access to data and who gains knowledge from the results; assessing what counts as harms and benefits and how these may be balanced; and determining to whom the researcher is accountable.

In the US, correctional services' control of research has led to what Reiter describes as a "pixelated" view of prisons, in that research has taken place, but has provided "at best, a blurry image of the institutions under scrutiny" (2014, p. 417). Sadly, in attempting to protect prisoners from coercive or manipulative practices, research ethics regulations have had perverse consequences. The principles and structures of research ethics have been used to protect correctional institutions from external scrutiny and it is this lack of external scrutiny that makes it far more likely that abuse of prisoners might occur.

Of course, research ethics review is just one part of a strategy of 'institutional protectionism' (Hannah-Moffatt 2011), a broad range of administrative practices and logistical difficulties deterring researchers from entering many correctional facilities. Bosworth and Palmer (2012) observed dryly that in the US "without being convicted it is not easy to learn about what occurs behind prison walls" (p. 495). There are many reasons why state agencies may block researchers' access. These explanations include: constraints of resources; potential disruption to the department or clients of the department; failure to see value to the agency in the chosen research agenda, methodology or expertise of the researcher; and a desire to avoid scrutiny. In the words of one public health researcher, "many correctional administrators may not see research as a priority and not want researchers 'poking around' for fear that they may discover something less flattering" (Arriola 2006, p. 138).

Unfortunately, the reason offered may not be the one that actually triggered the rejection. Research ethics regulations have enabled corrective services to portray their refusal to allow external researchers access to prisons as being in the best interest of prisoners. The ambition of corrective services to limit independent research might be less serious if it were not accompanied by a general lack of disclosure and transparency. Sadly, many American prisons also restrict access to data relating to prison operations, block access by journalists and advocacy groups, and operate free of oversight by national, state or independent agencies (Reiter 2014) such as those that exist in the UK and parts of Australia.

Outside the US, some researchers have responded to state control by disguising their activities in order to enter secure institutions. Covert research has been justified in limited circumstances on utilitarian grounds where it is necessary for the research to remain secret in order to maintain access to the research setting, perhaps in the face of the desire of powerful or secretive interests to resist external scrutiny. For example, Stanley Cohen and Laurie Taylor's (1972) classic study on the effects of long-term imprisonment on British offenders incarcerated in Durham prison in the late 1960s drew on information already gathered while they were running an adult education class in E-wing. When they sought formal permission to undertake research, the Home Office restricted access to prisoners and sought to control publication. Paweł Moczydłowski (1992), later to become director-general of prisons in post-Communist Poland, entered Polish prisons to undertake his research by joining study groups of questionnaire-wielding students. During her research on the illegal trade in human organs, Nancy Scheper-Hughes (2004) traveled incognito in Argentina "to enter a locked state facility for the profoundly mentally retarded … to investigate and ultimately to document allegations of tissue, blood, kidney and child theft from the neglected, emaciated, socially abandoned and unknown, so-called 'no-name' inmates" (p. 32).

Without covert research, Pearson (2009) argued, some aspects of society, including harms and injustices will remain "hidden or misunderstood" (p. 252) and the images powerful groups wish to project may go unchallenged. The value of covert studies has been accepted by British, Canadian, Australian, Norwegian and Swedish national codes and guidelines in exceptional circumstances. For example, the Framework for Research Ethics in the social sciences in the UK (Economic and Social Research Council 2015) considers covert research might be justified "if important issues are being addressed and if matters of social significance which cannot be uncovered in other ways are likely to be discovered" (p. 31).

It is unclear whether such provisions might allow covert research on institutions to expose, for example, state violence or corporate misconduct. It depends on whether the institution is considered a research participant. In Canada, the Tri-Council Policy Statement (Tri-Council 2010) suggests institutions should not be protected in this way. It recognizes that "social science research that critically probes the inner workings of publicly accountable institutions might never be conducted without limited recourse to partial disclosure" (p. 37). As a result, researchers are not required to obtain consent from those corporate or government organizations that they are researching, nor are such institutions entitled to veto projects, though private organizations may refuse researchers access to records or create rules governing the conduct of their employees that might make it difficult for those employees to cooperate with researchers. However, even in these situations, the research cannot involve more than minimal risk to participants (Article 3.7(a)), which might make it difficult for researchers to work with whistleblowers in those jurisdictions where whistleblowers are inadequately protected.

In the UK, the *Framework for Research Ethics* offers space for a similar argument to be made to avoid managerial vetoes (Economic and Social Research Council 2015, p. 28). The European Commission's draft Guidance Note for social science researchers, issued in 2010, warned against allowing powerful figures or organizations the right to withdraw or withhold consent for fear of leaving social scientists "without even the most basic rights to make enquiries by other social groups, such as investigative journalists, or even ordinary citizens who might confront such figures at public meetings" (p. 11). Despite these moves by research agencies to allow covert research under certain circumstances, the use of covert methodologies is in serious decline generally and it is not a methodology employed regularly within prison research.

Conclusion

Not only are criminologists being cut off from prisons, sadly we are also largely absent from the literature on prisons used by research ethics regulators. Part of this is our fault. Criminology has said little about the exploitation of prisoners by researchers. There are notable exceptions. Keramet Reiter (2009) explored the evolving regulation of experimentation on prisoners in the US, pointing out that prisoners have been used in research largely to further the interests both of big pharmaceutical companies and of researchers. Again, Kauzlarich and Kramer's (1998) study of state-corporate crime by the American nuclear state included a review of the irradiation of prisoners. But, overall criminologists are missing. We have failed to document a history of coercive practices in prison-based research. Given criminologists' interest in corrections, this seems an odd oversight. We could alert at least some research ethicists to the value of deploying critical theory to the analysis of vulnerability, victimization, state-organized and state-corporate crime, as well as institutional accountability.

If criminology has not entered the general research ethics literature, the converse appears also to be the case. There is an emerging criminological literature on at least some aspects of the ethics of research in prisons that goes well beyond the construction of the prisoner as the vulnerable object of research. For example, criminologists in various countries have explored the impact of power relations and emotions on research within prisons, the possibilities of offering greater agency to prisoners by rethinking traditional consent and reporting procedures, and the conflicts of interest faced by in-house or co-opted researchers (Palys & Lowman 2001; Waldram 1998). However, this work remains separate from the research ethics literature. Given the impact of research ethics regulations on our research, it would be sensible if criminologists engaged critically with the broader research ethics literature outside criminology.

The regulation of consent could operate in such a way that it protects the interests of vulnerable groups such as prisoners from harmful research carried out by government agencies and the corporations associated with private prisons. Alternatively, it could protect powerful agencies from scrutiny by external researchers (Murphy & Dingwall 2007). The intersection between these ethical and political matters should lie at the heart of criminology research. Paying more attention to them might help us to challenge current research ethics regulation. Instead, prison administrators continue to justify the shaping of methodology in criminology by pointing to the abuses of medical researchers in which correctional services themselves were complicit. Regulators continue to hold us responsible for the work by one psychologist in the 1970s on student volunteers. Even after 40 years, apparently, Zimbardo has still not done his time.

Acknowledgement

Some of the material in this chapter is drawn from Israel (2015).

References

Ackerman, S 2015, 'CIA torture appears to have broken spy agency rule on human experimentation', *The Guardian*, 15 June. www.theguardian.com/us-news/2015/jun/15/cia-torture-human-experimentation-doctors.

Advisory Committee on Human Radiation Experiments 1996, *The Human Radiation Experiments: Final Report of the President's Advisory Committee*, New York, Oxford University Press.

Alexander, L 1946, 'Countering the defense that Germans were experimenting on prisoners condemned to death', Memorandum, 23 December, Alexander Papers (n.34), box 4, file 34.

American Sociological Association 1999, *Code of Ethics*. www.asanet.org/images/asa/docs/pdf/CodeofEthics.pdf.

Annas, GJ & Grodin, MA eds 1992, *The Nazi Doctors and the Nuremberg Code*, New York, Oxford University Press.

Arriola, KRJ 2006, 'Debunking the myth of the safe haven', *Criminology & Public Policy*, vol. 5, no. 1, pp. 137–148.

Australian and New Zealand Society of Criminology 2000, *Code of Ethics*. www.law.ecel.uwa.edu.au/anzsoc/code_of_ethics.htm.

Berger, R 1990, 'Nazi science: The Dachau hypothermia experiments', *New England Journal of Medicine*, vol. 322, pp. 1435–1440.

Bosworth, M & Palmer, S 2012, 'Prisons: Securing the state' in *Handbook of Critical Criminology*, eds W DeKeseredy & M Dragiewicz, Abingdon, Routledge.

British Society of Criminology 2003, *Code of Ethics for Researchers in the Field of Criminology*. www.britsoccrim.org/docs/CodeofEthics.pdf.

British Sociological Association 2002, *Statement of Ethical Practice*. www.britsoc.co.uk/ Library/Ethicsguidelines2002.doc.

Carome, MA 2000, *Re: Human Research Subject Protections under Multiple Project Assurance M-1172*. Letter from Chief, Compliance Oversight Branch, Division of Human Subject Protections to Vice President for Research, University of Texas Medical Branch, 14 September.

Cohen, S & Taylor, L 1972, *Psychological Survival: The Experience of Long Term Imprisonment*, Harmondsworth, Penguin.

Cohen, S & Taylor, L 1977, 'Talking about prison blues', in *Doing Sociological Research*, eds C Bell & H Newby, London, Allen and Unwin, pp. 67–86.

Committee on Ethical Considerations for Revisions to DHHS Regulations for Protection of Prisoners Involved in Research 2006, *Ethical Considerations for Research Involving Prisoners*, Washington, DC, National Academy of Sciences. www.iom.edu/ CMS/3740/24594/35792.aspx.

Cordner, C & Thomson, C 2007, 'No need to go! Workplace studies and the resources of the Revised National Statement', *Monash Bioethics Review*, vol. 26, no. 3, pp. 37–48.

Council of Europe 2005, *Additional Protocol to the Convention on Human Rights and Biomedicine, concerning Biomedical Research*. Strasbourg. http://conventions.coe.int/Treaty/EN/ Treaties/Html/195.htm.

Department of Health, Education and Welfare 1976, *Protection of Human Subjects*, 42 Fed. Reg. 3076–91 (DHEW Jan. 14, 1977) (codified at 45 C.F.R. pt. 46). www.hhs.gov/ohrp/ policy/ohrpregulations.pdf.

Economic and Social Research Council (ESRC) 2015, *ESRC Framework for Research Ethics*. Swindon, Economic and Social Research Council. www.esrc.ac.uk/_images/ framework-for-research-ethics_tcm8-33470.pdf.

El Dorado Task Force 2002, *Final Report*, Arlington, VA, American Anthropological Association. http://anthroniche.com/darkness_documents/0598.pdf.

Evans, JH 2000, 'A sociological account of the growth of principlism', *Hastings Center Report*, vol. 30, no. 5, pp. 31–38.

Faden, RR & Beauchamp, TL 1986, *A History and Theory of Informed Consent*, New York, Oxford University Press.

Federman, DD, Hanna, KE & Rodriguez, LL eds 2002, *Responsible Research: A Systems Approach to Protecting Research Participants*, Washington, DC, National Academies Press.

Fleisher, MS 1989, *Warehousing Violence*, Newbury Park, CA, Sage.

Gillon, R 1994, 'Medical ethics: Four principles plus attention to scope', *British Medical Journal*, vol. 309, no. 6948, pp. 184–188.

Gontcharev, I 2013, 'Methodological crisis in the social sciences: The New Brunswick Declaration as a new paradigm in research ethics governance?', *Transnational Legal Theory*, vol. 4, no. 1, pp. 146–156. http://ssrn.com/abstract=2317435.

Grounds, A & Jamieson, R 2003, 'No sense of an ending: Researching the experience of imprisonment and release upon Republican ex-prisoners', *Theoretical Criminology*, vol. 7, no. 3, pp. 347–362.

Gunsalus, CK, Bruner, E, Burbules, N, Dash, L, Finkin, M, et al. 2005, *The Illinois White Paper, Improving the System for Protecting Human Subjects: Counteracting IRB 'Mission Creep'*, Center for Advanced Study Human Subject Protection Study Group, University of Illinois at Urbana-Champaign. http://gunsalus.net/assets/IllinoisWhitePaperMissionCreep.pdf.

Guttman, A & Wagner, J 2011, 'Letter to President Obama (undated)', in *Presidential Commission for the Study of Bioethical Issues, 'Ethically Impossible': STD Research in Guatemala from 1946 to 1948*. http://bioethics.gov/node/654#sthash.TR00BB3l.dpuf.

Hammersley, M 2013, 'A response to "Generic ethics principles in social science research" by David Carpenter', *Generic Ethics Principles in Social Science Research Symposium 1: Principles*. http://acss.org.uk/wp-content/uploads/2014/01/Hammersley-AcSS-Response-to-Carpenter-5-March-2013-Principles-for-Generic-Ethics-Principles-in-Social-Science-Research.pdf.

Hannah-Moffatt, K 2011, 'Criminological cliques: Narrowing dialogues, institutional protectionism, and the next generation', in *What is Criminology?*, eds M Bosworth & C Hoyle, Toronto, University of Toronto Press, pp. 440–455.

Harkness, JM 1996a, 'Nuremberg and the issue of wartime experiments on US prisoners: The Green Committee', *JAMA*, vol. 276, no. 20, pp. 1672–1675.

Harkness, JM 1996b, 'Research behind bars: A history of nontherapeutic research on American prisoners', thesis, Madison, University of Wisconsin-Madison.

Hoonaard, van den WC 2011, *The Seduction of Ethics: Transforming the Social Sciences*, Toronto, University of Toronto Press.

Hornblum, AM 1997, 'They were cheap and available: Prisoners as research subjects in twentieth century America', *British Medical Journal*, vol. 315, no. 7120, pp. 1437–1441.

Hornblum, AM 1998, *Acres of Skin: Human Experimentation at Holmesburg Prison*, New York, Routledge.

Humphreys, L 1970, *Tearoom Trade: Impersonal Sex in Public Places*, Chicago, IL, Aldine Publishing.

Israel, M 2004, *Ethics and the Governance of Criminological Research in Australia*, Sydney, New South Wales Bureau of Crime Statistics and Research. www.bocsar.nsw.gov.au/Documents/r55.pdf.

Israel, M 2015, *Research Ethics and Integrity for Social Scientists: Beyond Regulatory Compliance*, Sage, London.

Jacobs, BA & Wright, R 2006, *Street Justice: Retaliation in the Criminal Underworld*, New York, Cambridge University Press.

Jonsen, AR, Parker, ML, Carlson, RJ & Emmott, CB 1977, 'Biomedical experimentation on prisoners', *Ethics in Science and Medicine*, vol. 4, no. 1–2, pp. 1–28.

Kauzlarich, D & Kramer, RC 1998, *Crimes of the American Nuclear State: At Home and Abroad*, Boston, MA, Northeastern University Press.

Meyer, PB 1976, *Drug Experiments on Prisoners: Ethical, Economic, or Exploitative?*, Lexington, MA, Lexington Books.

Milgram, S 1974, *Obedience to Authority*, New York, Harper & Row.

Miller, MB 1970, 'Manipulation of the disenfranchised: Some notes on the ethical dilemma of experimentation using prison-subjects', unpublished paper, Department of Criminology, University of California, Berkeley.

Mitford, J 1972, 'Experiments behind bars: Doctors, drug companies, and prisoners', *Atlantic Monthly*, vol. 76, no. 1, pp. 64–73.

Mitford, J 1973, *Kind and Usual Punishment*, New York, Knopf.

Mobley, A, Henry, S & Plemmons, D 2007, 'Protecting prisoners from harmful research: Is "being heard" enough?', *Journal of Offender Rehabilitation*, vol. 45, no. 1–2, pp. 33–46.

Moczydłowski, P 1992, *The Hidden Life of Polish Prisons*, Bloomington, Indiana University Press. Originally published in Polish in 1982.

Moreno, JD 2000, *Undue Risk: Secret State Experiments on Humans*, New York, WH Freeman.

Morgan, R & Bronstein, A 1985, 'Prisoners and the courts: The US experience', in *Accountability and Prisons: Opening up a Closed World*, eds M Maguire, J Vagg & R Morgan, London, Tavistock, pp. 264–280.

Murphy, E & Dingwall, R 2007, 'Informed consent, anticipatory regulation and ethnographic practice', *Social Science & Medicine*, vol. 65, no. 11, pp. 2223–2234.

National Commission for the Protection of Human Subjects of Biomedical and Behavioral Research, United States 1976, *Report and Recommendations: Research Involving Prisoners*, Bethesda, MD, Department of Health, Education and Welfare.

Office for Human Research Protections 2003, *Guideline on the Involvement of Prisoners in Research*, Washington, DC, OHRP.

Osborne, GB 2006, 'Scientific experimentation on Canadian inmates, 1955 to 1975', *The Howard Journal*, vol. 45, no. 3, pp. 284–306.

Owen, B 1998, *'In the Mix': Struggle and Survival in a Women's Prison*, Albany, NY, SUNY Press.

Palys, T & Lowman, J 2001, 'Social research with eyes wide shut: The limited confidentiality dilemma', *Canadian Journal of Criminology*, vol. 43, no. 2, pp. 255–267.

Pearson, G 2009, 'The researcher as hooligan: Where "participant" observation means breaking the law', *International Journal of Social Research Methodology*, vol. 12, no. 3, pp. 243–255.

Presidential Commission for the Study of Bioethical Issues 2011, *'Ethically Impossible': STD Research in Guatemala from 1946 to 1948*, Washington, DC. http://bioethics.gov/node/654.

Quina, K, Garis, AV, Stevenson, J, Garrido, M, Brown, J, et al. 2007, 'Through the bullet-proof glass: Conducting research in prison settings', *Journal of Trauma & Dissociation*, vol. 8, no. 2, pp. 123–139.

Reiter, K 2009, 'Experimentation on prisoners: Persistent dilemmas in rights and regulations', *California Law Review*, vol. 97, no. 2, pp. 501–566.

Reiter, K 2014, 'Making windows in walls: Strategies for prison research', *Qualitative Inquiry*, vol. 20, no. 4, pp. 414–425.

Rugaber, W 1969, 'Prison drug and plasma projects leave fatal trail', *New York Times*, July 29, p. 1.

Scheper-Hughes, N 2004, 'Parts unknown: Undercover ethnography of the organs-trafficking underworld', *Ethnography*, vol. 5, no. 1, pp. 29–73.

Schneider, CE 2015, *The Censor's Hand: The Misregulation of Human-Subject Research*, Cambridge, MA MIT Press.

Shevell, M 1996, 'Neurology's witness to history: The Combined Intelligence Operative Sub-Committee Reports of Leo Alexander', *Neurology*, vol. 47, no. 4, pp. 1096–1103.

Shevell, M 1998, 'Neurology's witness to history (Part 2): Leo Alexander's contributions to the Nuremberg Code (1946–47)', *Neurology*, vol. 50, no. 1, pp. 274–278.

Sieber, JE & Tolich, MB 2013, *Planning Ethically Responsible Research* (2nd ed), Los Angeles, CA, Sage.

Smoyer, A, Blankenship, K & Belt, B 2009, 'Compensation for incarcerated research participants: Diverse state policies suggest a new research agenda', *American Journal of Public Health*, vol. 99, no. 10, pp. 1746–1752.

Tanaka, Y 1996, *Hidden Horrors: Japanese War Crimes of World War II*, Boulder, CO, Westview Press.

Tri-Council (Canadian Institutes of Health Research, National Science and Engineering Research Council of Canada, Social Sciences and Humanities Research Council of Canada 2010, *Tri-Council Policy Statement: Ethical Conduct for Research Involving Humans*, Ottawa: Public Works and Government Services. www.pre.ethics.gc.ca/pdf/eng/tcps2/TCPS_2_FINAL_Web.pdf.

Verdun-Jones, SN, Weisstub, DN & Arboleda-Florez, J 1998, 'Prisoners as subjects of biomedical experimentation: Examining the arguments for and against a total ban', in *Research on Human Subjects: Ethics, Law and Social Policy*, ed DN Weisstub, Oxford, Pergamon, pp. 503–530.

Waldram, JB 1998, 'Anthropology in prison: Negotiating consent and accountability with a "captured" population', *Human Organization*, vol. 57, no. 2, pp. 238–244.

Walker, T 2009. 'What principlism misses', *Journal of Medical Ethics*, vol. 35, no. 4, pp. 229–231.

Weindling, P 2001, 'The origins of informed consent: The International Scientific Commission on Medical War Crimes, and the Nuremberg Code', *Bulletin of the History of Medicine*, vol. 75, no. 1, pp. 37–71.

Wells, SH, Kennedy, PM, Kenny, J, Reznikoff, M & Sheard, MH 1975, *Pharmacological Testing in a Correctional Institution*, Springfield, IL, Charles C. Thomas.

Wolpe, PR 1998, 'The triumph of autonomy in American bioethics: A sociological view', in *Bioethics and Society: Constructing the Ethical Enterprise*, eds R DeVries & J Subedi, Upper Saddle River, NJ, Prentice Hall, pp. 38–59.

Wyman, BP 2000–01, 'Biomedical and behavioral research on juvenile inmates: Uninformed choices and coerced participation', *Journal of Law and Health*, vol. 15, no. 1, pp. 77–103.

Zimbardo, PG 2007, *The Lucifer Effect: Understanding How Good People Turn Evil*, New York, Random House.

Zimbardo, PG, Maslach C, & Haney, C 1999, 'Reflections on the Stanford Prison experiment: Genesis, transformations, consequences', in *Obedience to Authority: Current Perspectives on the Milgram Paradigm*, ed T Blass, Mahwah, NJ, Lawrence Erlbaum, pp. 193–237.

5

INDIGENOUS PEOPLES, RESEARCH AND ETHICS

Maggie Walter

Introduction

A heavy over-representation of Indigenous people within criminal justice and state welfare systems is a common factor of first-world colonized nation-states. In Australia, Aotearoa New Zealand, the US and Canada this over-representation positions Indigenous peoples as a group of key interest for criminological researchers and there is a significant body of criminological literature documenting this positioning in each country. This over-representation also positions Indigenous peoples as a disproportionately vulnerable group and highlights the criticality of ensuring that the conduct of research with Indigenous peoples meets high ethical standards. Conducting ethical research with, or about, Indigenous peoples, however requires much more than standard ethical approval from university or other institutional ethics committees.

Research with Indigenous peoples, particularly the ethical aspects of this research, is not neutral territory. Not only are there unique ethical principles, guidelines and needs associated with such research, the realm is also awash with racial, cultural, social and political assumptions. The signing of a consent form, for example, taken as evidence of a participant's voluntary informed participation in the research, may neither be culturally applicable nor meaningful for Indigenous participants. The complex realm of ethical Indigenous research practice in settler states, therefore, has to be examined from both ends of the research spectrum. The ethical principles and perspectives that the Indigenous subjects of research have articulated and the ethical dimensions of worldviews and values that researchers themselves bring to their research alongside the compatibility of these with Indigenous research ethics are central concerns of ethical research practice with Indigenous peoples.

The chapter begins with an overview of the shared positionality of Indigenous peoples on the hierarchy of socio-economic and cultural disadvantage and within criminal justice systems in their respective first-world colonized nation-states:

Australia, Aotearoa New Zealand, the US and Canada. The chapter then details Indigenous ethical perspectives, as they are conceived formally and informally, and their ramifications for criminology researchers in the practice of ethical research. For Indigenous peoples, ethical research is research that recognizes and respects Indigenous cultural values, norms, knowledges and sovereign rights. To this end most of our example first-world settler states have developed sets of ethical guidelines to inform researchers designing and conducting culturally appropriate and collaborative research. A cross-national comparative analysis of these demonstrates both the essential similarities across cultures and nation-states as well as national variations.

The chapter then addresses the ethical impact of the cultural, social and racial milieu of the researcher: the researcher's worldview. Even if the researcher is fully cognizant of Indigenous ethical dimensions, the outcome is not necessarily ethical research. If they do not understand their own social position and how this frames their research practice then a significant potential to do research harm remains. Researchers' worldview, and the value and belief systems that flow from this, shape and influence the research questions they regard as important, the way data are gathered, from whom, and, often most critically, the interpretation of those data. Criminological research is not purely a scholarly endeavor and those interpretations have social and public policy resonance. Far removed from researchers themselves, research findings have real life effects on Indigenous peoples and communities. An Australian research example is used to demonstrate such ethical issues.

Framing over-representation as a criminological research and ethics issue

A long history of Indigenous over-representation at all levels of the criminal justice system is a feature of Anglo settler states. This over-representation translates to Indigenous peoples and communities being a frequent focus of criminological research, in Australia, Canada, the US and Aotearoa New Zealand. The Australian Institute for Criminology, for example, has an Indigenous subset topic under their main heading of 'Criminal Justice' (AIC 2015) and the website features numerous articles on Indigenous interactions with the criminal justice system. Indigenous over-representation within the criminal justice system across our four example countries indicate a similar forward positioning of Indigenous peoples as the subject of criminological research.

First Nations, Métis, Native American, Alaskan Native, Aboriginal and Torres Strait Islander peoples and Māori peoples are all imprisoned at rates far higher than those of their respective settler majority populations. In the US, Native American and Alaskan Native people are imprisoned at a rate nearly five times that of White Americans (Hartney & Vuong 2009). In Aotearoa New Zealand, Māori make up around 13 per cent of the total population but 51 per cent of the prison population (58 per cent for women); a rate more than four times that of non-Māori (Ministry of Justice 2009). In Canada, Aboriginal adults are imprisoned at a rate roughly six times (18 per cent) that of their proportion in the Canadian population (3.1 per cent) (Statistics Canada 2009), and in Australia, the age-adjusted incarceration rate of Aboriginal and Torres Strait Islanders is 13 times that of the non-Indigenous population (SCRGSP 2014). Similar patterns can be found in arrest data, juvenile detention rates and other indicators of engagement with the criminal justice system. Critically, these disparate rates of interaction with the criminal justice system are not an historic artefact, or an issue that is resolving over time. In Australia, for example, Aboriginal and Torres Strait Islander imprisonment rates increased by 57 per cent between 2000 and 2013 (ibid) and in Canada, within the imprisoned population, the proportion of Aboriginal adults (including First Nations, Métis, Alaskan Native and Native American) grew from 13 to 18 per cent in the decade 1998–2008 (Statistics Canada 2009).

Indigenous populations in all these nations are also heavily over-represented on all indicators of socio-economic disadvantage and consequently within state welfare systems. The very different welfare systems across nations make direct comparison of the use of welfare services difficult but a comparative unemployment rate for each nation-state is evidence of a shared socio-economic position. Across Australia, the US, Canada and Aotearoa New Zealand, Indigenous people are unemployed at around double the rate of the dominant settler population. In 2013, unemployment rates for Native Americans were 11.3 per cent compared to 6.9 per cent for White Americans (Austin 2013). Similarly in Canada, the unemployment rate for the working-age Aboriginal population is more than twice that for other Canadians (13 versus 6 per cent) (Statistics Canada 2011). The unemployment rate for Māori was 14.1 per cent in 2013, compared with the 6.8 per cent unemployment rate for all people in New Zealand (Ministry of Business, Innovation and Employment 2013). In Australia the unemployment rate for Aboriginal and Torres Strait Islander people in 2011 was 9.6 per cent compared to 4.2 per cent for the general population (ABS 2013).

To be Indigenous, therefore, regardless of country, is to be far more likely to be poor and to have experienced negative interactions with the criminal justice system. The similarity of Indigenous positioning, across nation-states and continents, raises ethical questions. Why do such clear patterns of over-representation exist across a set of very different peoples who have, of themselves, very little in common, culturally or racially? What is it that they have in common besides poverty and high levels of imprisonment? Looking from the peoples themselves to their history of colonization and their settler majorities suggests at least a partial explanation. These Indigenous peoples share similar experiences of colonization. All are primarily Anglo-colonized and their contemporary nations' instruments of state still bear the standards of this legacy (Walter & Andersen 2013). All are also now living as minorities within first-world nations. This similar positioning is neatly summarized by Dyck's (1985) six-point definition of fourth-world peoples as those who:

1. Are Indigenous to the lands that now form the nation-state
2. Have had their sovereignty over those lands appropriated by settler colonialism

3. Constitute a minority of the population of that nation-state
4. Have had their culture stigmatized by their respective dominant cultures
5. Are struggling for social justice, self-determination and control of traditional lands and resources
6. Remain economically and politically marginalized

Indigenous populations in these first-world colonized nation-states are, therefore, not just another minority group. Their histories and contemporary realities provide a very specific social, racial, cultural and economic frame through which the over-representation of Indigenous peoples might be understood. This framework is also highly salient to criminological research for both researchers and Indigenous experiences as research participants.

Indigenous codes of ethics

Ethical criminological research with Indigenous peoples is further complicated by the deep suspicion with which many Indigenous peoples from these settler nation-states regard researchers. In all four countries identified above the Indigenous populations have long experiences of being the object of research, primarily by non-Indigenous researchers. Such experience has frequently not been positive. The major suspicion, often proved correct, is that the research aims and objectives as well as the distribution of research benefits and possible harms are uneven, with the ledger always disproportionately balanced toward the researcher, and the researcher's cultural and racial group. For example, Sahota (2007) details a lawsuit brought by the Havasupai people against the University of Arizona after blood samples taken ostensibly for research on diabetes were, without permission, also used in studies on schizophrenia and inbreeding.

Linda Tuhiwai Smith's (1999, p. 1) maxim that "research" is probably one of the dirtiest words in the Indigenous world's vocabulary, therefore, still rings true. The suspicions held by Indigenous peoples are deepened by the research burden they bear, then and now. Over-representation within negative indicators of social, economic and cultural wellbeing, combined with relative social, cultural and political powerlessness, leads to over-representation as research subjects. Being a young, poor, highly incarcerated population is to be criminologically 'interesting' as well as accessible, with little opportunity or resources to resist the research gaze. Yet, it is only in relatively recent times that Indigenous research concerns have been recognized as a discrete ethical issue. Since the 1990s, Australia, Aotearoa New Zealand and Canada have all instituted specific ethical guidelines for researchers working with Aboriginal peoples, with the US still in its beginning stages.

The following sections compare and contrast the most prominent Indigenous research ethics guidelines of each of these four settler nation-states. There are clear similarities between the various ethics guidelines. Each reflects ethics as seen through an Indigenous, rather than a Western, lens and each ensures that the research and its attendant ethical framework reflect Indigenous ethical perspectives and priorities. These perspectives challenge Eurocentric constructs and ways of knowing, privilege the Indigenous voice and reconceptualize research ethics to reflect Indigenous cultural positions. The results are ethical principles that are framed by the way Indigenous peoples see the world and the way Indigenous peoples organise within it (Tuhiwai Smith 1999). For criminological research, this means pushing the boundaries of standard ethical practice "to make intellectual space for Indigenous cultural knowledge systems that were denied in the past" (Rigney 2001, p. 9).

All frameworks also centre Indigenous cultural and epistemological positions as a guiding principle. This principle in itself, however, determines that there can be no pan-Indigenous ethical guidelines translatable across First Nation peoples. Criminological researchers, therefore, need to locate the Indigenous ethical guidelines relevant to their particular research. As an added dimension, the research ethics of working with Indigenous peoples within nation-states is also increasingly contested, with Indigenous groups within these nation-states developing their own expectations of what constitutes ethical research. This development complicates the field for researchers (see Drees 2001) but underscores the rights of Indigenous peoples and the ethical responsibilities of all researchers (Indigenous and non-Indigenous).

Australia

There are two major sets of Indigenous ethics guidelines operating in Australia. The earliest set, *Interim Guidelines on Ethical Matters in Aboriginal and Torres Strait Islander Health Research*, was developed by the National Health and Medical Research Council (NHMRC) in the late 1980s and released in 1991. These guidelines were developed through a series of meetings between Aboriginal and Torres Strait Islander health researchers and community members in response to the claim of both groups that the mainstream *National Statement of Ethical Conduct in Research Involving Humans* (National Statement) did not adequately address the ethical concerns of Aboriginal and Torres Strait Islander peoples as participants of research. A set of specific guidelines, rather than an Indigenous section of the National Statement, was preferred to emphasize to researchers that Indigenous ethical concerns are discrete and Indigenous-focused, not just an add-on to mainstream issues.

The guidelines have been updated over time. The most recent version, *Values and Ethics: Guidelines for Ethical Conduct in Aboriginal and Torres Strait Islander Health Research*, was endorsed by the NHMRC in 2003. These guidelines operate alongside the National Statement as the 'authoritative statement' on research involving Aboriginal and Torres Strait Islander people. Human research ethics committees, frequently including an Aboriginal member, are charged with ensuring that research practice and process involving Indigenous participants observes both the guidelines and the National Statement. The guidelines revolve around six key ethical values. These are outlined in Table 5.1.

TABLE 5.1 Six ethical values defined in *Values and Ethics: Guidelines for Ethical Conduct in Aboriginal and Torres Strait Islander Health Research*

Reciprocity	That the research is inclusive, demonstrates an equitable and respectful engagement with peoples, values and cultures and advances the interests of Australian Indigenous people in ways that are valued.
Respect	That the research acknowledges individual and collective contributions, interests and aspirations and acknowledges the right to have different values, norms and aspirations at all stages, including the consequences of research.
Equality	That the research recognizes the equality of and value of Aboriginal Torres Strait Islander knowledge and wisdom; that all partners are equal and there is an equal distribution of benefit.
Responsibility	That the research does no harm to Indigenous individuals/communities or things they value and is accountable to individuals, families and communities especially in relation to cultural and social dimensions.
Survival and protection	That the research recognizes and values Indigenous people; the importance of the personal and collective bond, and cultural distinctiveness and does not diminish the right to assert or enjoy that distinctiveness.
Spirit and integrity	The overarching value is that the research is approached with respect for the richness and integrity of the cultural inheritance and that negotiations exhibit credibility in intent and process.

Source: Adapted from NHMRC 2003, pp. 69–71

The Australian Institute of Aboriginal and Torres Strait Islander Studies (AIATSIS) also provides *Guidelines for Ethical Research in Australian Indigenous Studies*. These guidelines were originally developed for research within AIATSIS but are now used more widely. The 2012 updated guidelines include 14 principles divided between six overarching themes. These principles share attributes with the NHMRC six values but are expressed in terms of rights and are more prescriptive. The six overarching themes are: rights, respect, recognition; negotiation, consultation, agreement and mutual understanding; participation, collaboration and partnership; benefits, outcomes and giving back; managing research: use, storage and access; and reporting and compliance (AIATSIS 2012).

Aotearoa New Zealand

A range of ethical guidelines have been developed by Māori researchers and scholars since the early 1990s in Aorearoa New Zealand. The most recent, the *Te Ara Tika Guidelines for Māori Research Ethics: A Framework for Researchers and Ethics Committee Members*, were developed by the Putaiora (Māori Members of Ethics Committees) Working Group and released in 2010 (Hudson et al. 2010). The main ethical

TABLE 5.2 Principles of the Te Ara Tika framework

Minimum standard	*Good practice*	*Best practice*
Whakapapa – the quality of research relationships		
Consultation	Substantial and positive engagement	Kaitiaki – relationships that empower Māori to take a research-wide guardianship role for tangible outcomes
Tika – what is right and good and relates to the validity and design of the research		
Conforming to mainstream ethical standards, including how the research will impact Māori	Māori-centred practice –includes Māori as significant participants across full research process	Benefits Māori, is designed and conducted by Māori and uses Māori research methodologies
Manaakitanga – encompasses the notions of cultural and social responsibility and respect		
Cultural sensitivity – inherent dignity and right to confidentiality and privacy, for individuals and communities	Cultural safety – inclusive of Māori and broader Indigenous values and concepts and appropriate Māori protocols	Mahaki – respectful conduct that recognizes spiritual integrity and Māori philosophy
Mana – equity and distributive justice as related to rights, roles, risks, benefits and outcomes. Fully informed consent and oral consent as of equal value and culturally appropriate		
Open transparent consultation	Mana whenua – meaningful relationship with the mana whenua (iwi [tribe] and hapu (u) [kinship] group) to ensure equitable outcomes	Mana whakahaere, sharing of the power and control of the research relationships with hapu (u) iwi or the relevant Māori community

Source: Hudson et al. 2010

principles are drawn from tikanga Māori and its philosophical base of matauranga Māori (traditional knowledge). Tikanga are protocols and practices that reflect Māori values, belief systems and way of living in the world and ensure the preservation of mana, which is defined in the document as justice and equity, reflected through power and authority. These values are also integrated with understandings from the Treaty of Waitangi, the founding document defining the relationship between the Māori Indigenous people of Aotearoa and the British colonizing settlers. The guidelines also invoke the research framework of kaupapa Māori: research that is culturally relevant, rigorous and empowering to Māori people (Tuhiwai Smith 1999). The Te Ara Tika framework details four tikanga-based principles of ethical conduct for researchers working with Māori people, outlined across three levels of acceptable practice (see Table 5.2). Researchers are encouraged to frame their research within these principles by the presence of Māori research ethics boards at many universities in New Zealand which hold the authority to determine if the research meets ethical guidelines. To this end, the Te Ara Tika guidelines (Hudson et al. 2010) also provide a matrix for researchers and research ethics committees to use to assess the appropriateness of Māori consultation for any project.

Canada

National Indigenous research guidelines relating to research with Indigenous people are more recent in Canada. Until the late 1990s, the major research funding bodies, the Canadian Institute of Health Research (CIHR), the Social Sciences and Humanities Research Council of Canada (SSHRC) and the National Sciences and Engineering Research Council of Canada (NSERC) had separate guidelines. Harmonizing of mainstream ethics guidelines occurred during the 1990s with the *Tri-Council Policy Statement: Ethical Conduct for Research Involving Humans*, released in 1999. In 2004, the Interagency Advisory Panel on Research Ethics began to revise research guidelines in relation to Indigenous knowledge and Indigenous rights (Ermine et al. 2004). The Tri-Council Policy Statement now includes a separate section (1999, Chapter 9) that specifically addresses the topic of research involving Aboriginal Peoples.

Chapter 9, 'Research involving the First Nations, Inuit and Métis Peoples of Canada', recognizes in its introductory sections that previous research has not always reflected Aboriginal world views or benefited Aboriginal peoples and communities. It also states that the guidelines are not intended to replace ethical guidelines developed by Aboriginal peoples themselves but, rather, seek to ensure that research in this space is premised on respectful relationships and collaboration. The chapter's context section highlights the need to accord respect to Aboriginal peoples' knowledge systems and that the "various and distinct world views of Indian, Inuit and Métis peoples are represented in planning and decision making" (p. 10). The ethical guidelines for research with Indigenous peoples are set out across 22 articles, each accompanied by a section on how they should be applied. These are summarized in Table 5.3.

The United States

There is not (yet) a national set of ethics guidelines in the US that pertain exclusively to research with Native Americans and/or Alaskan Native peoples (Hamill 2015, personal communication, 24 April). Research on Indigenous peoples is covered, as is all research, by the 1974 National Research Act. This Act was prompted by the infamous Tuskegee Syphilis Study whereby researchers continued a study of the long-term effects of syphilis, using a sample of poor, African American men, for decades after a cure for syphilis was readily available (Heintzelman 2003). The 1974 National Research Act saw the creation of the National Commission for

TABLE 5.3 Articles from 'Research Involving the First Nations, Inuit and Métis Peoples of Canada'

Article	Description
9.1	**Requirement of Community Engagement in Aboriginal Research** – any research that involves Aboriginal people, communities
9.2	**Nature and Extent of Community Engagement** – determined jointly by researcher and the relevant community
9.3	**Respect for First Nations, Inuit and Métis Governing Authorities** – must be engaged before recruitment of individuals within communities
9.4	**Engagement with Organizations and Communities of Interest** – recognized through representation of their members in ethical review and oversight
9.5	**Complex Authority Structures** – alternatives to agreements with leaders to include documentation of community processes and measures taken
9.6	**Recognizing Diverse Interests within Communities** – take into account views of all relevant sectors, including individuals and sub-groups
9.7	**Critical Inquiry** – into public institutions, Indigenous organizations or those exercising authority over Indigenous peoples can be ethical
9.8	**Respect for Community Customs and Codes of Practice** – obligation for researchers to be informed of customs and codes of practice
9.9	**Institutional Research Ethics Review Required** – even when research approved by community research ethics boards
9.10	**Requirement to Advise the REB on a Plan for Community Engagement** – before ethical approval unless accepted rationale for non-engagement given
9.11	**Research Agreements** – formal engagement with a community to be set out in a formal research agreement
9.12	**Collaborative Research** – be considered by researchers and communities
9.13	**Mutual Benefits in Research** – where possible research should be relevant to community needs and priorities and extend knowledge
9.14	**Strengthening Research Capacity** – through enhancement of skills within the community on research methods, project management and ethical oversight
9.15	**Recognition of the Role of Elders and Other Knowledge Holders** – through participation in design and execution of research and within project
9.16	**Privacy and Confidentiality** – personal information not to be disclosed to community partners without participants' consent
9.17	**Interpretation and Dissemination of Research Results** – community to have opportunity to participate in interpretation of data and findings before final report
9.18	**Intellectual Property Related to Research** – how rights are to be assigned to be discussed and included in the research agreement
9.19	**Collection of Human Biological Material Involving Aboriginal Peoples** – how they are to be collected, used and stored in the research agreement
9.20	**Secondary Use of Information or Human Biological Materials Identifiable as Originating from Aboriginal Communities or Peoples** – must include engagement with community prior to initiating secondary use

TABLE 5.3 (*cont.*)

Article	Description
9.21	**Community Engagement is not Required if Information on Human Biological Materials is Legally or Publicly Available** – although recommended
9.22	**REB Review Required Where Research Involves Data Linkage of Two or More Anonymous Datasets Associated with Human Biological Materials**

Source: TCPS2 2014

the Protection of Human Subjects of Biomedical and Behavioral Research, which produced the Belmont Report (HHS 1979). The Belmont Report summarizes the ethical principles identified by the National Commission in three areas: the boundaries between practice and research; the ethical principles of respect for persons, beneficence and justice, with a focus on informed consent from autonomous individuals; and the requirement that research does no harm and maximizes benefits and minimizes harms.

The Belmont Report makes no mention of Native Americans or Alaskan Native peoples or Indigenous research dimensions. Indeed, it is only in the section on justice that the report mentions the Tuskegee Study to show how racially disadvantaged groups have been previously denied research justice. To overcome such injustices the report states that researchers should scrutinize their selection processes to see if some classes of people, citing examples of welfare patients and particular racial and ethnic minorities, are being selected on the grounds of availability or compromised situations. The application of the ethical guidelines in the Belmont Report focuses on informed (individual) consent, based on sufficient information, voluntariness and the distribution of risks and benefits (again, individually understood).

The failure of the Belmont Report to address Indigenous ethical dimensions has led to a growing effort on the part of Native American tribes to take control through tribal independent review boards (Hamill 2015, personal communication, 24 April). As sovereign nations, US Native communities have the right to regulate research on their peoples and lands and a number of Native American Nations have incorporated research regulation into their own laws (Sahota 2007). One such example is the Navajo Nation, which established the Navajo National Human Research Review Board in 1996 with the purpose of ensuring research involving Diné people was guaranteed to be ethical (see Navajo National Human Research Review Board 2009a, 2009b). They backed the work of the Human Research Review Board with the inclusion of the *Navajo Nation Human Research Code* within the Navajo Nation Council laws. This code sets out the conditions under which researchers can conduct research on human subjects within the territorial jurisdiction of the Navajo Nation and the role of the Board in ensuring these are followed. These are set out in Table 5.4.

Under these conditions, no research can proceed on Navajo lands without a Board-approved research permit. Within this, the Review Board has the power to

TABLE 5.4 Research conditions of the *Navajo Nation Human Research Code*

A.	Are consistent with the health and education goals and objectives of the Navajo Nation
B.	Do not detract from, nor interfere with, the provision of human services to the Navajo people
C.	Do not endanger the wellbeing of individuals or communities
D.	Require informed consent of all affected individuals or their legal representatives
E.	Are culturally relevant to the extent possible and are appropriate clinically, technically, epidemiologically and statistically
F.	Present only reasonable risks to subjects in relation to anticipated benefits, if any, and the knowledge that reasonably may be expected to result
G.	Selects subjects equitably. In making this assessment the Navajo Nation Human Research Review Board shall take into account the purposes of the research, the setting in which the research will be conducted, and the population from which subjects will be recruited

Source: *Navajo Nation Human Research Code*, Chapter 25, pp. 298–299

approve or disapprove projects and all their outputs, included theses and articles prior to publication, to review progress and negotiate additional or revised procedures or approaches. The evaluation process assures that the Nation is not only informed of all outcomes and findings but also owns any data emanating from the research (Becenti-Pigman et al. n.d.). The fact that the Board reviews the research at both ends of the process, start and finish, ensures researchers take their responsibility to adhere to the research conditions of the Navajo National Human Research Code very seriously. It also adds further protection for the Diné people so that they are not the subject of research that is not in their best interests.

Indigenous ethical guidelines in the US are less defined at the national level than in the other three comparator settler nation-states. The sovereign nation status of the Navajo Nation, however, arguably gives Diné people greater ethical protection than that provided by Indigenous peoples in other settler states. The right of the Review Board to both review and potentially deny publication of results is not present in the three other national codes. Such a right would probably not be possible under mainstream frameworks of academic freedom operating at the national level. These greater rights, however, are balanced by the lack of Indigenous research ethics protecting those Native American or Alaskan Native peoples and communities living in areas without nation status.

Ethical research and the standpoint of the researcher

So how do researchers respond to these guidelines? A minority actively resist. Rolls (2003, p. 2), for example, in explaining how non-Indigenous researchers cannot reasonably be expected to adhere to such guidelines, mocks the need to engage meaningfully with Indigenous communities: "[A]nother of the protocols we must adhere to if we are to be given a smiley stamp is that we must receive appropriate (and ongoing) community permission before proceeding with our research." Trigger (2014) takes a similar, although not quite as derisive, tone when he refers to the Australian NHRMC guidelines' value of spirit and integrity as mere tokenism. Resistance can also mean human research ethics committee Indigenous members encounter issues that are not faced by other members. Trudgett and Page (2014), for example, write of their experiences as Aboriginal members of an ethics committee at an Australian university during which they were singled out and accused of deliberately blocking research. Merely trying to ensure national guidelines are followed has resulted in the frequent disrespecting of their own scholarly expertise (both are well-credentialed education academics) alongside personalized and racialized commentary, including having their identity as Aboriginal scholars questioned by unhappy researchers.

The majority of researchers, however, understand the necessity of these guidelines and work with integrity to research within them. Yet, while contemporary guidelines articulate the key dimensions of Indigenous perspectives on ethics, these, on their own, are not enough. They are only half the story of ethical research with Indigenous peoples. Understanding the ethical dimensions of research through an Indigenous lens does not necessarily alter the worldview that informs, not always consciously, a researcher's practice. Indigenous ethical understandings, therefore, must be matched by a recognition of the positions the researcher themself brings to the research (Walter & Andersen 2013). A researcher's worldview is inclusive of that researcher's epistemological position, which shapes how they define, value and prioritize knowledge and knowledge sources. For example, how much weighting do we give statistical arrest data compared to oral testimonies by Indigenous prisoners? The researcher's axiological position reflects their values and belief systems. As shown by Indigenous ethical guidelines, the values defining what is an appropriate relationship between the researcher and researched are not culturally or racially universal. The researcher's ontological position reflects how they see the world and understand reality (ibid). For researchers such as Rolls (2003) cited above, Indigenous research ethical guidelines seemingly do not fit with their worldview on appropriate research practice with Indigenous peoples; leading in that case to open rejection of Indigenous understandings.

A researcher's social position sits above and frames that researcher's worldview. How we understand the world, including the research world, is not innate. These understandings are largely artefacts of our cultural, racial, class and gender positions. Take for example a criminologist who is a young Australian man of Anglo descent, raised in a middle-class professional family. No matter how non-sexist, non-racist and believing in social equality he is, these social attributes, the value systems implicit in them, alongside how they position him in his society, will influence *how* he understands the social phenomena of crime and the criminal justice system *and* the relationship between these and Indigenous peoples. His social position will influence the topic he is interested in, the research questions he poses and even the theoretical frameworks that make most sense to him (Walter 2013; Walter & Andersen 2013), shaping the who, what, when and how of the research. The ethical risk is that the researcher's standpoint can operate to limit the frame of the research, excluding other ways of knowing, understanding and conceptualizing the subjects and the research.

The ethics of research: a case study

The ethical dimensions of Indigenous research reach beyond those projects that interact directly with Indigenous people or communities. It is important to note that in the case study analyzed below the research data were drawn from statistical collections. In Australia, and most other jurisdictions, such secondary use of data usually negates the need to gain approval from a research ethics body. Yet, as shown here, administrative data analyzed outside of its social and cultural context is likely to produce results that are disconnected from the social phenomenon ostensibly being investigated. When such results are then used to reach criminological conclusions with real-life policy consequences there are significant ethical dimensions. The following section's examination of the research understood and interpreted through an Indigenous ethical lens raises questions about the ethical presumptions that inform the acceptance of this practice as ethically unproblematic.

In 2014, criminologist Don Weatherburn published *Arresting Incarceration: Pathways out of Indigenous Imprisonment*. The research base of the book is the analysis of arrest, incarceration, socio-economic and other statistics relating to Australian Indigenous people. The interpretation of the results supports the researcher's previously argued theory (see Weatherburn 2003) that the primary reason for over-representation of Australian Indigenous people in the criminal justice system is widespread criminality among Australian Indigenous peoples. The book notes that, "[A] high proportion of Indigenous Australians have become trapped in a cycle of arrest, conviction and imprisonment" (Weatherburn 2014, p. xiv) and the growth in Indigenous over-representation is related to the change in the relative rates of Indigenous and non-Indigenous involvement in serious crime. The impact of colonization is acknowledged but arguments related to its effects alongside dispossession, racism, disadvantage, systemic racism or bias in the criminal justice system are dismissed as weak and inadequate explanations. Weatherburn's theory of Indigenous incarceration has been subject to heavy critique from other criminologists. Cunneen (2005), for example, dismisses Weatherburn's analysis and interpretation as simplistic. It constructs, he argues, a "simple binary explanation for Aboriginal over-representation in prison as either the result of systemic bias *or* offending levels among Aboriginal people" (p. 334, emphasis in original). Cunneen argues that this approach negates the nuanced and complex historical, social, cultural and racialized elements of the structuring of crime and Indigenous interaction with the criminal justice system in favor of simple comparative arrest and incarceration statistics.

The point of this case study is not to critique the Weatherburn thesis *per se* but, rather, to analyze its ethical dimensions through the *Values and Ethics: Guidelines for Ethical Conduct in Aboriginal and Torres Strait Islander Health Research*.

Reciprocity

There is little evidence of an inclusive, equitable and respectful engagement with Indigenous culture and peoples in the Weatherburn analysis. Rather, Indigenous peoples are primarily present as the object of study. And where Aboriginal and Torres Strait Islander culture and values are engaged with, the author both decides what these are and then holds them responsible. Violence, for example, is posited as an Indigenous cultural value. Weatherburn (2014) argues that a "large part of the explanation for Aboriginal over-representation in prison, then, lies in Aboriginal over-representation in violence" (p. 57), citing research which it is argued demonstrates that Indigenous Australians have a propensity to respond aggressively to seemingly minor violations of social protocol (p. 58) and that Aboriginal children are encouraged to behave aggressively from a very young age (p. 59).

The absence of Indigenous engagement also renders invisible the longstanding Indigenous community and institutional activity in the field. Cunneen (2005, p. 337), in his critique of the Weatherburn thesis, points to the complete analytical exclusion of the role of Indigenous organizations in tackling issues related to over-representation. Night patrols, community-invoked bans or management of alcohol and other drugs, school engagement strategies, Aboriginal legal services, criminal justice workers and so on have been decades' long aspects of many, if not most, Aboriginal and Torres Strait Islander communities around Australia.

Respect

Respect, or lack of, refers ethically to how the research acknowledges Indigenous interests and aspirations and minimizes difference blindness. Weatherburn's research does differentiate Indigenous from non-Indigenous people, but pejoratively. Much of the Indigenous data is presented in comparison to data on non-Indigenous people, a practice I refer to as the orthodoxy of the dichotomy (see Walter 2010). The practice leads almost automatically to negative comparison, whereby the explanation behind an intractable social problem, in this case high Indigenous arrest rates, is to be found in the Indigenous peoples themselves. Criminality, in this research, is raced. Conversely, the research does not differentiate between Aboriginal and Torres Strait Islander peoples.

The analysis, which is confined to national and in some cases state-based aggregate data, treats its objects as one undifferentiated population. But the terms Indigenous, Aboriginal or Torres Strait Islander, Native American, Alaskan Native and First Nations are categories, not definitions. Indigenous peoples in Australia as elsewhere comprise many different Indigenous nations. They also comprise peoples with very different life circumstances: those remaining in homelands or on reservations; those living remotely – primarily in Indigenous-only communities; those living in urban and regional settings; those with treaty or other relationships with their nation-state and those without – the list goes on. Weatherburn's analysis, however, does not address any of these large cultural, locational and life world differences between Aboriginal and Torres Strait Islander peoples. This seems naïve.

Equality

What is the benefit of the research, how is it shared and how are Indigenous knowledges recognized? Under this dimension of ethical research, the researcher and the researched need to agree on what constitutes benefit and what is an acceptable share of the benefits that should flow to the research subjects. From this perspective it is hard to identify benefits that Aboriginal and Torres Strait Islander people would value and there is a complete absence of, or reference to, Indigenous knowledges. Weatherburn would no doubt sincerely consider his research as providing benefit, and perhaps point to his prescription to address Indigenous over-representation as set around six goals. These are (p. 155): improving Indigenous child development; reducing Indigenous substance abuse; increasing Indigenous school attendance and performance; increasing Indigenous workforce participation; reform of the law in relation to bail; and reducing Indigenous recidivism. These aspirations are worthy aims. The ethical issue is that achievement of these aims is situated in changing the problem behavior of Aboriginal and Torres Strait Islander people. The question is no longer how can we (non-Indigenous Australia) reduce Indigenous incarceration. From this perspective the real question is how can *they* (Indigenous people) be made less deficit and problematic?

Responsibility

Does the research do harm? Yes, it likely does, over and above the issues already discussed in the capacity to influence policy. The thesis that Indigenous over-representation in prison is caused by Indigenous criminality, which in turn is related to problematic behaviors by Indigenous peoples resonates with policy makers. The research extends the thesis to legal support services arguing that not only is there no evidence that lack of legal representation was a major cause of Indigenous over-representation in prison, there is no evidence to suggest that such services reduce Indigenous over-representation (Weatherburn 2014, p. 35). Although it cannot be directly linked, research such as this provides a rationale for policy actions such as the 2014 cutting of $13.4 million from Indigenous legal services (Law Council of Australia 2014).

Survival and protection

How does Weatherburn's research recognize and value sovereignty, cultural distinctiveness and the right to assert or enjoy that distinctiveness? It does not. There is a scant reflection on colonization, but no acknowledgment that Australian Indigenous peoples remain the traditional owners or that dispossession continues. The research does portray Indigenous communal bonds, but in depreciatory tones when Weatherburn argues for the normalization of criminality in communities, stating that as "Indigenous contact with the criminal justice system rose, the stigma of arrest and imprisonment would have reduced, robbing the criminal justice system of whatever deterrent effect it possessed" (p. x). The social capital strength of community bonds whereby community members gain their sense of belonging, the provision of a supportive environment, and the widespread sharing of resources are ignored.

Spirit and integrity

The research undermines, not supports, the spirit and integrity of Aboriginal and Torres Strait Islander peoples. The research does not accord with any of the six values described in the *Values and Ethics: Guidelines for Ethical Conduct in Aboriginal and Torres Strait Islander Health Research*. In this, the research is a continuation of, or a return to, the long tradition of the hegemonic Western gaze, which concerns itself primarily with the penetration and surveillance of the Indigenous 'other' (Tuhiwai Smith 2005).

Discussion

The overarching ethical problem of Weatherburn's research emanates from the power imbalance between the researcher and the researched. It is not suggested that the researcher intended the research to be unethical from an Indigenous perspective, but the power differential is reflected in the frameworks that inform the research. A key indicator of the power imbalance is the language used to describe Aboriginal and Torres Strait Islander people. As Cunneen (2005) argues in his earlier critique of the Weatherburn thesis, "[H]ow we speak, the language and categories we use, construct problems in particular ways, and imply certain solutions " (p. 329). Within the research Aboriginal and Torres Strait Islander people are distinguished as the problematic 'Other' and the language used in the discussion emphasizes and reemphasizes that otherness on almost every page. This raced and criminogenic positioning of the 'Aboriginal' in this research stands in contrast to the normative comparator: the race they are not, the 'non-Indigenous'. The result is a reassertion of the longstanding disrespected position of Aboriginal and Torres Strait Islander people in Australian society.

Weatherburn's language and presumptions, in turn, reflect a research worldview that directly aligns with the discourse of Aboriginal and Torres Strait Islander deficit. According to this discourse, both the cause and the remedy for over-incarceration can be found within Aboriginal people themselves. The fatal flaw in this reasoning is the uncritical acceptance of the stated social correlations of offending behavior, poor parenting, poor school performance, early school leaving, unemployment and drug and alcohol abuse as causes. But these phenomena are not social facts in and of themselves; they are indicators of inequality and as such cannot be the end point of an Indigenous over-representation explanation – they should be the starting point. Inequality does not just exist – it comes from somewhere. Inequality cannot be divorced from the social, cultural, racial, political and economic processes that create and maintain it. It is not that these things 'cause' offending but that offending, over-representation *and* these indicators are part of the same landscape of inequality.

Another indicator of the power differential is the presumption that the research can be undertaken without recourse to Indigenous perspectives. Moreover, the research presumes an analysis outside its historical and contemporary context. However, the positioning of Aboriginal and Torres Strait Islander peoples within their nation states has validity. As discussed in the opening sections of this chapter, Australian Indigenous people, along with those from Canada, Aotearoa New Zealand and the US, are colonized peoples, who are marginalized, stigmatized and economically and politically excluded within their own ancestral lands. Yet in Weatherburn's (2014) research the power differential and the author's own social position are elided through the claim of the research as 'objective'. The author states that other explanations of over-representation, including colonialism and dispossession, (unlike his own work it is implied) have not been "informed by a careful and dispassionate analysis of the facts" (p. 2).

Rather, such a question, asked from the Weatherburn perspective, functionally supports the social and cultural status quo. It maintains Indigenous inequality and allows the broader societal and structural dimensions of this inequality to remain unexamined, unquestioned and undisturbed. Such a question also fails to address the wider issue of why the Indigenous peoples of these countries are all heavily over-represented in incarceration rates within their individual nation states. If the answer is not somehow related to colonization and its aftermath, then the only other viable answer is that the British were just unlucky enough to colonize four discrete geographical locations where the Indigenous populations were naturally criminally inclined. Such an explanation is obviously ludicrous but such conclusions are the risk of analyses of criminological phenomena, such as those undertaken by Weatherburn, which are divorced from their social, cultural and racial locations.

How could it have been different? What if the researchers had asked, not why are Indigenous people criminals, but *what is it about the lived reality of fourth-world peoples in first-world Anglo colonized nation-states that leads to and results in their dramatic over-representation within their respective criminal justice systems?* A very different research question, with potentially very different outcomes, both in terms of results and ethically.

Conclusion

The vulnerable social and cultural position of first-world Indigenous populations means that they face numerous ethical risks within the research process. These have long been recognized by Indigenous peoples themselves and now are increasingly recognized by researchers and the institutions tasked with ensuring that human research is ethical research. But as shown in this chapter, criminologists also need to analyze the epistemological, ontological and axiological positions they themselves bring to their research and the compatibility or translatability of these within Indigenous research settings.

References

Austin, A 2013, *High Unemployment Means Native American are Still Waiting for an Economic Recovery. Report on Race and Ethnicity*, Economic Policy Institute. www.epi.org/publication/high-unemployment-means-native-americans/.

Australian Bureau of Statistics 2013, *Australian Social Trends*, Catalogue No. 4102.0, Canberra.

Australian Institute of Aboriginal and Torres Strait Islander Studies 2012, *Guidelines for Ethical Research in Australian Indigenous Studies*, Canberra, Australian Institute of Aboriginal and Torres Strait Islander Studies.

Australian Institute of Criminology, *Criminal Justice System*. www.aic.gov.au/criminal_justice_system.html.

Becenti-Pigman, B, White, K, Bowman, B, Duran, B, & Palmanteer-Holder, L n.d., *Research Policies, Processes and Protocol of the Navajo Nation Human Research Review Board (NNHRRB)*. www.nptao.arizona.edu/ProtocolPDFs/Navajo%20Nation%20Research%20Policies,%20Processes%20and%20Protocol0001.pdf.

Cunneen, C 2005 'Racism, discrimination and the over-representation of Indigenous people in the criminal justice system: Some conceptual and explanator issues', *Current Issues in Criminal Justice*, vol. 17, no. 3, pp. 329–246.

Drees, LM, 2001, 'Native studies and ethical guidelines for research: Dilemmas and solutions', *Native Studies Review*, vol. 14, pp. 83–104.

Dyck, N 1985, *Indigenous Peoples and the Nation-state: 'Fourth world' politics in Canada, Australia, and Norway*, St. Johns, NL, Institute of Social and Economic Research.

Ermine, W, Sinclair, R, & Jeffery, B 2004, *The Ethics of Research Invoving Indigenous Peoples, Report of the Indigenous Peoples' Health Research Centre to the Interagency Advisory Panel on Research Ethics*, Regina, Canada, Indigenous Peoples' Health Research Centre.

Hamill, C 2015, Personal communication, 24 April.

Hartney, C & Vuong, L 2009, *Created Equal: Racial and Ethnic Disparities in the US Criminal Justice System*. www.nccdglobal.org/sites/default/files/publication_pdf/created-equal.pdf.

Heintzelman, CA 2003 'The Tuskegee Syphilis Study and its implications for the 21st century', *New Social Worker*, vol. 10, no. 4. www.socialworker.com/feature-articles/ethics-articles/The_Tuskegee_Syphilis_Study_and_Its_Implications_for_the_21st_Century/.

Hudson, M, Milne, M, Reynolds, P, Russell, K, & Smith, B 2010, *Te Ara Tika Guidelines for Māori Research Ethics: A Framework for Researchers and Ethics Committee Members*, Health Research Council of New Zealand. www.hrc.govt.nz/sites/default/files/Te%20Ara%20Tika%20Guidelines%20for%20Māori%20Research%20Ethics.pdf.

Law Council of Australia 2014, *Law Council says Indigenous Imprisonment is a National Crisis*, MR# 1427. www.lawcouncil.asn.au/lawcouncil/.

Ministry of Business, Innovation and Employment 2013, *Māori Labour Market Factsheet March 2013*. www.dol.govt.nz/publications/lmr/quick-facts.

Ministry of Justice 2009, *Over-representation of Māori in Prison*. www.justice.govt.nz/policy/constitutional-law-and-human-rights/human-rights/international-human-rights-instruments/international-human-rights-instruments-1/convention-against-torture/united-nations-convention-against-torture-and-other-cruel-inhuman-or-degrding-treatment-or-punishment-new-zealand-periodic-report-6/article-11/18-over-representation-of-maori-in-prison.

Navajo Nation Council n.d., *Navajo Nation Human Research Code*, Chapter 5. www.nptao.arizona.edu/research/docs/Navajo_Nation_Human_SubjectsCode.pdf.

Navajo National Human Research Review Board 2009a, www.nnhrrb.navajo-nsn.gov/.

Navajo National Human Research Review Board 2009b, www.nnhrrb.navajo-nsn.gov/pdf/NavNatHumResCode.pdf.

Rolls, M 2003, 'Why I don't want to be an ethical researcher: A polemical paper', *Australian Humanities Review*. www.australianhumanitiesreview.org/archive/Issue-Jan-2003/rolls1.html.

Sahota, PC 2007, *Research Regulation in American Indian/Alaskan Native Communities: Policy and Practice Considerations*, Washington, DC, NCAI Policy Research Center, National Congress of American Indians.

Smith, LI 1999, *Decolonizing Methodologies, Research and Indigenous Peoples*, London and New York, Zed Books.

Smith, LT 2005, On tricky ground: Researching the native in the age of uncertainty, in *The Sage Handbook of Quantitative Research* (3rd ed), eds N Denzin & YS Lincoln, Los Angeles, Sage.

Statistics Canada 2009, *The Incarceration of Aboriginal People in Adult Correctional Services*. www.statcan.gc.ca/pub/85-002-x/2009003/article/10903-eng.htm.

Statistics Canada 2011, *Fact Sheet – 2011 National Household Survey Aboriginal Demographics, Education Attainment and Labour Market outcomes*. www.aadnc-aandc.gccca/eng/.

Steering Committee for the Review of Government Services Provision 2014, *Overcoming Indigenous Disadvantage: Key Indicators*, Canberra, Steering Committee for the Review of Government Services Provision, Productivity Commission.

Tri-Council Policy Statement CPS2 2014, *Tri-Council Policy Statement: Ethical Conduct for Research Involving Humans*, Ottawa, Secretariat on the Responsible Conduct of Research.

Trigger, D 2014 'Ethics and politics', *Australian Journal of Anthropology*, vol. 25, no. 3, pp. 387–388.

Trudgett, M & Page, S 2014, 'When the anths come marching in', *Australian Journal of Anthropology*, vol. 25, no. 3, pp. 388–390.

United States Department of Health and Human Services (HSS) 1979, *The Belmont Report*, US Department of Health and Human Services. www.hhs.gov/ohrp/humansubjects/guidance/belmont.html.

Walter, M 2010 'The politics of the data: How the statistical indigene is constructed', *International Journal of Critical Indigenous Studies*, vol. 3, no. 2, pp. 45–56.

Walter, M (ed.) 2013, *Social Research Methods* (3rd ed), Oxford, Melbourne, Oxford University Press.

Walter, M & Andersen, C 2013, *Indigenous Statistics: A Quantitative Methodology*, Walnut Creek, Left Coast Press.

Weatherburn, D 2014, *Arresting Incarceration: Pathways out of Indigenous Imprisonment*, Canberra, Aboriginal Studies Press.

Weatherburn, D, Fitzgerald, J, & Hua, J 2003, 'Reducing Aboriginal over-representing in prison', *Australian Journal of Public Administration*, vol. 62, no. 3, pp. 65–73.

6

ETHICS AS WITNESSING

'Science', research ethics and victimization

Dale C. Spencer

Introduction

This chapter engages with the 'problem' of ethics in criminological research on victimized populations. The aim of this chapter is to interrogate the biomedical model[1] of research ethics boards that increasingly governs social scientific research (Haggerty 2004, reproduced in this volume) and to provide an ethics of witnessing apposite to the study of victims of crime. Here I am in agreement with Maurice Punch (1998) when he states that the

> generality of codes [related to ethics boards] often does not help us to make the fine distinctions that arise at the *interactional* level in participant observation studies, where the reality of the field setting may feel far removed from the refinements of scholarly debate and ethical niceties. (Emphasis added, p. 168)

I would add that, in addition to studies using participant observation, any corporeal engagement with research participants is often at odds with ethical challenges, especially in cases where those being interviewed have been subjected to extreme levels of violence. The core question of this chapter is: what are ethics in relation to crime, criminal justice and victimization? Drawing from the work of Giorgio Agamben (1998, 1999, 2003, 2005, 2010), Adriana Cavarrero (2010), and Jacques Derrida (1995, 1998, 2001), I propose what *ethics* is when confronting those suffering from trauma related to victimization. I engage with an ethics of witnessing, consisting of three modes by which witnessing is practiced in research on victims and victimization.

This chapter begins by discussing some of the mass victimizations of the twentieth century that spurred the creation of research ethics boards and how some social scientists contributed to the angsts regarding fieldwork. I demonstrate how research ethics boards are haunted by the 'specter of experimentation' and argue that ethics must be transformed to be specific to the aims and inquiry inherent to the social sciences. I then engage with the specifics of research ethics boards and ethics in criminology. Next, this chapter outlines an ethics of witnessing that is integral to victimological inquiry. Drawing on a recent project on homeless masculinities and victimization, I explore an ethics of witnessing that is integral to working with victims.

Clearing a space for ethics: knowledge production and research ethics boards

In this section, I explore the distinctions between ethics in social scientific research and biomedical research. The biomedical ethical model has enframed how research ethics boards operate and governs how both social scientific and biomedical research are conducted (Haggerty 2004; van den Hoonaard 2002, 2011). In this chapter, I demonstrate that ethics in biomedical research and criminological research is a matter of difference in *kind* and not degree. I illustrate this difference with regards to the history of these *kinds* of research that have been carried out in the name of the respective projects and show how these two approaches produce very different *kinds* of knowledge.

Research ethics and ethics boards, as we have them today, exist because of the legacy of experimentation (in the name of scientific inquiry) that took place during the Second World War (Flicker et al. 2007; Haggerty 2004; van den Hoonaard 2002). Nazi human experimentation consisted of a series of medical experiments on concentration camp prisoners, primarily Jews, but also Soviet prisoners of war, homosexuals, Romani, Poles, and disabled Germans. Josef Mengele experimented on over 1,500 unwilling twins without informed consent. Eduard Wirths exposed prisoners to hazardous chemicals, while Carl Vaernet conducted experiments on homosexual prisoners in an attempt to 'cure' homosexuality. Research 'participants' were, inter alia, subjected to water, hammer, and other forms of torture. At the same time, Unit 731 was established in Manchuria, China by order of Japanese emperor Hirohito. Under Commander Shiro Ishi, Unit 731 served as the site of experiments that involved vivisections and amputations without anesthesia and testing biological weapons on Chinese civilians (Williams & Wallace 1989). The story is the same: no consent and the physical welfare of participants was sacrificed in the name of scientific knowledge production. Moreover, the researchers at Unit 731 were provided immunity (and their findings inadmissible as war crimes evidence) in exchange for the results of their studies on human experimentation, which the US then used as information to develop its own biological warfare program (Gold 2004). The victims' voices – those subjected to vivisections and weapons testing – were thus silenced, as such messages were considered to be Communist propaganda in the West (Rapoport 2001).

In relation to the social sciences, Laud Humphreys' (1970) *Tearoom Trade* stands as a paradigmatic case of social research that raised ethical questions regarding the relationship of the researcher to his or her study participants. As an ethnographic study of anonymous male-to-male sexual encounters in public bathrooms in the 1960s, it was controversial to say the least. Humphreys argued that these males engaged in a number of public efforts to conceal their deviation from social norms and, in the end, these encounters were victimless. Because Humphreys chose to conceal his identity from his participants, he was criticized for failing to acquire research subjects' consent. While Humphreys was careful not to identify his participants in his published work, he has been criticized for privacy violations and deceit.

As an inheritance and by-product of the atrocities of the Second World War, Maurice Punch (1998, p. 167, emphasis in original) states, "the attempt to control *biomedical* research, and to protect its subjects, has also become the model for the social sciences." That is, the model of scientific knowledge construction and the application of ethics in the biomedical sciences and the social sciences is asserted as if it is a matter of differences of degree. The atrocities that transpired during the Second World War under the auspices of biomedical research invariably get placed along a continuum with what could be seen as social scientific research blunders, in cases like Zimbardo's prison experiment (Zimbardo 2008) and Humphreys' (1970) tearoom trade.

Speaking to the division between social and natural sciences, Bent Flyvbjerg (2001) suggests that the nature and aims of the respective sciences is different in kind. Drawing on Aristotle, he contends that social practice is commonly involved with *phronesis*, rather than *episteme*. The natural sciences (the model that biomedical sciences subsume) are associated with *episteme*; that is, analytical scientific knowledge associated with explanation and prediction. The latter serve as the basis under which knowledge in the social sciences is judged, despite the reality, as Flyvbjerg (ibid, p. 4) avers, that this is an ideal and hallmark that will never be reached in the social sciences. The greatest of the intellectual virtues, *phronesis*, is associated with practical wisdom, which is the necessary basis for social and political inquiry. *Phronesis* is the most salient because it is "that activity by which instrumental rationality is balanced by value-rationality, and because such balancing is crucial to the sustained happiness of the citizens in any society" (ibid). According to Flyvbjerg, phronesis is the context-dependent knowledge that is and should be produced in the social sciences and allows for consideration of power and values in social inquiry.

While it may be difficult, if not impossible, to disentangle and extricate notions derived from the natural sciences that have made their way into the social sciences, what can be taken from the previous discussion is that the ends of the respective projects are different in kind. The ways in which the world is viewed within these paradigms leads to differences in the ways in which ethics pertains to the respective scientific paradigms. Be that as it may, Haggerty (2004) has demonstrated that, in relation to research ethics boards, harms and risk are figured in ways that coincide with the biomedical model and are, as the story goes, imposed on social scientific research (see also, van den Hoonaard 2002, 2006). This is despite the fact that the biomedical model, which enframes the ways in which ethics boards view research in the English-speaking West, remains haunted by the potentiality for the production of 'bare life' (Agamben 1998, 2003, 2005, p. 87) – that is, life without form and value – engendered by deadly forms of experimentation that manifested during the Second World War and continues today.

This *specter of experimentation* haunts the biomedical sciences insofar as experimentation on animals (be it humans or other species) remains ongoing. This is problematic, if not deadly, in at least two respects. First, the biomedical sciences directly contribute to the ongoing reduction of persons to naked life in the contemporary era, insofar as they reduce that life to no more than its biological substance through the extraction of biomedical data from massive populations. This, in turn, contributes to a basis of identity that is no more than its *biological datum* (cf. Agamben 2010, p. 52). A second way in which the specter of experimentation remains problematic is that, while ethics boards in the social sciences are subjected to far more stringent conceptions of harm and risk in research on human animal subjects, the biomedical sciences continue unabated in experimentation on non-human animals. This is justified by an anthropological machine – manifested both within the biomedical sciences and broader conceptions of the relationship between humans and animals – that continuously reaffirms the hierarchy between humans and animals (cf. Spencer & Fitzgerald 2015).

The danger here is that genocides and mass killings of humans (as well as animals in biomedical research) have been and continue to be justified on the hierarchy of intelligence along ethnic and 'racial' lines *and* species (see Baird 1991; Marcus 2005; Patterson 2002). This justification can be, under the auspices of ethics boards, reconfigured in such a way as to depoliticize any and all forms of research within the sciences. Clearly, Satoshi Ishi and Josef Mengele and the totalitarian regimes that they belonged to began from the presupposition that the Chinese and Jewish prisoners, respectively, were less-than-human animals and therefore experimentation and widespread killing was justified in the name of the advancement of science and progress. The naming of victims of genocide as animals or animal-like remains a primary justification for mass extermination of a people, as seen in the mass extermination of Tutsis by the Hutus in Rwanda in the 1990s (Straus 2013). Today, the experimentation and mass consumption of animals is continually justified in the name of betterment of humanity and advancement of science (Baird 1991; Beirne 2007; Marcus 2005; Patterson 2002). The specter of experimentation looms.

In the words of ethicist Simon Blackburn, an "ethic gone wrong is an essential preliminary to the sweat-shop or the concentration camp and the death march" (2002, p. 8). The question, then, is how do we jam the anthropological machine and the presumed hierarchy between humans and animals (Calarco 2007), and establish ethics and research ethics boards apposite to criminology and the study of victims and victimization, specifically? Surely criminological research cannot be guided by the technocratic guidelines of the biomedical sciences. While learning the lessons derived from the studies of Milgram, Humphreys, and Zimbardo, criminological research must be guided by a different ethic, that which is calibrated by and attuned to the power dynamics of the carceral and traumatized worlds of those that the researcher seeks to understand. For researchers, especially criminologists who research victims of crime, to sit back in their Archimedean ivory tower arm-chairs and fail to respond to the pain and anguish of their research participants is, to quote Denzin and Giardina (2006, p. xxiii), as "morally indefensible" as the natural scientist that sacrifices rabbits in the name of producing a tear free eye make-up remover. In the remainder of this chapter, I engage in a form of phenomenological 'epoche' (Derrida 1998), a suspension and deconstruction of ethics as it is defined by research ethics boards. In addition, I will ground this analysis in envisaging of ethics-as-witnessing and analyze data from a project on homeless masculinities and victimization.

Ethics boards, ethics, and criminology

As a graduate student, postdoctoral fellow, and faculty member, I have applied for ethics approval for over a dozen research projects at four Canadian universities. In the course of these research ethics applications I have received a variety of responses ranging from informative to odd. In relation to the former, ethics board review-ers have made suggestions regarding strategies for recruitment, which in the case of marginalized and oft-hidden populations, is particularly invaluable. In relation to the latter, in a study on police responses to the sexual victimization of children and youth, I was required to change my consent form (the form that participating police officers had to sign) to note that, if they informed me in the interview of a child being abused, be it physical, sexual or psychological, I had to report it to the authorities! After some back and forth with the research ethics board at this univer-sity, I acquiesced to their authority and decided to insert the sentence in the consent form, knowing how meaningless the sentence would be in speaking with police officers, who in their positions as authority figures, regularly respond to the sex-ual victimization of children and youth. Essentially I would have to report back to the officers what they had just told me in the course of the interview! What I have found, especially in cases of moving to another university and submitting for ethics approval from the new university research ethics board, is that continuity does not necessarily exist between ethics board reviewers' responses to the same applications (cf. Haggerty 2004).

Concomitantly, the Canadian "Tri-Council Policy Statement on Ethical Conduct for Research Involving Humans" attempts to maintain a 'common standard' of research. However, as Grayson and Myles (2005, p. 294) argue, each university in Canada can have a different interpretation of the same research proposal: "while a research project or practice may be acceptable in one uni-versity, it may be totally unacceptable in another". In relation to the interpret-ations of 'potential' harms and risks related to a given project, this is significant. As Haggerty (2004, p. 400) states, the "range of potential research related harms envisioned by REBs at times seem to be limited only by the imagination of different reviewers". Roth (2005) further demonstrates that arbitrariness, power, and institutional control are inconsistent with the democratic values of transparency and accountability. Because of the tremendous amount of power REBs yield in determining what can be studied, Haggerty (2004) avers that research ethics boards hold a monopoly over research decisions at any given Canadian university. Outside of Canada, American sociolegal scholar Malcolm Feeley (2007) furthers this argument by suggesting that research ethics boards violate notions of legality and the rule of law given the fact that they are the final decision-makers and yield a tremendous amount of power that is not subject to public scrutiny. They can and do, without question, determine what can and cannot be studied. Research ethics boards, as Hamburger (2004, 2007) has argued in the same context, 'license' research that amounts to prior restraint and hence contravene the American constitutional tradition of free expression. Regardless of national background, due to the arbitrariness of ethics boards and the lack of coherence in terms of their decision making, the 'ethics' of research ethics boards is, to an extent, vacuous and amounts to bureaucratic risk management and a mechanism used by universities to govern research.

As previous commentaries on research ethics boards have shown (see Haggerty, this volume; van den Hoonaard 2002, 2011), research ethics boards impose a biomedical or scientific model of ethics on all forms of research that is, among other things, at odds with the values and practicalities of social scientific research, including matters of informed consent and confidentiality in the social sciences. Due to the specter of experimentation and the lack of coherence between the research processes and ends of biomedical sciences and social sciences, there has been an evisceration of choice *and* content regarding the 'ethics' of research ethics boards (cf. Feeley 2007). Social scientists are left without a real definition and sense of what ethics is in relation to research practice. Specifically, what is ethics in relation to crime, criminal justice and victimization? In *Ethics, Crime, and Criminal Justice*, Williams and Arrigo (2011, p. xvii) argue that the purpose of criminal justice ethics is to "help us become 'good' people and to make 'good' decisions". Ethics offers a basis for discussing how we are to treat others in manifold situations. That said, any inquiry into the lives of victimized others opens researchers up to a number of questions regarding and considerations of ethical commitments to participants, including their relationship to victims and the situationally appropriate ethical guidelines for conducting research on and with victims.

Ethics, then, in relation to victims is far more complicated than just 'being good' and 'making good decisions'. What is required, especially in the study of victims and victimization, is an ethics specific to this line of inquiry and area of criminological research. Relying on resources derived from the work of such Continental philosophers as Giorgio Agamben (1998, 1999, 2003, 2005, 2010), Adriana Cavarrero (2010), and Jacques Derrida (1995, 1998, 2001), here I offer a conceptualization of what ethics *should* look like in research on victims and victimization with an eye to dilemmas experienced by those conducting research on victimized others.

Ethics as 'witnessing'

Outside of criminology, Continental philosophy offers a number of resources for thinking about ethics and our relationship to others. For Immanuel Kant (1785), a foundational thinker in terms of the metaphysics of ethics, the treatment of morals as a system of ethics is grounded in the language of means and ends. He states that,

> [M]an [sic], and in general every rational being, exists as an end in himself and not merely as a means to be arbitrarily used by this or that will. He must in all his actions, whether directed to himself or to other rational beings, always be regarded at the same time as an end. (Kant 1785, p. 35)

Here, Kant argues that the foundation of ethics is to treat others not as a means to our own ends, but as an end unto themselves. This maxim offers something of an approach to treating criminological research participants, but offers little in terms of the position of the researcher in relation to traumatized victims. That is, it offers criminologists little in terms of the shifting conceptual frameworks (see Guillemin & Gillam 2004) necessary for engaging with victimized others; specifically, those who have experienced extreme levels of violence and victimization.

Adrianna Cavarero (2010) argues that, when we shift our point of view in witnessing massacres, genocides and other atrocities from the position of the warrior to the victim, the scenes of violence change. The means becomes substance and the ends of violence vanish. The primary reaction is no longer terror, but horror. On the other hand, the location of research and researcher implies that any project always carries within itself an epistemology (see Usher & Edwards 1994). This epistemology is never 'innocent' as it contains within itself a set of values, which means there is always a *politics of victimology research*. Inquiry implies particular ends and has particular implications for those who are studied.

In relation to victims, taking on 'impersonal' categories ('the researcher', 'the victim') implies certain prior ethical commitments. That is, to be 'the researcher' implies a hierarchy in relation to and a commitment to 'know' research 'subjects', and the label of 'the victim' connotes a universal acceptance of the category of 'the victim'. To engage in the type of 'social engineering' that is the goal of some positivistic approaches implies a universal sense of justice and law (one that is at odds with the one advocated in this chapter). The following section carves out an ethical and epistemological position for the study of victimization that does not reduce the experience of victimization to a category.

Three modes of witnessing emerge in relation to the event of victimization. The first position is being a witness to oneself within the experience of victimization (Agamben 1999). The second witnessing position is being a witness to others being victimized. The third position is being a witness to the *process* of witnessing. Based on these three levels of witnessing, various moments in the chain of victimization can be posited, starting from the event of victimization itself. The researcher, it should be understood, can take on a range of *possible* research positions as a witness to the event of victimization (not necessarily concomitantly, nor necessarily in the same project). As a point of inquiry, research focuses on the *narratives* of those experiencing the trauma of victimization, which can involve both the researcher as a witness in the first and second positions. This involves illumination, through rich description (Katz 2002), the event of victimization itself and the often-devastating effects of trauma on the bodies and minds of victims. For example, the researcher may follow the victimized through their engagement with police and the ways in which they experience the continual reverberations of the event of victimization. Conducting such research also requires that researchers engage with voluntary and professional victim service organizations and correctional agencies, taking on the third position as being a witness to the process of witnessing itself.

The interview encounter takes on a particular character in relation to victimization. The interviewer takes on the ethical responsibility for bearing witness to their traumatic narrative that previously the narrator felt she or he bore alone. It is the encounter and the coming together between the survivor and the interviewer that makes possible something like a repossession of the act of witnessing (see Laub 1995). In some cases, those who have experienced an event of victimization and the interviewer enter into an encounter whereby the victimized *survives to tell their story but also tells their story to survive.* The ethical challenge is to listen and respond to the traumatic stories in ways that ensure they do not lose their impact, and that does not reduce them to clichés or turn them into versions of the same story (see Caruth 1995).

While recognizing the unique experience of the event of victimization, this is not to say that, in its totality, the singular experience of the event of victimization is ever recollected. Details can and will vanish into memory (Derrida 2001). This is, in Derrida's (1995, pp. 207, 209) term, the "experience of cinders": the experience of forgetting. Cinders are the traces of a disintegrated past, which, in part, is consumed by the fire of time. While the researcher bears witness to the existence of an event of victimization, that event in its totality is never revealed. Because there is loss in the act of remembering, testifying and inscribing (writing) an event of the past, the work of the researcher is always a work of mourning. If memory testifies to the fact that one can never fully recollect the past, then mourning affirms that victims are never finished with the past: that the task of comprehending the past always lays ahead (Derrida 1995).

As an ethics of witnessing, the focus may also be on the ways in which stories are produced, the ways they are read, the work they perform in wider worlds, how they change, and their role in the political process (cf. Holstein & Miller 1990). Further, the focus is on how particular victimized individuals are put forth as the face of a particular type of event of victimization. A case in point in this regard is the victimization of Megan Kanka and the resulting proliferation of Megan's Law in the US (Simon 2000). As Deleuze and Guattari (1987) warn, despotic regimes require a particular face to *overcode* other signs and stand as representations of people, things and actions. In the case of Megan Kanka, her face has come to overcode other experiences of the pain and suffering associated with sexual offenses. Any attempts to challenge the unconstitutional nature of Megan's Law are seen as challenges to the victimization of Megan Kanka (Simon 2000; Spencer 2009). In addition, such regimes, at times, lead to victims victimizing others vis-à-vis taking vengeance on offenders (Pratt 2000). The focus on the singularity of experience of the event of victimization advocated here requires an ethics of witnessing that emphasizes the *polyvocality* of the experiences of such traumatic events of victimization as child sexual assault and murder. Such an ethics of witnessing is resolute in highlighting marginalized voices and experiences of victims overlooked in mediatized discourses (see following section) and refrains from assumptions regarding what victims want after victimization (i.e. retribution, restitution, etc.).

Integral to an ethics of witnessing is understanding the experiences of victimized others by focusing on the narratives of those victimized, rather than subject them to the symbolic violence characteristic of reducing experiences of trauma to number(s). The narration of a life story offers an alternative sense to politics because it deals with unique persons and illustrates the interaction between people (Cavarero 2000). Narration reveals the finite in its fragile uniqueness. In the researcher's exposure to victimized others we are open to their harm and to being *horrified* by their stories of victimization (Cavarero 2010). Through the opening of stories we come to be exposed to the events of victimization. Victimization, then, is comprehended in terms of the impact of victimization on the existence of a singularity,[2] irrespective of the type of harm. Through narrative, each event of victimization can be understood as starting from the potential upheavals in the lives of individual victims that victimization triggers. We come to understand the transmogrification of lives that occurs through victimization. Such an analytic also allows for consideration of the relations engaged in as a result of events of victimization (criminal justice agencies, other victims, etc.) and how these relations are made meaningful to each singularity. In addition, such an approach considers the embodiment of victimization and the corporeal effects of trauma that, in a recursive way, point to the salience of the event of victimization to the individual singularity (Spencer 2011, 2015). Lastly, an ethics of witnessing also brings the possibility for vicarious trauma to be experienced by the researcher in and through their engagement with their research participants, which, arguably, challenges the myopic concern of research ethics boards (with participants and risk) to a much broader evaluation of how victim-related research is a thoroughly traumatic endeavor.

Researcher as witness: studying homeless masculinities and victimization

In early 2013, after reviewing the vast literature on gender, violence and victimization, I noted that there was a significant lacuna in research on arguably the most violence-saturated cohort in society: street-involved and homeless males who are scattered across the contemporary urban landscape. At the same time, I began this project as a witness, a testifier to the unbelievable number of males in

Winnipeg, Manitoba panhandling and sleeping on the streets that I encountered on an everyday basis. While in itself this social fact is violent – at the very least at the symbolic level – as a victimology scholar I was left wondering what forms of violence and trauma these men experience. Ethics as witnessing matters insofar as the narratives of seemingly powerless homeless and street-involved males go unheard and, more broadly, are silenced due to the shame associated with speaking of pain and suffering even amongst the most subaltern masculinities. There is a failure to expose the extreme levels of violence and victimization experienced by this cohort. And so, positioned as a researcher as witness, I began a comparative case study of homeless masculinities and victimization in Winnipeg, Manitoba and Chicago, Illinois. Between April 2013 and April 2014, I conducted 70 semi-structured interviews with males who were patrons of local drop-in centres and homeless shelters or clients of housing organizations dedicated to aiding marginalized and homeless people. Winnipeg and Chicago were chosen as cases or sites for data collection for manifold reasons, one of which is worth mentioning here. At the time of selection of research sites, both Winnipeg and Chicago had the highest number of murders in major cities in their respective countries (Coutts 2012; Wilson 2013). They are violent cities. The interviews focused on their life stories and were intentionally wide-ranging and covered such topics as participants' experiences of homelessness, (un)employment, violence, victimization and exclusion. Below, I engage with the embodiment of victimization and the corporeal effects of trauma experienced by an overwhelming majority of the 70 males I interviewed. The following analysis is not an exhaustive analysis of narratives from this project; rather, I utilize the narratives of four men to illustrate the ethics of witnessing as it figures in the study of victims and victimization. Keeping with the ethics of witnessing, pseudonyms have been assigned to reduce retraumatization and create the conditions whereby participants feel able to open up and tell their life stories.

Within the research act, qualitative and ethnographic criminologists are witnesses to the stories of their participants but also exposed to their corporeal co-presence in the encounter that is registered at the affective, emotional and sensory levels (Harris & Guillemin 2012; Pink 2009; Spencer 2014). In the research encounter, our bodies are in an ongoing way immersed in and among the world's obstinacies and rhythms (Gregg & Seigworth 2010; Massumi 2014). We are affected by and we affect our participants. In our exposure to the other, we are exposed to their skin, that which reveals the pain and trauma of past events. Our historiated skin possesses and displays a particular history (Serres 2009, p. 55). Our skin makes visible the wear and tear, revealing scars from wounds. Memory is inscribed on the skin. Memories, here, are not passive records, but shape a sense of bodily self and ground that sense of self into experienced and re-livable sensations (Seremetakis 1994; Spencer 2014; Waskul et al. 2009). Scars across the surface of the skin serve as reminders of events of victimization (Spencer 2011). My encounter with 21-year-old Sigmund, a Cree homeless male, exemplifies this aspect of witnessing:

Uh I got stabbed in uh … [names location] under the underpass, it happened by the big bus depot there … I was heading down to my friend's party, and they stopped me and said, "Oh, give us your beer," and I said. "No," and then they pulled out a knife. I just fuckin … I threw the beer at them. They said, "Okay, now give us your bank card." I said, "No, I don't want to." I said, "Why?" And well, "We want it, we want your numbers." … They tried to get my bank card, I punched one in the face, they held me down, they put me on the ground, they asked me, "Are you going to give us your number?" and I said, "No." They cut me once down here [points to the left side of his neck], then he said, "Are you going to give us your number," and I spit in his face, he, he did it up again [cutting him up his neck]. And then his friend took over and it's like, "Okay, I'm going to cut your throat." It's like, "Okay, are you going to give us your number?" I spit blood at him too, and he just went all the way around, and they just left me there. I got up, I tried to make it to my friend's but I blacked out and … when they found me like I was just covered in my blood everywhere, and uh I woke up in the hospital about a day later. It, I really didn't know what was going on at first, and I was scared.

Sigmund's neck, with scarification traceable from one side to the other, reveals the moment of victimization. To the onlooker, it calls for more explanation. This scar signifies an attempt on his life and physically embeds memories of the past, of trauma that cannot be hidden from view. While telling the story, Sigmund runs his fingers across the scar that, in contradistinction to the clean line of a surgeon, meanders across his neck. Throughout my interview with Sigmund, he tells his narrative in a matter of fact way, as if being sliced open is part of his ordinary experience. It is his vision of everyday life. As a witness to Sigmund's narrative, I am affected by his strength and resilience, his ability in the face of death to fight for life and maintain self-respect. I come to see his victimization through his eyes. Concomitantly, remembering him run his fingers along his scar, I was and am horrified by his experience, a horror that has still not left me. This form of vicarious trauma is part of the ethics of witnessing.

Witnessing qua seeing takes place within a political, social and cultural framework that defines the limits of intelligibility. An essential component of this process involves determining who possesses the ability to constitute what counts as intelligible (Weiss 2008). It is impossible to approach the question of how violence is experienced and is constituted in and through particular horizons of significance without acknowledging that for some people ordinary experience, in opposition to its disruption, is itself defined by extreme suffering and misery. Gail Weiss (2008) writes that for those whom "deprivation and degradation is a way of life, the disruption of the ordinary can be a hope, a fantasy, or even a prayer" (p. 5). In this way, the sedimentation of everyday experience into intelligible patterns may serve to codify domination, violence, and victimization and provide a sense of existential stability. The following excerpts demonstrate how suffering and misery can be the dominant experience of everyday life:

It's, it's a brutality; it's a brutal reality I guess you could say. Like um I don't know, it kind of, it's a very traumatic experience. I mean years of that it starts building up into your lifestyle and it almost seems like the best thing you got you know like, you feel like you've already ruined your life to a point where you can't really uh live like most other people do and uh it's that sense of helplessness I guess. (Daniel)

Violence towards me, I got a black eye from my stepdad a few times, violence at school, fighting and stuff, violence on the streets: one time I seen this guy, he dragged another guy to the curb and then put this teeth on the curb and then jumped on the back of his head; we call it curb stomping. (Jerome)

Daniel's response reveals a life of continuous abuse. Everyday life in this sense seems an impossible ideal. A son of abusive, alcoholic parents, extreme forms of violence characterize his existence; levels of violence and trauma that leave a lasting impression on his habitus (Bourdieu 1992; Merleau-Ponty 1982; Sanchez Garcia & Spencer 2013). Similarly, Jerome points to the various institutions in his life and only finds violence. He notes an extreme vision of violence that dominates his memory of the past. In relation to Daniel and Jerome, I serve as a witness to their particular horizons of significance and how suffering and violence are focal, rather than disruptive, elements of their everyday life. Through telling his story, Daniel moves away from a sense of helplessness to reaffirm his narrative, to which it is incumbent upon me as a witness to retell and make known to broader audiences. In relation to Jerome, I am also positioned as a witness to his visions of violence that comprise life on the streets.

Similarly, Dustin reveals an everyday life littered with visions of violence and victimization:

Um, well when I was a kid my mom dated uh an older man, he was very abusive, he tried to kill her eight times in front of us. ... When I was ten years old, a little younger, probably nine, I seen him try and slit my mom's throat so I called the cops and the cops came and then we got out of there ... but uh as soon as we got out of the house she, she dated a lot of people and they weren't very good men, one guy raped her in front of me and like choked her one time until she was like blue and then uh we got out of that relationship. ... When I was like ten years old, like grade three, and I never really realized why I was like acting up and like getting in to so many fights until nowadays.... I never had a dad; my mom and him broke up when I was a kid. He pushed her into a door knob when I was in her stomach still. I was six days early; I was suppose to be a Christmas baby, but I was born December 19th.

The spaces of survival that made and continue to make up Dustin's everyday life are characterized by moments of acute violence. Viewed from the point of view of the victim, the scenes of horror in Dustin's narrative blend together as means rather than ends. They are strewn together as part of his everyday life; they are relived as traumatizing moments. As I sensed/witnessed throughout the interview with Dustin, his ontological dignity is shattered, reflected in his face as he recounted the many scenes of violence. The reclamation of dignity becomes the key point of struggle and resistance, which the researcher qua witness has an ethical responsibility to take part in. In this case, I am a witness not only to his victimization but also to his witnessing of the extreme violence experienced by his mother. In addition, the witnessing of a narrative in this way involves seeing and listening, and in relation to the latter, to the amplitude, density, and vibration of how words are said (Nancy 2007). Long after witnessing the telling of this narrative, I am haunted by this story. Dustin experienced and continues to experience trauma related to these violent incidences and I can vividly recall Dustin's shaking hands, his intense eye contact, his oft-quivering voice, and the grin he gave me as we concluded the interview. In the end, the encounter involves reclamation of a narrative and an affective event, leaving its mark on the researcher and participant.

Conclusion

In a short essay entitled "Ethics", Giorgio Agamben (2005, p. 43) asserts, "the point of departure for any discourse on ethics is that there is no essence, no historical or spiritual vocation, no biological destiny that humans must enact or realize". The ethical experience is only possible because we lack a substance that determines our existence; that is, what we are as humans is not presupposed by a predefined essence (see Crewe & Lippens 2009). The challenge, then, is that ethics is the realm of the possible, the potentiality to be or not to be, to determine being one way or another. Returning to the discussion of research ethics boards, we can think of this institutional procedure, regardless of type of social scientific endeavor, as an unfinished project. That is, research ethics boards should be seen as the realm of the possible, as possessing the potential-to-be-otherwise than they now exist and operate. In relation to criminology, scholars should not conceive of and approach research ethics boards as fixed entities, but rather as an iterative process that can and should be changed at the local and national levels in ways that are apposite to the criminological project. At the local level, criminologists should engage with reform of their universities' research ethics boards to make them more understanding of the vagaries that arise in the processes of doing criminological research. For example, criminologists may sit on ethics boards and/or consult with their university ethics boards through presentations and/or submission of position papers to outline the *nature* of fieldwork and research on victims and victimization. At the national level, criminological researchers should advocate for change to research ethics protocols that view social scientific research not as different in degree from their biomedical science counterparts, but as different in kind, possessing their own ends, dilemmas, and ethical responsibilities. Moreover, in this potential-to-be-otherwise, research ethics and research ethics boards could be attuned to the fact that victim-related research is a thoroughly traumatizing endeavor and, as such, could proceed by being oriented to care (rather than risk) and a commitment to proffering of a multitude of voices related to diverse forms of victimization.

In this chapter, I have introduced an ethics of witnessing as a way of thinking about and ethically relating to victims and victimization. From the three levels of witnessing prescribed here, victimology can develop ethical positions specific to its subject matter and serious thinking about the implications of engaging with the narratives of victimized others. Moreover, through the project on homeless mas-culinities and victimization, I illustrate how this ethics of witnessing plays a vital role in the interview encounter and always involves more than the telling of stories. An ethics of witnessing possesses the potential for a repoliticized subdiscipline of victimology through a focus on narrative and embodiment. This is a move away from accumulating 'official' crime statistics on victimization and towards a critical victimology that engages with marginalized populations and hidden forms of vic-timization that are all too often ignored.

Notes

1   Here, I am referring to the biomedical scientific model that consists of a set of applied sciences that are used to develop knowledge and technology interventions in healthcare and/or public health.
2   By singularity, I am pointing to the haecceity of humans. In the work of Charles Sanders Peirce (1974) and those who follow him, it is meant to denote the extreme individuality of humans, unique in gait, disposition, etc., which biological mapping cannot capture.

References

Agamben, G 1998, *Homo Sacer: Sovereign Power and Bare Life*, trans. D Heller-Roazen, Palo Alto, CA, Stanford University Press.

Agamben, G 1999, *Remnants of Auschwitz: The Witness and the Archive*, trans. D Heller-Roazen, New York, Zone Books.

Agamben, G 2003, *The Open: Man and Animal*, trans. K Attell, Palo Alto, CA, Stanford University Press.

Agamben, G 2005, *Coming Community*, trans. M Hardt, Minneapolis, University of Minnesota Press.

Agamben, G 2010, *Nudities*, trans. D Kishik & S Pedatella, Palo Alto, CA, Stanford University Press.

Baird, RM 1991, *Animal Experimentation*, Buffalo, NY, Prometheus Books.

Beirne, P 2007, 'Animal rights, animal abuse and green criminology', in *Issues in Green Criminology: Confronting Harms against Environments, Humanity and Other Animals*, ed P Beirne, Cullompton, UK, Willan, pp. 55–83.

Blackburn, S 2002, *Being Good: A Short Introduction to Ethics*, Oxford, Oxford University Press.

Bourdieu, P 1992, *The Logic of Practice*, Palo Alto, CA, Stanford University Press.

Calarco, M 2007, 'Jamming the anthropological machine', in *Giorgio Agamben: Sovereignty and Life*, eds M Calarco & S DeCaroli, Palo Alto, CA, Stanford University Press, pp. 163–179.

Caruth, C 1995, 'Introduction' in *Trauma: Explorations in Memory*, ed C Caruth, Baltimore, MD, Johns Hopkins University Press, pp. 3–12.

Cavarero, A 2000, *Relating Narratives: Storytelling and Selfhood*, trans. P Kottman, New York, Routledge.

Cavarero, A 2010, *Horrorism: Naming Contemporary Violence*, trans. W McCuaig, New York, Columbia University Press.

Coutts, M 2012, 'Latest numbers crown Winnipeg as Canada's murder capital', *Yahoo News Canada*. https://ca.news.yahoo.com/blogs/dailybrew/latest-numbers-crown-winnipeg-canada-murder-capital-214530106.html.

Crewe, D & Lippens, R 2009, 'Existentialism – freedom, being and crime', in *Existentialist Criminology*, eds R Lippens & D Crewe, New York, Routledge-Cavendish, pp. 1–11.

Deleuze, G & Guattari, F 1987, *Thousand Plateaus: Capitalism and Schizophrenia*, trans. B Massumi, Minneapolis, University of Minnesota Press.

Denzin, NK & Giardina, M 2006, 'Introduction', in *Qualitative Inquiry and the Conservative Challenge*, eds NK Denzin & M Giardina, Walnut Creek, CA, Left Coast Press, pp. ix–xxx.

Derrida, J 1995, *Points... Interviews, 1974–1994*, trans. P Kamuf, Palo Alto, CA, Stanford University Press.

Derrida, J 1998, *Of Grammatology*, trans. GC Spivak, Baltimore, MD, Johns Hopkins University Press.

Derrida, J 2001, *A Taste for the Secret*, Cambridge, Polity.

Feeley, M 2007, 'Legality, social research, and the challenge of institutional review boards', *Law & Society Review*, vol. 41, no. 4, pp. 757–776.

Flicker, S, Travers, R, Guta, A, McDonald, S, & Meagher, A 2007, 'Ethical dilemmas in community-based participatory research: Recommendations for institutional review boards', *Journal of Urban Health: Bulletin of the New York Academy of Medicine*, vol. 84, no. 4, pp. 478–493.

Flyvbjerg, B 2001, *Making Social Science Matter: Why Social Inquiry Fails and How it Can Succeed Again*, trans. S Sampson, Cambridge, Cambridge University Press.

Gold, H 2004, *Unit 731 Testimony: Japan's Wartime Human Experimentation Program*, Boston, MA, Tuttle.

Grayson, JP & Myles, R 2005, 'How research ethics boards are undermining survey research on Canadian university students', *Journal of Academic Ethics*, vol. 2, no. 4, pp. 293–314.

Guillemin, M & Gillam, L 2004, 'Ethics, reflexivity, and "ethically important moments" in research', *Qualitative Inquiry*, vol. 10, no. 2, pp. 261–280.

Haggerty, KD 2004, 'Ethics creep: Governing social science research in the name of ethics', *Qualitative Sociology*, vol. 27, no.4, pp. 391–414.

Hamburger, P 2004, 'The new censorship: Institutional review boards', *Supreme Court Review*, vol. 271, pp. 290–306.

Hamburger, P 2007, 'Getting Permission', *Northwestern University Law Review*, vol. 101, pp. 405–492.

Harris, A & Guillemin, M 2012, 'Developing sensory awareness in qualitative interviewing a portal into the otherwise unexplored', *Qualitative Health Research*, vol. 22, no. 5, pp. 689–699.

Holstein, JA & Miller, G 1990, 'Rethinking victimization: An interactional approach to victimology', *Symbolic Interaction*, vol. 13, no. 1, pp. 103–122.

Hoonaard, W van den 2002, *Walking the Tightrope: Ethical Issues for Qualitative Researchers*, Toronto, University of Toronto Press.

Hoonaard, W van den 2006, 'New angles and tangles in the ethics review of research', *Journal of Academic Ethics*, vol. 4, no. 1–4, pp. 261–274.

Hoonaard, W van den 2011, *Seduction of Ethics: Transforming the Social Sciences*, Toronto, University of Toronto Press.

Humphreys, L 1970, *Tearoom Trade: Impersonal Sex in Public Places*, Piscataway, NJ, Transaction Publishers.

Kant, I 1785, *Grounding for the Metaphysics of Morals,* trans. JW Ellington, Indianapolis and Cambridge, Hackett Publishing Company.

Katz, J 2002, 'Start here: Social ontology and research strategy', *Theoretical Criminology*, vol. 6, no. 3, pp. 255–278.

Laub, D 1995, 'Truth and testimony: The process and the struggle', in *Trauma: Explorations in Memory*, ed C Caruth, Baltimore, MD, Johns Hopkins University Press, pp. 61–75.

Marcus, E 2005, *Meat Market: Animals, Ethics, & Money,* Minneapolis, MN, Brio Press.

Massumi, B 2014, *The Power at the End of the Economy*, Durham, NC, Duke University Press.

Merleau-Ponty, M 1982, *Phenomenology of Perception*, London and New York, Routledge.

Nancy, JL 2007, *Listening*, trans. C Mandell, New York, Fordham University Press.

Patterson, C 2002, *Eternal Treblinka: Our Treatment of Animals and the Holocaust*, New York, Lantern Books.

Peirce, CS 1974, *Collected Papers of Charles Sanders Peirce*, Cambridge, MA, Harvard University Press.

Pink, S 2009, *Doing Sensory Ethnography*, Thousand Oaks, CA, Sage.

Pratt, J 2000, 'Emotive and ostentatious punishment: Its decline and resurgence in modern society', *Punishment & Society*, vol. 2, no. 4, pp. 417–439.

Punch, M 1998, 'Politics and ethics in qualitative research', in *The Landscape of Qualitative Research: Theories and Issues*, eds NK Denzin & YS Lincoln, London and New Delhi, Sage, pp. 156–184.

Rapoport, D.C. 2001, 'Terrorism and weapons of the apocalypse', in *Twenty-First Century Weapons Proliferation: Are We Ready?* eds JM Ludes & H Sokolski, London, Routledge, pp. 14–32.

Roth, WM 2005, 'Ethics as social practice: Introducing the debate on qualitative research and ethics', *Forum Qualitative Sozialforschung / Forum: Qualitative Social Research*, vol. 6, no. 1. www.qualitative-research.net/index.php/fqs/article/view/526.

Sanchez-Garcia, R & Spencer, D 2013, 'Introduction: Carnal ethnography as path to embodied knowledge', in *Fighting Scholars: Ethnographies of Habitus in Martial Arts and Combat Sports*, eds R Sanchez-Garcia & D Spencer, London and New York, Anthem, pp. 1–18.

Seremetakis, CN 1994, *The Senses Still*, Chicago, IL, University Of Chicago Press.

Serres, M 2009, *The Five Senses: A Philosophy of Mingled Bodies*, trans. M Sankey & P Cowley, New York, Continuum.

Seigworth, GJ & Gregg, M 2010, 'Introduction', in *The Affect Theory Reader*, eds M Gregg & GJ Seigworth, Durham, NC, Duke University Press.

Simon, J 2000, 'Megan's Law: Crime and democracy in late modern America', *Law & Social Inquiry*, vol. 25, no. 4, pp. 1111–1150.

Spencer, DC 2009, 'Sex offender as homo sacer', *Punishment and Society*, vol. 11, no. 2, pp. 219–240.

Spencer, DC 2011, 'Event and victimization', *Criminal Law and Philosophy*, vol. 5, no. 1, pp. 39–52.

Spencer, DC 2014, 'Sensing violence: An ethnography of mixed martial arts', *Ethnography*, vol. 15, no. 2, pp. 232–254.

Spencer, DC 2015, 'Corporeal realism and victimology', *International Review of Victimology*, vol. 21, no. 1, pp. 31–44.

Spencer, DC and Fitzgerald, A 2015, 'Criminology and Animality: Stupidity and the Anthropological Machine', *Contemporary Justice Review*, vol. 18, no. 4, pp. 407–420.

Straus, S 2013, *The Order of Genocide: Race, Power, and War in Rwanda*, Ithaca, NY, Cornell University Press.

Usher, R & Edwards, R 1994, *Postmodernism and Education: Different Voices, Different Worlds*, New York and London, Routledge.

Waskul, DD, Vannini, P & Wilson, J 2009, 'The aroma of recollection: Olfaction, nostalgia, and the shaping of the sensuous self', *The Senses and Society*, vol. 4, no. 1, pp. 5–22.

Weiss, G 2008, *Refiguring the Ordinary*, Bloomington, Indiana University Press.

Williams, CR & Arrigo, BA 2011, *Ethics, Crime, and Criminal Justice*, Upper Saddle River, NJ, Prentice Hall.

Williams, P & Wallace, D 1989, *Unit 731: Japan's Secret Biological Warfare in World War II*, New York, Free Press.

Wilson, R 2013, 'FBI: Chicago passes New York as murder capital of US', *Washington Post*, September 18. www.washingtonpost.com/blogs/govbeat/wp/2013/09/18/fbi-chicago-passes-new-york-as-murder-capital-of-u-s/.

Zimbardo, P 2008, *The Lucifer Effect: Understanding How Good People Turn Evil* (reprint), New York, Random House Trade Paperbacks.

PART III

Research on and with police

7

NAVIGATING RESEARCH RELATIONSHIPS

Academia and criminal justice agencies

Erin Gibbs Van Brunschot

Introduction

In the summer of 2011, my colleagues and I were awarded a research grant by the judicial branch of a provincial government. So began a three-and-a-half-year collaborative research project involving university researchers, local and provincial police forces, as well as various social and welfare service agencies. The funding supported a research project investigating the application of Global Positioning System (GPS) electronic monitoring (EM) to different types of offenders in various locations across the province. Importantly, certain parameters of the project were predetermined by the funder, but also by legislation. For example, the funding was for the purpose of investigating GPS-EM; other forms of community supervision were of less concern (though were considered as part of the project). The funder determined, at least initially, which other government agencies and stakeholders would be represented on the advisory committee. Given the length of the project, the advisory committee membership often shifted to accommodate changes in personnel at the partner agencies, resulting in new members on the committee. Early committee members were replaced with others, each of whom had varying interests in the project. Legislative boundaries were also placed on the project as the research team and advisory committee had no say in who would wear the GPS-EM units – this was determined by judges – which set limits on the research design and questions that could be answered.

The collaboration involved navigating differing expectations among and between stakeholders about what the research was about, what it could be about and the opportunities associated with collaboration, as well as the limitations associated with these types of projects. The experience shed much light on the nature of research collaborations and how it is that academics may define and participate in research somewhat differently than do those with whom they collaborate.

For example, academics and public agency stakeholders have different bureaucratic structures that require different permissions (such as ethics approval, in the case of university research, and executive permission, in the case of agency participation) in order to launch and undertake research. Alongside the substantive research questions, the experience proved invaluable in terms of understanding – or at least appreciating! – how organizational structures and goals impact the way research moves forward in collaborative projects. Overarching organizational philosophies, for example, impact the perceived (and real) value of research and its use.

In this chapter, I describe and explore issues related to the production of 'useful' research when involving stakeholders who may hold very different expectations about what central questions are and what constitutes research that is valued and valuable. In particular, I highlight the issues involved in collaborations between policing agencies and academics. I begin by exploring the changing nature of policing and police philosophies and how changing paradigms are central to the willingness and desire of policing agencies to collaborate with academics. I then describe the context in which academics work and how research is defined within a university context. Having established the contexts in which research collaborations may emerge, I consider the opportunities and challenges associated with these collaborations.

The evolution of policing

Sir Robert Peel, often referred to as the 'father of modern policing',[1] produced the *Principles of Law Enforcement* (1829), which provides both a historical and philosophical context to North American policing. While his principles may appear somewhat dated, his emphasis on crime prevention, public approval, public cooperation, limited use of force, and "persuasion, advice and warning"[2] have been given considerable (although variable) weight over the course of the last 185 years. In some instances, such as in recent situations marked by police over-use of force (as demonstrated in Ferguson, Missouri in 2014, for example), it may be argued that these principles have been completely over-ridden by the contingencies of policing in the modern era.[3]

Today, we see increasingly complicated uses of technology by police and the public; increasingly complicated types of crime and expectations for police to be 'global' as well as local (dealing with terrorism and local break and enters, for example); and increasing calls for public accountability in policing (again, incidents such as Ferguson and North Charleston, South Carolina come to mind) (Yilmaz 2013). Social climates create differing pressures on policing environments, which, in turn, make policing agencies differentially receptive to collaboration with non-policing agencies. While much policing philosophy is underpinned by Peel's principles, policing in 2016 occurs in a very different social and technological context than Peel could have imagined when he provided his guidance.

While 'community' is mentioned by Peel in the *Principles of Law Enforcement*, the concept of 'community policing' is relatively new, evolving from dissatisfaction with traditional policing paradigms. Shifts in policing paradigms are the result of answers to questions such as: "What is policing?" and "What do police do?" (Shearing 1998, p. 1). While the answers at first seem obvious, answers are dependent upon the contexts in which these questions are asked. As Shearing explains, police have traditionally tended to work with basic premises: people continue to commit crime because rewards outweigh costs; punishing people will make them stop committing crime (specific deterrence); when criminals are punished, it will be clear to others that crime does not pay (general deterrence); and society will be more secure when it is obvious that crime does not pay (ibid p. 2). The challenge for traditional policing efforts has been how to address these premises: what policing strategies will ensure, for example, that the costs of crime are greater than the rewards? How can 'offenders' be caught and punished?

But are criminals caught and punished? Do residents feel secure? The former Canadian federal government's increasingly animated "get tough" responses to crime suggest that criminals are not caught and adequately punished and residents feel increasingly insecure. A traditional approach to the 'crime problem' is that greater efficiencies should be sought in the practice and application of strategies and legislation that deal with catching criminals and ensuring their punishment. In other words, both the police and the criminal justice system must be made more effective and have the legislative (and practical) tools at their disposal to better deal with crime. Shearing (1998) notes that, "upgrad[ing] resources, management and training" (p. 3) are frequently suggested as strategies to address failures and deficiencies. The challenge from a traditional policing perspective is to come up with strategies that more effectively address the underlying issues; for instance, crime cannot be seen to pay. In particular locations across North America, this has resulted in the increased militarization of police agencies and greater use of military-style equipment such as tanks, full-body armor, Kevlar vests, shotguns, etc. (see, for example, Kappeler & Kraska 2013; Kraska 2007; Kraska & Kappeler 1997). As a result of the spate of police shootings primarily against unarmed victims, US President Obama recently prohibited the use of specific military equipment, suggesting that its use alienates and intimidates more than it provokes feelings of security.[4]

Rather than bolster police and criminal justice system resources, a second approach to dealing with these issues has been identified. As Shearing (1998) explains, and Obama and his taskforce appear to support, the alternative 'community policing' model is based on a different, non-traditional set of assumptions. First, rather than a focus on offenders, the focus is on opportunities. Second, the police are recognized as not in the best position to reduce and eliminate crime opportunities. Finally, physical force and intimidation are not seen as the best means to eliminate crime. Ultimately, police are very limited in their ability to address crime and must form partnerships with other agencies and institutions to address crime-related issues (ibid, p. 4).

Recognizing that traditional models of policing have failed to provide security and deter crime, as well as that crime is caused by a number of factors – economic, social and political – over which the police have no control, alternatives to traditional models of policing have emerged over the past few decades. The police, essentially, cannot resolve public safety issues on their own (Scheider 2013). Yilmaz (2013) notes that, since the 1980s, police agencies have begun to decentralize and to increasingly become partners with the public – much as Peel originally imagined the relationship between police and the public. Embracing this community policing model involves rethinking what police do and with whom policing is practiced. Rather than 'bandit catching', Shearing (1998) explains that, under the community policing model, police are required to shift to a problem-solving orientation often directly involving community members who work together with the police to find solutions to crime issues (p. 4). The terminology associated with 'community policing' may vary by location – including variants such as problem-oriented policing, 'quality of life' policing or neighborhood policing – all of which generally refer to paradigms that involve the non-traditional premises noted above.

While bandit-catching remains a large part of the policing function, the community policing philosophy enables police agencies and communities to think differently about crime problems and solutions and, more specifically, the role and function of police. The attraction of community policing for academics – as members of the public and as field experts – is the expectation that the community policing philosophy will better employ the use of the skills, resources and expertise that the public and academics have to offer. For example, the inclusion of academics in the crime-solving puzzle enables the provision of evidence-based answers to crime problems (Guillame et al. 2012), which may be larger than the jurisdiction of any particular criminal justice agency. Further, if police are willing to see that crime problems are not exclusively 'owned' by the police – problems are not theirs alone to address – room is potentially made for considering how the criminal justice system itself, including what police do, contributes to various crime issues. What a community policing philosophy does is open the door for discussions about how best to move forward – even if solutions may require shifts in police practice. When the police understand that crime problems are not theirs alone to resolve, more critical approaches may be brought forward as the spotlight shifts to include not only what the police do but also what others (can) do to address crime issues, with room for moving in directions favorable to particular communities.

While the involvement of the community in policing efforts is the mainstay of the community policing paradigm, there is no 'community policing 101' course that dictates the essential components of this paradigm. Critics suggest that the actual practice of community policing is open to interpretation and may be present in specific policing realms but not others (police homicide units, for example, may be less likely to engage in community policing initiatives than a property crimes unit). What is clear, however, is the likelihood of engaging and working with academics to answer policing and crime issues is unlikely with police agencies that exclusively favor traditional approaches to seeking solutions to crime.

Academics often have particular views about which questions need to be asked and how one might generate answers to those questions. Before considering how collaborations between police agencies and academics might be accomplished, we first consider the parameters of research in a university setting.

Research, university-style

It comes as little surprise that for many academics who study crime and deviance, the data that the police hold is a veritable gold mine. Initially as a doctoral student investigating assault, I was drawn to the range and type of information the police possess (and grateful to have the access that I initially gained to police files detailing incidents of assault). While policing data is by no means perfect, any data source that deals with offending and victimization will be limited in some way by the data collection method, as well as by the researcher who analyzes the data. Regarding policing data, the police historically capture data that will contribute to their own investigations. Carefully recording data of interest to sociologists – such as specific education levels, family background variables, interactions between police and the public, etc. – is not always on the police radar. At the same time, researchers may ignore various types of data that they feel are not central to the questions they want to generate.

Inculcated in our graduate studies, young researchers learn that research with value results in publication. Mainstream research training consists of learning to pose theoretically-driven research questions and to seek suitable evidence when investigating these questions and, in many cases, testing our hypotheses. We learn about research design and the pros and cons of setting up projects according to discipline-specific standards. We ensure that our research protects and anonymizes those we study; often elaborate ethics procedures precede our studies. We submit our results to peer-reviewed journals with the expectation that our study and interpretations of our data and research questions will pass the scientific rigors of peer review. We strive to advance our disciplines by undertaking research that poses new questions and cutting edge analyses, or we revisit older questions with new data and new insights. Importantly, advancing the field does not necessarily mean that there are practical applications that result from the research we conduct.

Fascination with policing data aside, what an academic considers excellent use and application of police data does not necessarily address the burning questions that police agencies wish to have answered. In their article describing a collaboration with the Buffalo Police Department (BPD) and the University of Buffalo regarding 'action research', Beal and Kerlikowske (2010) suggest that the type and nature of research that is of interest to police (and other stakeholders) is, understandably, that which may be translated into action or practical applications. Whereas academics tend to focus on advancing their respective disciplines and contributing to knowledge more generally – and getting published in peer-reviewed journals – action research is oriented first toward problem solving at the local level. This means that the kind of research in which police are most interested is often not the research that academics may be interested in nor rewarded for. In fact, Beal and Kerlikowske suggest "it may be that research universities with their focus on 'pure research' are not the best fit for partnerships or action research" (p. 118). Instead, they suggest that smaller, less research-intensive universities may be better able to address the concerns of police and other local community stakeholders than universities which advance and reward other types of research.

Despite the differences in how academics and police view research, the Buffalo project provides helpful observations regarding how these orientations to research may coalesce. Beal and Kerlikowske (2015) suggest that collaborative projects must take into account the needs of all parties and work together from the outset, from the determination of the research questions and the methods the study will employ, to the ability of the partnering organizations to act upon and reward research efforts. Rather than viewing the 'research dissonance logic' between academics and police as a barrier to collaboration, such dissonance may be a means of leveraging the respective impact that collaborators can have on each other.

The Buffalo project represents an ideal that may be somewhat difficult to achieve in less collaborative contexts. Where the research questions and processes are mutually determined through collaborative decision making, there is less chance of misunderstandings occurring along the way, especially when it comes to interpretation of results. Truly mutual collaborations require openness to interpretations that partners may resist or not expect. Of particular importance is the way in which the research is framed: when framed as 'solution-oriented', research findings that might otherwise be seen as unfavorable can be interpreted as part of a solution-based approach rather than as a means of placing blame. Research partnerships with police often come to fruition based on improving practices, cost savings and improving public perceptions of police. Having said this, in an era of heightened liability, it would be difficult to navigate collaborations involving policing data without the benefit of the expertise that university and police legal teams can provide regarding ownership and use of data.

It is clear that different expectations of research are based on the variable contexts associated with policing agencies and academics. Policing agencies that have embraced a community policing philosophy not only view partnerships with the community as central to addressing crime issues but also view themselves as one of many agencies capable of addressing crime issues. These policing agencies are more likely to be amenable to research that studies both specific as well as broader questions than those posed by traditional policing concerns. Similarly, university-based researchers may not always be as willing to collaborate on research projects if their home institutions only reward and value studies likely to be published in peer-reviewed outlets geared toward pushing disciplines and general research forward.

So, then, why collaborate?

Engel and Whalen (2010) specifically ask, "why should police listen to [partner with] academics?" (p. 106). They list four reasons, including, first, operational effectiveness and efficiency. Engel and Whalen observe that police budgets tend to be regularly strapped for resources and taking advantage of the expertise that academics have to offer simply makes sense based on cost-effectiveness. Associated with this point, Kelman and Hong (2014) suggest that doing things right costs less in the long run than having to change to accommodate best practices later on. A second reason has to do with external validity (Engel & Whalen 2010, p. 106). Engel and Whalen, for example, argue that academics serve as an independent means of assessing police practices. A third reason is that partnering with academics serves the purpose of 'cooperative transparency' (ibid). By partnering with academics, the police are able to increase their perceived legitimacy with the public, which in turn is believed to positively impact police–public relations. As Engel and Whalen (2010) observe, "a police–academic partnership can create a bridge between the often divided police and public" (p. 107). Finally, another reason to partner with academics is due to the information technology revolution. The demand for information has significantly expanded, as has the creation of data. Further, technological advances continue to result in increasing opportunities for the application of technology in policing practice. Related to this is increasing pressure on police agencies, especially by vendors of new technology, to embrace the technologies that vendors are selling. At the same time, it is very difficult for police agencies to create the in-house expertise required to assess data or technology. Partnering with academics enables police to take advantage of the expertise that academics have to offer without necessarily having to hire their own analysts and engineers – also, police may be less likely to be influenced by vendors who may exaggerate claims in order to make sales.

A similar question must be asked of academics: "why should academics listen to [partner with] police?" (Engel & Whalen 2010, p. 107). Engel and Whalen suggest three reasons. First, academics who collaborate with police are likely to see more immediate impacts of their research. The claims that 'ivory tower' research has little to do with actual policing practice may be reversed when working directly with police. Rather than expecting police agencies to read the studies published in (to them) obscure and jargon-laden journals, creating research that takes local policing contexts into account is much more likely to have an immediate effect. Knowing the specific contexts in which police work often sheds much light: "most academics know so little of the idiosyncrasies and politics operating within police agencies that their recommendations are often difficult if not impossible to implement" (ibid). A second, related reason why academics should collaborate with police is that their research will be enhanced by fostering partnerships. Engel and Whalen explain that, most often, researchers launch research projects based on their own 'academic' understanding of the phenomenon at hand. Yet the basis of academics' understanding is likely to be studies conducted by other academics that may also be missing a critical piece of the puzzle – which is knowing and appreciating the policing culture and context (Sherman 2015, p. 20). For example, it would be difficult for an academic to truly appreciate citizen–police encounters without ever having witnessed a citizen–police encounter first-hand.

A third reason for academics to collaborate with police has to do with accessibility (Engel & Whalen 2010, p. 108). As mentioned earlier, for many, access to police data allows for the possibility of asking questions that simply cannot be addressed in any other way. As Engel and Whalen observe, the public increasingly has access to official forms of policing data as found on government and some police agency websites, yet this publicly accessible data may not allow for addressing the most compelling research questions. By directly accessing police data, academics are allowed increasingly more access to other types of policing data that "provide[s] better understandings of the nuances associated with the publicly available data" (ibid).

Challenges to effective collaboration

Engel and Whalen's (2010) Cincinnati project and Beal and Kerlikowske's (2010) Buffalo collaboration provide convincing examples of effective collaborations between police agencies and academics. My own experience with collaboration came with some unanticipated challenges. In the past, I had successfully worked with and accessed policing data. I anticipated that working with more than one policing agency at the same time would simply be a matter of 'more of the same'. As it turned out, there were far greater differences between participating police agencies than expected – some of which may be the result of the varying policing philosophies that each embraced (as described above). Further, the range of stakeholder expectations varied considerably – primarily in terms of how 'success' might be measured and the resources that each of the respective stakeholders put into the project.

In the discussion that follows, I highlight the challenges that collaborative projects with policing agencies may face and how these may be addressed. The four primary challenges I identify are: the importance of shared meanings; internal barriers and pressures; investment; and external pressures.

Shared meanings

When parties come together in a project it is critical that everyone understands their role – and feels comfortable with it. In our collaboration, a proposal was put forward to study a specific topic in a specific way – much of this framed, at least initially and not unlike other granting agencies, by the funder. Time was required to sort out the respective input that various parties would make to the project. During the early phases of the project, discussions involved establishing the guidance that stakeholders would provide to the project – stakeholders consisted of various units within the respective justice department, probation, and police representatives. Together with the stakeholders, terms of reference were drafted and approved establishing stakeholders as 'advisory' to the project. After these terms were agreed to, one stakeholder suggested significant changes to the document, including the idea that "decisions will be reached through a consensus". This was felt by the academics on the team to conflict with academic freedom and to undermine the advisory capacity that had been agreed to by all. Eventually these issues were sorted out, but much negotiation was required to address central concerns regarding academic freedom, data access and publication rights. The university's legal team played a central role in these deliberations.

In hindsight, there were elements of our project that might have been handled differently had there been greater collaboration from the outset. First, rather than the identification of stakeholders being predetermined by the funder, we should have undergone a process of exploration to identify relevant stakeholders, which would have included making calls to parties deemed well-suited to participate. The predefined identification of stakeholders resulted in some parties simply not having vested interests in the project; rather, they were part of the advisory group simply as a result of their positions in the government bureaucracy. Second, the collaboration was plagued at the early stages by references to various teams: the research team, the stakeholder team and the executive team. Much of this was based on the funder's past experiences with research, yet required sorting out for this particular project. Eventually an advisory team was established, consisting of interested stakeholders and the research team, the latter consisting of academics who gathered and analyzed the data. As noted earlier, given the length of this project, members of the advisory committee changed substantially from the initial to the end stages.

Further problematizing how collaboration would be defined was the differing use of particular language among the stakeholders. As identified earlier, partners in a collaborative research project must come to terms with potentially varying definitions of central concepts, such as 'collaboration', 'research' and 'outcomes'. During the early stages of our project, stakeholders made reference to research in ways that were less familiar to the research team: 'research' was used interchangeably by the funder with 'pilot project', for example. For some, research was not seen as a process, but was equated with data collection or results. Further, research implied a practical application with specific recommendations as the outcome. There may have been some sense of frustration when results were eventually presented with a lengthy list of limitations.[5]

Internal barriers and pressures

Collaborations face the reality of uneven internal organizational pressures that can either undermine or support working with outside others. As described above, there are differing orientations to policing that vary in their support for community partnerships. Police agencies today are perhaps less homogenous than in the past, with local (and global) pressures playing a role in the types of priorities police set and the types of partnerships they feel are valuable to them. Aside from general orientations to policing, there are also organizational structures that play a role in how collaborations unfold – though these structural features are by no means specific to policing. The often hierarchical structure of many policing organizations means that attraction to collaborations is likely to vary across the organization. As Cordner and White (2010, p. 92) indicate, good relations with police executive may not directly impact on the relationships that can be built with those in the lower ranks who may have more to do with certain projects than the executive.

In my own experience, support at the executive level is critical to any collaboration's success. By way of illustration, in one police agency, the collaboration had the full support of the chief, which translated into full support at all levels of the policing organization. In another police agency, however, while there was enthusiasm for the project at the unit level, these individuals did not have the power to endorse the project and move things forward (such as access to data). Without the executive level backing the research, we came to a standstill very quickly at this particular site.

Academics and policing organizations operate under different models for career placement and advancement. In academia, individuals are hired for their expertise in a particular discipline. Tenure often ensures that an academic spends nearly his or her entire career in one department, with promotion decisions based upon the continuing demonstrated expertise in one area as evidenced through scholarly output. In policing, officers tend to be placed in varying units based on need, but move around the organization and work in different units to maximize their exposure to various police operations and investigations to ensure promotion. One can see the rationale for the policing model. When it comes to longer-term research collaborations, however, this model may inhibit forming relationships that last the entire duration of research projects. For example, over the course of our three-and-a-half-year collaboration, four individuals in one particular agency were in the position of staff sergeant – a critical role for the continuation of our project as this position enabled various permissions at the 'local level'. As others have noted (i.e. Beal & Kerlikowske 2010), the support of the supervisory level is central to the success of collaborations.

An issue related to the movement of officers throughout the police agency concerns the assignment of project 'ownership'. In the policing agency with the changing staff sergeants, the ownership of the project was at the unit level and the changing personnel at the supervisory level did not, fortunately, negatively impact our project whatsoever. In another policing agency, ownership of the project was initially undertaken by a specific individual. His subsequent transfer out of the unit at an early stage of the project, without a similarly keen individual replacing him, resulted in no internal advocate for the project. With no individual or unit claiming ownership of the project, and without achieving endorsement at the executive level, the project never really got off the ground at this location.

While the pressures that police executives face are both internal and external, Engle and Whalen (2010, p. 109) explain why it is that police chiefs, in particular, have been reluctant to take advice from and collaborate with academics. First, they suggest that chiefs are ultimately responsible for the direction that police operations and initiatives take. Academics often have little responsibility for applied operations and therefore the risks involved in implementing research are borne by the chief. A second reason, addressed below, is that expectations for executive performance are not entirely set internally, but rather are impacted by relationships with local and provincial politicians. Third, Engle and Whalen note some hesitation to implement strategies when the police can seemingly readily take credit (and also assume blame) for their results. For example, suggesting that a drop in the crime rate is the result of a new practice is fine until the crime rate swings upward – credit must clearly be taken for both outcomes. Finally, Engle and Whalen note that due to differing expectations of research, it is often difficult for police agencies to successfully implement research as academics may move on to other projects, feeling that they have done their job, leaving police at the implementation phase essentially unassisted.

Investment

The issues of shared meanings and ownership are related to challenges regarding investment in particular research projects. Bringing partners to similar understandings about the nature and point of the research process is crucial. Collaboration in research projects also brings with it different points of view about what defines success, for example, and what kinds of investment in the research are reasonable from collaborators' perspectives. From the outside, it sometimes appears as though agencies that work within the same criminal justice system make similar assumptions about the nature of the work they do. This simply may not be the case. In our collaborative experience, for example, it became clear that success was very differently defined by probation and police officers. For probation officers, the primary orientation to those who commit crimes is 'rehabilitation'. The application of GPS monitors to these offenders, they explained, is partly a way of reminding offenders of their previous crimes and to be better people. The police, on the other hand, were perhaps less interested in the 'rehabilitative' component of this technology than they were in the ability of these devices to simply deter recidivism and establish wrongdoing. Partner agencies start with very different assumptions about the work they do and how to facilitate that work. Investment can therefore vary depending upon whether collaborators feel that their needs will be addressed by the project.

Investment may be relational or substantive and may be evidence of commitment to the project (although not always). Relational investment refers to the support that partners are willing to provide to the project by way of feedback and engagement in the process. For example, relational investment in our project was evinced in the support and advice consistently provided by the Crown's office regarding legal interpretations and matters. Substantive investment refers to resources both in terms of hardware and people. In one police agency, we were given excellent desk space and access to specific information on their server that monumentally facilitated our research. Further, once we had been security cleared, we were given access to come and go as our schedules allowed. In another agency, while direct access to data was not provided, research analysts employed by the policing agency dedicated time to the project. In a third policing agency, very limited access to data was allowed and only under strict supervision at times convenient to specific officers. The levels and types of investment in the project impact the results of the project and its utility for partner agencies.

Resource issues ultimately relate to accountability and who is to answer for the ideas that the research ultimately puts forward. If collaborators' investments and resources are withdrawn or reduced, accountability for the research findings is increasingly withdrawn as well. Should this occur, the research team must be very precise in terms of what reduced involvement may mean for the interpretation of findings. For example, if 'partners' are not engaged with the decision-making process along the way, this will impact the degree to which findings will be presented with all interests in mind. While it is natural for interests to ebb and flow with personnel changes and over a project's duration, those most closely associated with the research are accountable for its findings.

Investment at the project level will also be determined, to a certain extent, by the ability of agencies to afford research and make use of research findings. In times of budgetary constraints, enthusiasm may wane for research that never results in specific applications. Most funding for the criminal justice system is based on federal and provincial coffers, and economic declines may result in projects stalling or being abandoned.

External pressures

In his assessment of the differences between fire-fighting and policing, Hoover (2010) laments the fact that the public appears happy to see firefighters sleep between emergencies, but is intolerant of the idea that police could simply be on emergency stand-by between emergencies. The expectations of police, he argues, are that they must make use of 'uncommitted patrol time' (p. 162). While little public (or academic) inquiry has been devoted to firefighters' down time, there is little doubt that Hoover correctly identifies public pressure on police. Of course, as emergency responders, firefighters deal with a very different type of emergency to than police (even if they often appear on the same scene). As identified by Shearing (1998), the police and the public have similarly begun to view police as but one element in dealing with crime, recognizing that crime is the product of a number of individual and societal factors.

The public appear fascinated with crime and are, in turn, fascinated with the police and continuously scrutinize them. Incidents of police brutality and police shootings reignite discussions about how the police do their jobs and if they are doing their jobs in the best way possible. Because they are publicly-funded, it is difficult for policing agencies to ignore the public and to set goals and initiatives that are entirely independent of public opinion. A potential challenge is that police may be more interested in research that addresses public opinion than in research topics germane to broader areas of policing.

But is it police who are more driven by public opinion, or politicians? As Punch (2010) has observed in the UK, different political parties increasingly take similar stands on crime policy and assume a 'law and order' stance that trickles into policing practice and support (or lack thereof) for research. Punch further notes that barriers to research collaborations between police and academics are related more to "short-sighted, populist-oriented governments who want the police organization to be a servile agency" (p. 159). In Canada, there is no stable stream of core funding for police research at the federal or provincial levels (Griffiths 2014) and the 'tough on crime' mantra remains prominent. There is no doubt that legislators and legislation substantially influence policing, and thus influence the nature and type of research collaborations. There are many examples of legislation created specifically in the face of heinous crimes that are passed as a means by which governments plan to 'do something' about a specific type of threat that society faces – but police are responsible for working with such legislation. Along with not wanting to appear soft on crime, Brandon and Farrington (2005) observe that politicians tend to have very short time horizons, "which make programs that show results only in the longer run less appealing to those who are trying to get elected every few years" (p. 339).

Beyond winning public popularity, politicians also face economic realities that can change their priorities over time. For example, our research project was launched in 2010 during a time when the province was experiencing an economic boom and when a minister held a specific interest in the project. The minister eventually moved to another government portfolio and the new minister had different priorities. Further, the funding initiative that housed the project dissolved when the economy began its downturn. Promises regarding continued funding for partner agencies also dissolved – although funding was reconsidered when the media reported on the story.

Conclusions: making collaborations work

At this point, it is clear that collaborative research between police agencies and academics are rarely boiler-plate undertakings and require that specific attention be paid to the capacities and goals of the collaborators. In a collaborative project between the University of Buffalo School of Management and the Buffalo Police Department, Hunt and Beal (1999) describe how the parties launched their mutual project. The goal of the project was to "help the BPD build effective strategies for community policing" (p. iii). The team followed a number of general guidelines in order to develop specific strategies: the research agenda was to be determined primarily by police/practitioners; regular feedback was to be provided in order to ensure that issues were addressed quickly; and changes would be led from the middle. Regarding the research agenda, the researchers had not predetermined the strategies that would be developed or the specific questions that would guide their research. Rather, the researchers "had purposely left the strategies unspecified so that the steering committee could design them to fit the particular needs and capacities" of the police department (p. iv). In our project, the research team provided the advisory committee with a research strategy and sought feedback on a regular basis.

The Buffalo project included researchers as part of the steering committee, along with supervisory-level members from across the police department. The purpose of the steering committee was to provide a forum for determining the specific research agenda and feedback, but also for sustaining both a short- and long-term focus. As Hunt and Beal explain, the steering committee discussed issues that were important but "which managers seldom have the time to address in the heat of other pressing problems" (1999, p. v). Regular contact through the steering committee venue provides some intangible benefits as well. Academics are better able to understand the nature of the issues that the police face and are better able to learn about local police cultures as a result of regular contact. As Bradley and Nixon (2009, p. 430) have observed, one of the reasons why research is not taken up by police is because research has tended to ignore or discount the "morally complex and sociologically embedded nature of police practices and contexts". Through creating more opportunities for academics to learn about and hear of issues central to the police, the more likely it is that researchers can produce findings meaningful to them.

But are collaborations undertaken when the research questions and process may bring the police under close scrutiny and/or find fault with their practices and procedures? In collaborative research projects where research questions are determined together and are framed as a means by which solutions are sought, such findings do not necessarily present an insurmountable problem. Collaboratively framing research questions assumes a certain degree of agreement about identified issues and problems, as well as assumes a level of trust (as implied by the term 'collaboration'). If the police are not part of framing the research questions, it is unlikely that their cooperation for the project can be effectively secured. Similarly, if academics are asked to consider research questions in ways that limit their ability to fully answer questions (i.e. through lack of access to data or ignoring findings), the project is unlikely to result in any meaningful conclusions.

The subject matter of our project was 'predefined' by the granting agency. Perhaps an advantage of this situation is that, substantively, all stakeholders were generally on the same page – we knew what the focus of study would be. On the other hand, interest in this project varied because of that predetermination; the involved agencies showed different levels of interest in this substantive topic. For example, one police agency enthusiastically embraced the project and, as a result, the researchers knew considerably more about that particular policing culture than about the cultures of the other policing agencies. Less frequent contact with the other policing agencies impacted the ways in which the researchers were able to know their local cultures, geographically and relationally, and vice versa. Trust was not as effectively developed. Having a local academic at each location to ensure regular contact would likely have made our work at each location much more effective.

We observed earlier that barriers to collaboration may be due to differences in partners' resources. An alternative way to look at these differences is to conceive of them as opportunities for pooling resources and assembling a team that mutually provides what each does not have alone. Given the reality of public scrutiny of the police and public pressures regarding police accountability, the police are well positioned to take full advantage of the reputation typically associated with academics. For example, the appearance of neutrality is a resource that the police are simply not able to generate internally, but is a reputational mainstay of most university researchers. Rather than be swayed by organizational goals and public demands, research projects involving academics provide a source of external validation in a way that police agencies cannot generate on their own. As noted earlier, a strength of university expertise is cutting-edge research – policing agencies can be advantaged by partnerships that may offer very specific types of expertise otherwise not available to them. Our own research team included an engineer who is a GPS expert – a resource that policing agencies would not otherwise have had ready access to. This expertise was far more objective than the advice of vendors who hoped to sell GPS equipment to police agencies.

As noted above, the resources that the police have to offer researchers are most specifically evident in terms of, first, access to data and, second, access to police culture. The police have vast amounts of data of great interest to researchers. Collaborating with police exponentially increases the likelihood of access to that data. With regard to police culture, insight into the 'realities' of policing is often only revealed after having access to the organization and to the officers themselves. The physical presence of researchers and the willingness to share information beyond the specific context of a single project are resources that the police bring to the table and which are not available through other means. Learning about police culture and the everyday circumstances of police work not only brought 'color' to our work with the police, but also enabled us to better understand the gray zones within which police often work. For example, while working at one agency, officers would often chat about the cases they were working on and the cases we were reading about in their files. Their observations on offenders' behavior provided us with information that simply could not be gleaned from the files themselves, or through any other means. These discussions revealed the idiosyncrasies of the offenders, and gave us much greater insight into how offender characteristics interacted with their social and physical environments.

Bumbarger and Campbell (2012) explain that successful collaborations rely on keeping partners' goals and needs clearly in mind. They explain that while there are overlapping goals in collaborations, other goals and understandings clearly do not overlap. Collaborations that are most successful have an awareness of where, how and why overlaps occur but also an awareness of where there is much less common ground. Bumbarger and Campbell also remind us that "mission drift" is possible when collaborators' overlapping needs and goals take a back seat to those that do not overlap. Being aware of the contexts from which partnerships emerge reduces the likelihood that collaborations will drift and instead provides greater appreciation for the pressures, capacities and knowledge that collaborating parties bring to the table resulting in research all parties view as important and worthy.

Notes

1 See, for example, http://thelawdogfiles.blogspot.ca/2008/04/police-are-public-and-public-are-police.html;
2 www.durham.police.uk/About-Us/Documents/Peels_Principles_Of_Law_Enforcement.pdf.
3 www.theglobeandmail.com/globe-debate/editorials/the-nine-commandments-of-polic-ing-and-how-ferguson-police-forgot-them/article20076106/.
4 www.theguardian.com/us-news/2015/may/18/president-obama-limits-supply-military-style-equipment-police.
5 This list of limitations was the result of having to work within specific predefined legis-lative boundaries that made a research design of our choice not feasible.

References

Beal, P & Kerlikowske, RG 2010, 'Action research in Buffalo and Seattle', *Police Practice and Research: An International Journal*, vol. 11, no. 2, pp. 117–121.

Bradley, D & Nixon, C 2009, 'Ending the "dialogue of the deaf": Evidence and policing pol-icies and practices. An Australian case study', *Police Practice and Research: An International Journal*, vol. 10, no. 5–6, pp. 423–435.

Brandon, CW & Farrington, DP 2005, 'Evidence-based crime prevention: Conclusions and directions for a safer society', *Canadian Journal of Criminology and Criminal Justice*, vol. 47, no. 2, pp. 337–354.

Bumbarger, BK & Campbell, EM 2012, 'A state agency–university partnership for transla-tional research and the dissemination of evidence-based prevention and intervention', *Administration in Policy and Mental Health*, vol. 39, pp. 268–277.

Cordner, G & Shain, C 2011, 'The changing landscape of police education and training', *Police Practice and Research: An International Journal*, vol. 12, no. 4, pp. 281–285.

Cordner, G & White, S 2010, 'The evolving relationship between police research and police practice', *Police Practice and Research: An International Journal*, vol. 11, no. 2, pp. 90–94.

Engel, RS & Whalen, JL 2010, 'Police–academic partnerships: Ending the dialogue of the deaf, the Cincinnati experience', *Police Practice and Research: An International Journal*, vol. 11, no. 2, pp. 105–116.

Griffiths, CT 2014, 'Economics of policing: Baseline for policing research in Canada', *Public Safety Canada*, Cat. No. PS14-30/2014E-PDF.

Guillaume, P. Sidebottom, A, & Tilley, N 2012, 'On police and university collabora-tions: A problem-oriented policing case study', *Police Practice and Research: An International Journal*, vol. 13, no. 4, pp. 389–401.

Hoover, LT 2010, 'Rethinking our expectations', *Police Practice and Research: An International Journal*, vol. 11, no. 2, pp. 160–165.

Hunt, RG & Beal, PK 2000, 'Developing a partnership between a university and a police department: The UBSOM-BPD Partnership Project', Paper produced from Award 95-IJ-CX-0081.

Kappeler, VE & Kraska, PB 2013, 'Normalizing police militarization, living in denial', *Policing and Society*, vol. 25, no. 3, pp. 268–275.

Kelman, S & Hong, S 2014, 'This could be the start of something big: Linking early manager-ial choices with subsequent organizational performance', *Journal of Public Administration Research and Theory*, vol. 25, pp. 135–164.

Kraska, P 2007, 'Militarization and policing: Its relevance to 21st century police', *Policing*, vol. 1, no. 4, pp. 501–513.

Kraska, P & Kappeler, VE 1997, 'Militarizing American police: The rise and normalization of paramilitary units', *Social Problems*, vol. 44, no. 1, pp. 1–18.

Punch, M 2010, 'Policing and police research in the age of the smart cop', *Police Practice and Research: An International Journal*, vol. 11, no. 2, pp. 155–159.

Roberts, JM Jr, Roberts, A, & Brewer, DD 2014, 'Network contacts and activity domains: Information-sharing among police agencies', *Human Organization*, vol. 73, no. 1, pp. 13–24.

Rossi, PH 1980, 'The Presidential Address: The challenge and opportunities of applied social research', *American Sociological Review*, vol. 45, no. 6, pp. 889–904.

Ryan, BJ 2013, 'Reasonable force: The emergence of global policing power', *Review of International Studies*, vol. 39, pp. 435–457.

Scheider, MC 2013, 'Commentary: Community policing and public housing authorities', *Cityscape: A Journal of Policy Development and Research*, vol. 15, no. 3, pp. 153–157.

Shearing, C 1998, 'Changing paradigms in policing: The significance of community policing for the governance of security', Institute for Security Studies. Occasional Paper No. 34, pp. 1–8. http://dspace.africaportal.org/jspui/bitstream/123456789/31569/1/paper34.pdf?1

Sherman, L 2015, 'A tipping point for "totally evidenced policing": Ten ideas for building an evidence-based police agency', *International Criminal Justice Review*, vol. 25, no. 1, pp. 11–29.

Welsh, BC & Farrington, DP 2005, 'Evidence-based crime prevention: Conclusions and directions for a safer society', *Canadian Journal of Criminology and Criminal Justice*, vol. 47, no. 2, pp. 337–354.

Yilmaz, S 2013, 'Tailoring model in reforming police organizations towards community policing', *Journal of Organizational Change Management*, vol. 26, no. 5, pp. 897–924.

8

BRIDGING THE SOLITUDES

A grounded look at how to create meaningful police–academic research partnerships

Rose Ricciardelli, Laura Huey, Hayley Crichton and Tracy Hardy

Introduction

It is almost axiomatic within criminal justice literature to refer to relations between police and academic researchers in terms that invoke 'two solitudes' – that is, as entities who chronically misunderstand and distrust each other because they lack a common language or cultural bonds. For evidence in support of this claim, we can simply turn to a wealth of academic literature in which policing scholars either reflect on the difficulties of working with police organizations (Bradley & Nixon 2009; Cockcroft 2014; Fleming 2010; Stanko 2009) or, conversely, document the many ways in which police see academic researchers as failing to provide tangible outcomes that may "allow the organization to move forward and identify the things that are required to make the shift in policing" (Griffiths et al. 2014, p. 39). Regardless of perspective, it is clear that a multitude of barriers to successful collaborations between academics and police have existed, with both parties highlighting the apparent disconnect between diverse institutions – a gap intensified by differences in research methods, interests, and world views (Amabile et al. 2001; Bradley & Nixon 2009; Buerger 2010; Canter 2004; Cockcroft 2014; Cordner & White 2010; Fleming 2010; Foster & Bailey 2010; Marks et al. 2010; Rosenbaum 2014; Scott 2010; Wuestewald & Steinheider 2010). As a result, interactions between police and researchers have been described as infrequent (Sanders & Fields 2009), unplanned and disorderly (Marks et al. 2010), and challenging by police and academics, who equally report uncertain, often limited, understandings of the *other* party's objectives and how to seek clarification about said objectives (Wood et al. 2008). Further, research requires attention to the ethical challenges involved with remaining attentive to the desires of upper management, the positions of the members, and the research objectives without compromising the integrity of any party involved, of the research outcomes, or breaching growing trust between parties.

As we note in invoking the 'two solitudes' metaphor above, different languages (including professional or discipline-related jargon) that reflect different professional cultures, ethical considerations, systems, and organization have also compromised potentially successful and ongoing research relationships between police and academics (Cordner & White 2010). For example, police research is often viewed by academics as unsystematic and undisciplined (Birzer 2002; Canter 2004), and complicated by the exclusive and cliquish nature of police culture (Sklansky 2006; Wood et al. 2008) recognizing that policing is shaped by intergroup loyalties (Skolnick 1994) which are entrenched in the strong social indoctrination practices apparent in policing (Reuss-Ianni 1983). Overall, Dennis Rosenbaum (2014) eloquently summarized academic barriers to full partnerships between academics and police agencies as being rooted in scholars having limited incentive to carry out applied research (in light of the tenure system and funding availability), their failure to understand police organizational constraints that determine what information can be disclosed and how research can be conducted, and the inhibited nature of any police agency that lacks a learning organizational culture. Barriers to partnerships with law enforcement agencies, he explained, are additionally rooted in their rigid hierarchical authority and communication structures as well as their suspicion of outsiders, need for immediate actionable findings, the low priority placed on research given a "crisis-management style of leadership", and the perceived unintelligible, non-local and non-generalizable content of publications.

To this end, collaborative research between the police and academics needs to be interdependent and, although the two groups may not always work well together, their combined efforts toward developing empirically sound research to inform efficient and effective policy and practice are essential (Wilkinson 2010). Not only are they essential, but they can be achieved and, with mutual understanding and respect, have great effects on policing practice and academic scholarship. To illustrate this point, we draw on our own experiences as stakeholders when engaging in police–academic collaborative research and draw attention to our unique experiences working on a fairly complex, applied research project. These experiences are shared from two different perspectives: those of the academic researchers (as represented by the primary investigator) and those of the police officers (represented by the then-commanding officer, the assistant commissioner). Further, these observations developed through the advancement and maintenance of a multi-part, large-scale research partnership between an Eastern Canadian university, as facilitated by the primary researcher, multiple researchers at other Canadian universities, and a division of the Royal Canadian Mounted Police. As such, all impressions noted in this chapter reflect on important encounters experienced by key stakeholders in the research project. Using an auto-ethnographical approach, we facilitate an open discussion of the experiences associated with an ongoing, successful and collaborative research project involving academics and police officers across ranks.

In simple terms, the objectives of the multi-faceted project are to inform youth policing and, more broadly, relationships between youth and police while implementing extrajudicial measures in the province. We are developing methods of police work and community involvement that may address current challenges associated with policing youth in a province with a unique cultural landscape and provide officers with more options when trying to divert youth from the criminal justice system. This research project has thus far included presentations, participation in training initiatives, focus groups, interviews and additional, more informal, interactions with police, youth, and the community. In sharing insights gleaned from these experiences, we hope to highlight the need for transparency when conducting cross-disciplinary work, and the value of building trust, overcoming questions of ethics, and recognizing that just as some officers have been thought (by outsiders) to be close-minded, 'old school', or negative, so too have diverse academics whose work is further criticized for being inapplicable to police practice or simply incomprehensible (Wuestewald & Steinheider 2010, see also Gibbs Van Brunschot, this volume). Thus, we put forth how both police and academics can be viewed as hard to work with, particularly when stakeholders are inexperienced in either the practical application of such work (e.g. they fail to recognize that 'in theory' can too often amount to nothing in practice) or the slower processes involved in conducting research (e.g. the need for empirical evidence alongside theoretical understanding prior to progressing). We speak of the need to listen and give voice to all parties involved in collaborative research, and to be able and willing to hear criticism and provide feedback – even when we appear not to all be speaking the 'same' language.

Further, we highlight the introspection required to maintain a collaborative research approach while understanding that negative findings can undermine the trust previously developed. In other words, transparency is required when addressing the ethical dilemmas related to opening an institution's doors to 'outside' researchers, whose findings may not be wholly favorable and who may request access to confidential information. Indeed, perhaps much of the distrust felt by police toward researchers as reported in previous literature lies in police officers' assumptions that academic research is entirely antagonistically critical (Bradley & Nixon 2009; Wuestewald & Steinheider 2010). Thus, a memorandum of understanding was developed early in the research project in order to ensure that the findings produced were immune from censorship and always protected the participants using methodologies that were in line with agreed-upon objectives.

Research: identifying the need for change

Research conducted in policing institutions has been largely internal (e.g. contracted out to specific individuals or carried out in-house) and restricted (e.g. only accessible by police and police management) (Kelty & Julian 2010, 2012; Rojek et al. 2012). This may be a result of conceptual gaps in the perceived value of research apparent between police, who may read academic research as overly theoretical and impractical, and academics, who may view police agencies as cliquish, riddled with intergroup loyalties, and who generally oppose, even distrust, other authorities (Alarid 1999; Tan & Heraclesous 2001; Wuestewald & Steinheider 2010).

Further intensifying the disconnect between researchers and the police agencies they wish to study is the fact that more critical police research often functions to inform government and legislation through publication rather than changing police structure and practice (Bradley & Nixon 2009). Not surprisingly, in a report for the National Research Council on the status of policing in the US, Skogan and Frydl (2004) concluded that discouraging gaps in our understanding of policing may be the result of a lack of good scientific research. This was recently reiterated by Dennis Rosenbaum at the University of Chicago (2013). Their findings support the need for evidence-based policing, which has gained popularity in recent decades, specifically in the US, the UK, and Australia. The effectiveness of engaging police in research and the value of designing research projects that generate evidence to inform policy and practices are now recognized (Bradley & Nixon 2009). In light of this push for more evidence-based (and thus efficient) researcher–police collaborations, these projects are becoming more common or at least there appears to be more openness among stakeholders to establish such projects (Kelty & Julian 2012). However, collaborative research projects specific to the operation of Canadian law enforcement agencies are, and have been, rare.

Canadian research has generally involved research *on* policing institutions rather than research *with* Canadian police agencies or officers (Jain et al. 2000; Shulenberg 2014; Yuille 1984). A stakeholder in our recent project, Commanding Officer Hardy, however, took a different approach, as she explains:

> Indeed, the tendency in policing, from my perspective, is to focus on crisis management and thus prioritize reactive policing efforts by responding and investigating offences and apprehending offenders. Participation in crime prevention activities, despite best efforts, is often constrained by limited resources and support for such programs. Nonetheless, I recognized the need for evidence-based research to inform future policy decisions on police expenditures and resource utilization and wanted to utilize all resources for the betterment of the policing my division provides to the province and greater communities. The primary goal of this research, then, is to proactively, rather than reactively, create sustainable crime prevention programs that reflect the diversity of our communities and improve relationships between the RCMP and the community.

Her views fall in line with those of Innes (2010), who revealed the value of localized and focused approaches to police research that include both researchers and police in the analyses of specific problems and implementation of possible solutions. As Fleming (2010) noted, successful collaborations between police and academics must be founded on the production of applied research that can be practically harnessed and implemented by police practitioners (see White 2010). This requires research to be conducted *with* police instead of *on* police to ensure research remains effective, timely and practical for implementation.

Collaborative efforts: organizational challenges and knowledge needs

Studies of police agencies frequently document barriers and challenges grounded in differing interests between stakeholders that impact data collection (see inter alia Banton 1964; Bradley & Nixon 2009; Brown & Waters 1993; MacDonald 1986; Young 1991). To successfully traverse such potential divides, a number of experienced researchers have suggested having both parties state upfront their desired objectives (Kelty & Julian 2012; Marks et al. 2010). Scott (2010) goes further in arguing that both academic and police practitioners should not only disclose their research interests from the beginning, but also their reasons for participating in the project and any and all expectations prior to commencing research. As policing research is a complex undertaking, it follows that expectations from both parties will be multifaceted. Thus, transparency becomes an intrinsic part of successful police research such that all parties believe their objectives are being met, or at least a substantial effort is being made to do so.

In developing our own project, we followed Scott's (2010) approach. As Commanding Officer Hardy explains:

> In order to retain commitment from my team and invest in such research, it was important to demonstrate the relevance of our project as it pertained to our policing priorities. During each step of the first phase of the project our input, as research partners and law enforcement professionals, was sought and all of the generated material closely scrutinized, debated and even contested for accuracy and applicability. From the start of this collaboration it was clear that the interests of the police were reflected in the project objectives and we were able to contribute significantly to the project design and delivery. It was indeed a collaborative effort and this reality in itself allowed trust to build.

As Hardy notes above, transparency in objectives was central to the partnership's development. In particular, what researchers learned about transparency was that we make a central assumption when entering research relationships: that our motives are not always well understood and that we need to sometimes answer a question that may underlie police concerns; 'What do researchers have to gain?' To academics the answer might seem obvious: we do research because that is our job, not unlike how we expect police officers to engage in policing. However, we sometimes forget that outside of academia the nature of what we do and why is not always apparent – particularly when dealing with an institutional culture that is known to be rather cynical about the motives of outsiders (e.g. Caplan 2003). Ricciardelli, the primary researcher in the current project, explains:

> I also realized that my seemingly transparent motivation for participating in the research was unclear to members. It was genuinely hard to explain that

I was participating because the project fell in line with my research interests and greater research objectives. I explained that the nature of my occupational role was structured around research as well as the more publically recognized teaching component. As much as I needed to learn about the interworkings of the RCMP culture, they too needed information about the structures and practices of the academy.

Clarifying motives does not mean, however, that there is never a need to revisit research objectives or to make efforts to maintain open, ongoing dialogue in order to retain transparency. On this project, transparency was facilitated through meetings, routinely held, that allowed all parties to discuss project developments, both positive and negative. As an example, to determine if research would be actively informing practice, or would simply be documenting new and existing practices in the field, we met as a collective many times in order to come to an agreement. These meetings were particularly vital as different officers and researchers were brought into new roles in the research project. Regardless of the particular substantive issue, the point was always to ensure that all parties were on the same page. This consensus building was essential to ensure that friction did not develop and begin to interfere with relationship building. Meetings at which issues and roles were clarified allowed stakeholders to revisit their roles and to reconfirm how the overall objectives were being met. Of course, this also meant that amendments to ethical protocols needed to be submitted with each project change or addition of a new researcher. As a result, the primary researcher has developed a rather friendly relationship with the faculty and staff in the ethics office in her institution.

Although police agencies are becoming increasingly decentralized, as an institution policing remains fairly hierarchical (Buerger 2010; Wuestewald & Steinheider 2010). At times, researchers found the task of navigating the complexities of this hierarchical structure difficult. The difficulties arose from a lack of deeper understanding of police culture and its relationship to rank structure. What researchers often encountered were officers concerned with how they might be viewed by their superiors. Their actions, or more often inactions, were sometimes perceived by researchers as indecision or a lack of commitment or understanding. At other times, officers basically jumped to fulfill requests. What became clear over time was that both sets of circumstances were borne of the desire to satisfy rules and orders given by superiors in order to avoid reprimands.

Working directly with the commanding officer provided further insight. When the 'CO' makes a decision, it is acted on. To illustrate, when traveling the province for research purposes, the direct line of communication between the researcher and commanding officer was discovered to be a source of both intimidation and respect. On one side, this open communication channel allowed the researchers to garner the support and respect of police members. However, knowledge that researchers had a conduit to the CO also meant that researchers sometimes had to work harder to convince lower ranking officers that what they said and did would be treated confidentially, and would not be reported back to the CO. Further, CO public support for the project, given the hierarchical structure of the organization, meant researchers also had to be sure to inform officers that participation in any sources of data collection (interviews, focus groups or surveys) was voluntary and *not* tied to the CO's role in or support for the research project(s). To do so, the researchers exhaustively explained processes of consent and anonymity, the project scope, roles of different members, how data would be used, stored and analyzed, and who would have access to the raw data.

It is also worth noting that the presence of the researchers, itself, is a direct breach in the normative authority structure of the institutional hierarchy, a breach that requires a new mode of navigation. Put another way, members of the research team had to learn how to negotiate the position of research 'outsiders' who are suddenly on the 'inside'. In fact, even first inviting the researchers to 'be on the inside' was not an easy task, as Commanding Officer Hardy explains:

> I had some apprehensions initially launching into this partnership with the university. Some of my past experiences, as they related to the academic community, had been fraught with mutual suspicion and mistrust. Analyses of past policing operations by academic experts was, and is, too often unbalanced and critical; merely appraisals and opinions without providing recommendations for improving service delivery or recognizing the limitations inherent [in] our role as police in provisions of public safety. Further, there exists [a] very limited organizational framework within the RCMP to support collaborative partnerships with the academic community.

Yet, it was the actions of the primary investigator, Ricciardelli, which encouraged Hardy to continue to take steps toward developing the partnership:

> Ricciardelli did not arrive at our work site with any apparent preconceived notions about the organizational culture of the RCMP; she understood that as this was a new experience for my team, we would require her guidance and flexibility in order to achieve successful outcomes. She was genuinely interested in our perspective of current and potential policing practices that relate to youth crime prevention. In order to retain commitment from my team and invest in such research, it was important to demonstrate the relevance of our project as it pertained to our policing priorities.

As Hardy notes, it was essential that, as collaborators, all stakeholders learned about the dynamics of the hierarchical law enforcement agency in order to ensure that institutional culture, while respected, would also not compromise the nature or quality of data collected. The ethical challenge, then, is how to be true to the desires of upper management, the positions of the members, and the research objectives without compromising any promises made or breaching growing trust between parties.

Clear intentions: disseminating knowledge

From the outset, both parties should commit to a memorandum of agreement that clearly sets out the purpose of the research and the desired objectives, the method to be employed, and the timeline within which goals are to be achieved. This is essential given, as Cordner and White (2010) found, differences in police and academic organizational structures can and have led to deal-breaking differences in timelines for deliverables. They argue that *key* to successful research initiatives between police and academics is a wholly collaborative research methodology that takes into consideration these organizational differences. In essence, this includes the incorporation of consistent and immediate deliverables that benefit the police agency and subsequently normalize the existence of researchers within the policing environment through communication and visibility in the research design (Innes 2010).

The memorandum of agreement must also provide specific parameters around what can be done with the knowledge produced and how it can be disseminated. These details need to be set out from the beginning in order to avoid later conflict over, among other possible points of contention, whether data is published for academic or professional audiences, or intended strictly for internal use (Kelty & Julian 2012). An additional related issue is whether, and, if so, to what extent, study outcomes may be censored (unless, of course, findings may create undue risk to research participants or violate their confidentiality or anonymity).

In our study, the academics needed to verify that all research could be conducted openly, without prejudice, and that the findings would be uncensored. In return, the police wanted research results that were within their desired knowledge needs and were produced through methods that were not only conducted in a timely fashion but also did not impede safety, security, and institutional policies. Further, it was required that study findings be reported back to the RCMP in clear language, with specific recommendations and outcomes. In essence, then, data collected was useable for peer-review journal articles, as long as the RCMP were provided with results in the form of non-technical, jargon-free reports – basically, two sets of 'deliverables'.

Openness to uncensored publication not only helped to strengthen the relationship, but also spoke to the interest of police leaders in contributing to research aimed at improving practice and policy within the division and in policing more generally. Indeed, Commanding Officer Hardy was well aware of knowledge and practical gaps in policing practices that she believed could and should be addressed through empirical study. Further, over time, as confidence in the partnership grew, she was able to trust in the researchers' abilities to know where appropriate boundaries existed, and to avoid crossing them. For example, the fact that researchers did not want access to confidential case data was key to ensuring that police members would not be placed in positions whereby they felt their occupational responsibilities and public safety could be compromised. If researchers wanted, without clear justification, access to files outlining how members have dealt with specific cases – open or closed case files – this could breach mutual trust by suggesting their actions required review or, worse yet, expose practices that could possibly impair community and officer safety. As researchers, we had no need to cross such lines, and this recognition was paramount to garnering the respect of the membership and the persons overseeing the partnership's development. Of course, if or when such needs arise the same prior discussions and clarified objectives would guide such research endeavors (i.e. the need to bar the censorship of findings). The police officers involved knew, or grew to know, that the researchers would protect their personal, professional, and institutional safety.

Conclusion

The successes from this partnership shed light on what can 'work' when doing research *with* – and not *on* – the police. Recognizing the many documented barriers to successful collaborative research between academics and police in the constitution of a 'partnership', our experiences demonstrate how such barriers can be overcome if project objectives are shared and transparent, communication is direct and trust is carefully cultivated. As this project did not require researchers to first aggressively cross lines that result in breaches of trust, it may be that the topic of interest facilitated a more positive relationship from the outset. However, as the research progressed we did experience some less favorable processes or findings that did impair trust with select officers. The value in establishing trust is that it did not impair faith in the research team nor in the membership more broadly; such occurrences were individualized (e.g. not everyone can be in agreement or on the same page!). What worked here is building police–academic collaborative relationships based on transparency, trust, and clear objectives. Further, what reveals to us that this partnership approach is working is that, as RCMP members, including CO Hardy who provided the impetus for this project, retire or transfer, the project continues to grow with continued support from those who move into said positions.

One thing the researchers were clear on from the beginning is that police organizational constraints, including the need for approval from headquarters, must be respected and any desire to obtain information that could compromise security or reputation should be avoided unless there are clear methodological justifications for such activities. The researchers on this project were fortunate, however, in that such issues were largely irrelevant: our focus was instead on learning about frontline officers' beliefs, thoughts, insights and practices in relation to working with young people. While it was the case that, in some instances, the academics needed to be briefed on certain political factors shaping policing practice – which can be a somewhat delicate set of discussions – this knowledge was provided when necessary to move research forward and always with respect for confidence, reasoning, applicability, and in ways that would not compromise the security and safety of participants or stakeholders. Correspondingly, academic issues that might have served as barriers to an effective partnership were also disclosed openly, including issues related to institutional practices, protocols, and other complexities (such as the process of navigating research ethics across multiple institutions). Thus, transparency meant that both parties knew and understood some of the organizational and other constraints faced by the other and could adjust expectations accordingly. The research process was further helped, as documented above, by a detailed memorandum of understanding, which served as a contract between parties. It was, however, approached as a flexible contract, subject to amendment as circumstances changed or exigencies arose.

Over a decade ago, Stanko (2002) asserted the need for "a greater commitment on behalf of both academics and the police organization to find a common evidence-based language with which to debate the police and to be inspired by the effort that is required to bring systematic academic knowledge together with police problem solving and strategic/tactical thinking" (p. 309). She further argued that researchers and police need to re-examine their professional relationships with the other in order to begin developing truly collaborative, productive partnerships. Her words remain as true today as they were over ten years ago.

Based on our experiences as members of such a collaboration, it is possible to develop mutually beneficial relationships in which both sides not only learn from the other, but learn to co-generate useful results. Among lessons learned through the partnership discussed here, is the need for open and shared objectives between partners, and respect and empathy for all parties. Without these key ingredients, we remain two solitudes.

References

Alarid, LF 1999, 'Law enforcement departments as learning organizations: Argyris's theory as a framework for implementing community policing', *Police Quarterly* vol. 2, no. 3, pp. 321–337.

Amabile, T, Patterson, C, & Mueller, J 2001, 'Academic–practitioner collaboration in management research: A case of cross professional collaboration', *Academy of Management Journal*, vol. 44, no. 2, pp. 418–431.

Banton, M 1964, *The Policeman in the Community*, London, Tavistock.

Birzer, M 2002, 'Writing partnerships between police practitioners and researchers', *Police Practice and Research*, vol. 3, no. 2, pp. 149–156.

Bradley, D & Nixon, C 2009, 'Ending the "dialogue of the deaf": Evidence and policing policies and practices. An Australian case study', *Police Practice and Research: An International Journal*, vol. 10, no. 5/6, pp. 423–435.

Bradley, D, Marks, M, & Nixon, C 2006, 'What works, what doesn't work and what looks promising in police research networks', in eds J Fleming & J Wood, *Fighting Crime Together: The Challenges of Policing and Security Networks*, Sydney, New South Wales Press, pp. 170–194.

Brown, J & Waters, I 1993, 'Professional police research', *Policing*, vol. 9, no. 4, pp. 323–334.

Buerger, ME 2010, 'Policing and research: Two cultures separated by an almost-common language', *Police Practice and Research*, vol. 11, no. 2, pp. 135–143.

Canadian Policing Research Network 2014, *A community building Canada's policing research*. www.cprncriminology.com/.

Canter, D 2004, 'A tale of two cultures: A comparison of the cultures of police and of academia', in *Policing of a Safe, Just, Tolerant Society: An International Model for Policing*, eds R Adlam & P Villiers., Winchester, Waterside Press, pp. 109–121.

Caplan, J 2003, 'Police cynicism: Police survival tool?', *Police Journal*, vol. 76, no. 4, pp. 304–313.

Cockcroft, T 2014, 'Police culture and transformational leadership: Outlining the contours of a troubled relationship', *Policing*, vol. 8, no. 1, pp. 1–9.

Cordner, G & White, S 2010, 'The evolving relationship between police research and police practice', *Police Practice and Research,* vol. 11, no. 2, pp. 90–94.

Fleming, J 2010, 'Learning to work together: Police and academics', *Policing: A Journal of Policy and Practice*, vol. 4, no. 2, pp. 139–145.

Foster, J & Bailey, S 2010, 'Joining forces: Maximizing ways of making a difference in policing', *Policing*, vol. 4, no. 2, pp. 95–103.

Griffiths, C, Murphy, C, & Snow, S 2014, 'Police culture and transformational leadership: Outlining the contours of a troubled relationship', prepared for Community Safety and Countering Crime Branch, Public Safety Canada. ISBN: 978-1-100-24574-4.

Innes, M 2010, 'A "mirror" and a "motor": Researching and reforming policing in an age of austerity', *Policing*, vol. 4, no. 2, pp. 127–134.

Jain, HC, Singh, P, & Agocs, C 2000, 'Recruitment, selection and promotion of visible- minority police officers in selected Canadian police services', *Canadian Public Administration*, vol. 42, no. 3, pp. 46–74.

Kelty, SF & Julian, R 2010, 'Identifying the skills and attributes of good crime scene personnel', *Australasian Policing: A Journal of Professional Practice and Research*, vol. 2, no. 2, pp. 40–41.

Kelty, SF & Julian, R 2012, 'Looking through the crystal ball: Do others know what you expect from research projects?' *Policing*, vol. 6, no. 4, pp. 408–417.

MacDonald, B, 1986, 'Research and action in the context of policing: An analysis of the problem and a programme proposal', Unpublished document of the Police Foundation of England and Wales.

Marks, M, Woods, J, Ally, F, Walsh, T, & Witbooi, A 2010, 'Worlds apart? On the possibilities of police/academic collaboration', *Policing*, vol. 4, no. 3, pp. 112–118.

National Police Research Platform 2014, *Advancing Knowledge and Practice in Policing*. www.nationalpoliceresearch.org/background.

Neyroud, P & Weisburd, D 2014, 'Transforming the police through science: The challenge of ownership', *Policing*, vol. 8, no. 4, pp. 287–293.

Reuss-Ianni, E 1983, *The Two Cultures of Policing*, New York, Transaction.

Rojek, J, Alpert, G, & Smith, H 2012, 'The utilization of research by the police', *Police Practice and Research: An International Journal*, vol. 13, no. 4, pp. 329–341.

Rosenbaum, D 2014, *Police–research Partnerships: Contributions of the National Police Research Platform*, presentation at the Economics of Policing: National Policing Research Symposium, Department of Public Safety, Vancouver, BC.

Sanders, B & Fields, M 2009, 'Partnerships with university-based researchers', *Police Chief*, vol. 76, no. 6, pp. 58–61.

Scott, MS 2010, 'Policing and police research: Learning to listen, with a Wisconsin case study', *Police Practice and Research*, vol. 11, no. 2, pp. 95–104.

Sherman, L & Murray, A 2015, 'Evidence-based policing: From academics to professionals', *International Criminal Justice Review*, vol. 25, no. 1, pp. 7–10.

Shulenberg, JL 2014, 'Systematic social observation of police behaviour: The process, logistics, and challenges in a Canadian context', *Quality & Quantity: International Journal of Methodology*, vol. 48, no. 1, pp. 297–315.

Sklansky, D 2006, 'Not your father's police department: Making sense of the new demographics of law enforcement', *Journal of Criminal Law and Criminology*, vol. 96, no. 3, pp. 1209–1243.

Skogan, WG & Frydl, K eds 2004, *Fairness and Effectiveness in Policing: The Evidence*, Washington, DC, National Academies Press.

Stanko, E.A. 2009, 'Improving policing through research', *Policing*, vol. 3, no. 4, pp. 306–309.

Tan, T & Heracleous, L 2001, 'Teaching old dogs new tricks: Implementing organizational learning in an Asian National Police Force', *Journal of Applied Behavioral Science*, vol. 37, no. 3, pp. 361–380.

White, A 2010, *The Politics of Private Security: Regulation, Reform and Re-legitimation*, Basingstoke, Palgrave Macmillan.

Wilkinson, S 2010, 'Research and policing: Looking to the future', *Policing: A Journal of Policy and Practice*, vol. 4, no. 2, pp. 146–148.

Wood, J, Fleming, J, & Marks, M 2008, 'Building the capacity of police change agents: The nexus policing project', *Policing and Society*, vol. 18, no. 1, pp. 72–87.

Wuestewald, T & Steinheider, B 2010, 'Practitioner–researcher collaborations in policing: A case of close encounters?', *Policing*, vol. 4, no. 2, pp. 104–111.

Young, M 1991, *Inside Job: Policing and Police Culture in Britain*, Oxford, Oxford University Press.

Yuille, J 1984, 'Research and teaching with police: A Canadian example', *Applied Psychology*, vol. 33, no. 1, pp. 5–22.

9

CRIMINOLOGIZING EVERYDAY LIFE AND CONDUCTING POLICING ETHNOGRAPHY IN CHINA

Jianhua Xu

Introduction

In his recent book *Democratic Policing in a Changing World*, Peter Manning (2010) argues that recent policing researchers in democratic countries have come too close to the research subject. This policing scholarship often focuses on issues of "what works" and "what can the police do?" rather than examining the moral, political and social consequences of police action (ibid, p. 106). In this sense, some scholars argue that sociological inquiry into the discipline of policing in Western countries has become "sociology for policing" instead of "sociology of policing" (Loader 2011). If policing research in democratic countries is "too close" to its research subject, then policing research in authoritarian China is best described as an even more unilateral spokesperson for its research subject. In a review of articles in Chinese academic journals on policing, Lo (2010) points out that many research articles are simply "worshippers" and "flatterers" of the Chinese party-state's ideology, with the content merely reflecting authors' adherence to existing political lines and slogans. While some articles discuss some practical conditions of Chinese policing such as public relations or crime control (Chen 2015; Li 1998), a critical discourse is largely absent. In addition, policing research in China, like many other topics within the field of criminology, remains at the level of general discussion and speculation without a sound framework and empirical evidence (Zhang 2011, p. 83). In this chapter, based on my recent research on police/business and crime solicitation posters in Guangzhou, I reflect on the challenges and opportunities one faces in conducting policing research in China. In addition, I examine the ethical nature of these challenges and its relevance for policing research in other authoritarian countries.

Challenges of and opportunities for policing research in China

Researchers have faced several challenges in studying policing in China. The first relates to the general difficulty of studying policing. In modern society, the police are one of a few government agencies legally authorized to use force. Further, the secret nature of much police work facilitates the formation of a conservative police culture which prevents police from sharing information about their work with the public and researchers (Manning 2004). Compared with those targeted by police, usually young, poor and underclass citizens, the police are in a position of power. And indeed, criminological research of the powerful is much more difficult to conduct than of the powerless (Lumsden & Winter 2014). Some scholars even argue that criminology, the umbrella discipline under which policing falls, has become a tool of social control due to its unbalanced selection of research targets, especially low status offenders (Jacques & Wright 2010). Chinese policing studies are not immune to this problem, and seldom question the philosophy, method and consequences of policing strategy (Lo 2010).

The second challenge of researching police is related to academic freedom in China. Although Chinese society has undergone unprecedented changes over the past three decades, China remains under one party rule; that of the Chinese Communist Party (CCP), which actively preempts any possible challenges to its rule. An independent and critical discourse of the cornerstone of the CCP's repressive force, the police, would be regarded as challenging the legitimacy of the party-state and is therefore actively suppressed. Critical researchers may suffer from various punishments, ranging from losing their jobs to being imprisoned, if they are regarded as posing a threat to the rule of the Communist party-state (Xu & Liu 2015).

After Xi Jingping took power in 2012, what limited academic freedom existed was further eroded and control over universities also strengthened. In 2013, the party-state launched a campaign to ban universities and media from talking about seven topics deemed to be "dangerous Western influences". The infamous "seven speak-nots" include universal values, freedom of speech, civil society, civil rights, the historical errors of the Chinese Communist Party, crony capitalism and judicial independence (Carlson 2013). In 2015, foreign textbooks were further banned from use in Chinese universities to stem infiltration of "Western values" (Chen & Zhuang 2015). If the visible hand of political control on academic freedom affects the production of knowledge on Chinese society in general and on policing in particular, the invisible hand of self-censorship affects Chinese policing research in a more subtle way. Researchers will avoid many 'sensitive' topics if they believe there is no chance to get their work published for political reasons. As such, these research topics certainly cannot garner financial support through grants, as the government controls most grants. Researchers must also be cautious in drawing their conclusions according to certain political lines. And indeed, my personal experience of reviewing Chinese journal articles on crime and policing is also illuminating. For many academic journals, when they solicit my comments on submitted articles, the first criteria in the review form is "whether the article is politically correct or not", which means not being critical towards the government, and particularly not being critical towards the CCP. Although I can dismiss these instructions by indicating that articles are politically correct, other reviewers may act differently. In addition, the existence of this political criteria itself illuminates the lack of academic freedom in China, which greatly affects the formation of a critical analysis of policing among Chinese scholars.

The third difficulty for policing studies in China is scholars' lack of experience and skills in terms of conducting empirical studies. In the 1950s, soon after the CCP took power in China, all social science disciplines were banned from universities as a result of their alleged political incorrectness. It was not until the 1980s, when China started economic reform and opened up to the outside world, that the social science disciplines were re-established. The absence of social sciences for three decades deprived almost two generations of scholars of advancement in empirical studies, both theoretically and critically. During the last two decades, although Chinese scholars have started to catch up and develop their ability to conduct empirical research on topics such as the family, juveniles and migration, the legacy of a lack of training and experience in social science research still greatly limits the production of knowledge in policing. As a result, much research is based on unsupported speculation and without a theoretical framework, despite a few exceptions in recent years (Hu 2015).

Since the 1990s, due to the growing impact of China in the world and increasing interest in Chinese policing internationally, a small body of literature on Chinese policing began to emerge in the English-speaking world (Dai 2008). Although this body of research covers a wide range of topics and offers a critical examination that includes the philosophy and practice of Chinese policing (Bakken 2000, 2005; Dutton 2005; Fu 2005; Tanner 2005; Wong 2002; Xu 2012, 2014a), most researchers conduct studies using archival and secondary data. Empirical study of Chinese policing in the English-speaking world is also underdeveloped. While Chinese scholars have to face the problems of limited academic freedom and training in conducting empirical policing scholarship, the major challenge for international scholars is the problem of access to research participants. Scoggins (2014, p. 394) recently reflected on the challenges tied to her identity as an American scholar when conducting policing research in China and concluded that the most difficult part of the research was the recruitment of police for interview.

Facing these challenges, some international scholars resort to different strategies to conduct empirical studies on Chinese policing. On the one hand, some avoid studying police officers and policing strategies directly. Instead, they focus on people's perceptions of the police and analyze factors affecting different populations' trust in and satisfaction with the police (Sun et al. 2013; Wu & Sun 2009). However, given the difficulty of studying policing in general and the authoritarian nature of Chinese policing in particular, an independent and large-scale survey of police officers has yet to emerge.

On the other hand, some international scholars utilize their simultaneous insider and outsider identities to facilitate empirical data collection while avoiding political interference in publishing research findings. In recent decades an increasing number of Chinese scholars have obtained their PhD in sociology, criminology or political science in the US, the UK, Australia and Hong Kong.[1] These scholars enjoy a hybrid semi-foreigner and semi-Chinese identity, which facilities their primary data collection in policing research (Xu et al. 2013). Their outsider identity helps avoid political intervention and self-censorship in publishing their research findings. For instance, based on published materials and fieldwork data from two Chinese cities, Wang Peng, a UK trained, Hong Kong-based Chinese scholar, explored how Guanxi, a Chinese version of personal connection, affected police corruption by facilitating the selling and buying of senior police positions and promoting formation of corrupt networks between the police and criminals (Wang 2014). Using archival material and interviews with police officers, Zhou Kai and Yan Xiaojun, two Hong Kong-based Chinese scholars, examined how local police used information strategies, persuasive strategies and coercive strategies to control protests and maintain social stability in a city of northern China (Zhou & Yan 2014). My previous ethnographic research into robbery of motorcycle taxi drivers in southern China also offered a critical analysis of how a discriminative motorcycle ban policy affected the working time of local and migrant drivers and, by extension, their differential risk of robbery (Xu 2009). Despite various challenges, these researchers opened new possibilities for conducting empirical research on Chinese policing, although scholars inside mainland China (including those returned from training overseas) may still face many difficulties in exploring these possibilities. In the next section, I will reflect on how my identity as both insider and outsider affects research design, data collection, publications and ethics involved in the process of researching the police in China.

Political sensitivity and the alternative way of entering the policing field in China

The most challenging aspect of conducting policing ethnography in China is obtaining access to the police for fieldwork, given its conservative political environment towards policing research (Scoggins 2014). However, observation of police work is of vital importance to advance our understanding of policing. The founder of the Chicago School of Sociology, Robert Park, informed his students about the importance of fieldwork and first-hand observation:

> You have been told to go grubbing in the library, thereby accumulating a mass of notes and liberal coating of grime. You have been told to choose problems wherever you can find musty stacks of routine records based on trivial schedules prepared by tired bureaucrats and filled out by reluctant applicants for fussy do-gooders or indifferent clerks. This is called "getting your hands

dirty in real research." Those who counsel you are wise and honorable; the reasons they offer are of great value. But one more thing is needful: first hand observation. Go and sit in the lounges of luxury hotels and on the doorsteps of flophouses; sit on the Gold Coast settees and the slum shakedowns, sit in the orchestra hall and in the Star and Garter burlesque. In short, gentlemen, go and get the seat of your pants dirty in real research. (cited in McKinney 1966, p. 71)

Almost one century later, in a speech at a British Society of Criminology lifetime awards ceremony, the British sociologist and criminologist Stanley Cohen reiterated the importance of getting "out there" in the field for researchers. Cohen counseled, "beware of the people … who are always grabbing you to tell you … how things work 'out there'. The criminological version of 'out there' is sitting in the back of a police van" (cited in Hall 2011).

   Although 'sitting in the back of a police van' has been a long tradition for policing researchers in democratic societies (Black 1970; Martin 2007; Reiss 1971a), such a practice has not yet been possible in authoritarian China. However, my research experience reveals that there are also other possibilities in terms of conducting policing ethnography research by studying the traces left behind by police activity or the evidence of what the police fail to do in the public space. One of the strengths of ethnography is that it allows researchers to examine traces of human activity in their natural settings. Although many aspects of police work such as crime investigation and intelligence gathering are secretive and out of sight for the public, some police work, including traffic control, stop and check and the production of policing posters for crime prevention, must be conducted or shown in public spaces. These forms of publically performed police work provide possibilities for researchers to observe police behaviors directly or to study the behavior of police through observing the traces of police work indirectly. While directly observing law enforcement might be methodologically challenging, posing certain risks to researchers and being ethically complicated, studying the traces left behind by police activities raises no such concern. My research experience reveals that widely existing policing posters, banners as well as crime solicitation posters in urban China, provide a unique window through which to study various aspects of Chinese police and policing. Looking through this window, we can examine police business relations, commodification of policing, modernization of policing, police culture and the soft-authoritarian nature of policing in a rapidly changing China (Xu 2013, 2015).

Criminologizing the everyday life: insider/outsider identity and the selection of research subjects

In his recent book, *Criminological Imagination*, Jock Young (2011, pp. 79–80) warns against three major problems existing in the current production of criminological knowledge that severely restrict its imagination: (1) male, working-class crime is described as all criminality; (2) descriptions of crime in advanced industrial countries are used to describe crime in general; and (3) the Americanization of criminology. In order to regain its imagination, Young (2011, p. 222) calls for bringing currently marginalized ethnography back to criminology, and making critical ethnography the mainstream. Indeed, there is an increasing recognition of the need to develop criminological ethnography in non-Western societies (Fraser 2013), and to expand the vision of criminology in general and policing studies in particular by drawing inspiration from everyday life in non-Western contexts. Sociologists have long called for integration of research and their personal lives to make the latter a source of inspiration in knowledge production. The American sociologist C. Wright Mills instructed sociology students on the art of intellectual craftsmanship in his classic book, *The Sociological Imagination*:

> The most admirable thinkers within the scholarly community you have chosen to join do not split their work from their lives … what this means is that you must learn to use your life experience in your intellectual work: continually to examine and interpret it. (1959, pp. 195–196)

For me, police/business and crime solicitation posters are part of my everyday life experience and have also become a subject of criminological inquiry: a process of criminologizing everyday life (Felson & Santos 2010; Naughton 2014).

My identity as a semi-insider and semi-outsider in different cities contributed to the process of criminologizing everyday life. Over the past 15 years, I have been studying, working, living and conducting research in three different cities in southern China: Guangzhou, Hong Kong and Macau. Guangzhou is the capital of Guangdong, the richest province as a result of its leading role in China's economic reform since the 1980s. At the end of 2014, Guangzhou had a population of roughly 17 million, where half the populous included rural-to-urban migrant workers; Hong Kong had a population of 7 million and Macau 0.5 million. Hong Kong and Macau are Special Administrative Regions of the People's Republic of China, former colonies of the British and Portuguese, respectively. Under China's one-country two-systems policy, Hong Kong and Macau enjoy a highly autonomous position. Despite the increasing influence of mainland China and the political pressure of mainlandization in recent years (Lo 2012), Hong Kong and Macau still maintain very distinctive urban landscapes and cultures that differ from those of Guangzhou. Spending much time traveling and living in these three cities makes me aware of the sharp differences that exist in the use of urban space by the police for the purpose of crime prevention. While various types of policing posters and banners promoting crime prevention are omnipresent on the streets of Guangzhou, they are much less popular in Hong Kong and Macau. In addition, some posters and banners have uniquely Chinese characteristics, such as police/business posters and police slogan banners.

I was born and raised in mainland China, where I received a Master's degree and worked as a police officer (in Guangzhou) for five years before moving to Hong Kong, where I completed my PhD and postdoctoral work. Since 2013, I have been teaching in Macau while regularly visiting Hong Kong and Guangzhou. Across all these cities I enjoy both an insider and outsider identity. This status increases my sensitivity to the unique use of public space by Guangzhou police and facilitates the selection of police/business and crime solicitation banners as a research subject. These omnipresent police posters/banners and crime solicitation posters are part of everyday life for residents in Guangzhou but have never become the subject of criminological inquiry. Let me now examine how I adopted this alternative method to criminologize my life experience and study Chinese policing through systematically observing police/business and crime solicitation posters.

Systematic social observation of police/business and crime solicitation posters in Guangzhou

Systematic social observation is the direct observation of social phenomena in their natural settings to generate quantitative variables for analysis. Although this method proves to be very useful in policing research (Reiss 1971a), compared with other research methods such as interviews and surveys, systematic social observation is underdeveloped. Observing public places, however, is one of the hallmarks of the Chicago School (Park & Burgess 1921), and direct observation is fundamental to the advancement of knowledge (Sampson & Raudenbush 1999; Taylor et al. 1985). Reiss (1971b) advocated systematic social observation as a key measurement strategy for natural social phenomena. In recent years there has been a renewed interest in applying this method with the assistance of new technology such as videotaping (Sampson & Raudenbush 1999) and Google Street View (Hwang & Sampson 2014). This method has seldom been used in studying Chinese policing except in one of my earlier research projects examining how policing affected differential risks of criminal victimization between migrant workers and local residents in China (Xu 2009). This method was further developed in my study of police/business and crime solicitation posters in Guangzhou.

Since 2009, I have been systematically collecting policing posters and banners in Guangzhou. Wherever I go, I take my professional camera or smart phone with camera function with me. I take pictures of anything related to crime and policing. I largely visit urban villages where most residents are rural-to-urban migrant workers. Urban villages, the Chinese version of urban slums, have also been regarded as the centre of "prostitution, gambling and drugs" and crime hotspots by the police (Xu 2014b). Interestingly, the public space of urban villages has become a contested space between the police and criminals. On the one hand, the police post numerous warning posters with the aim of crime prevention, such as listing typical tricks of tele-communication fraud and reminders to lock doors properly. On the other hand, urban villages are also hotspots of crime solicitation posters posted by criminals on which information on various illegal activities is provided, such as the creation of fake documents and certificates, recruiting sex workers and selling sex, loan sharking, selling fake invoices, guns or stolen cars and motorcycles. There are 138 urban villages in Guangzhou and I have visited almost all of them on foot or by bicycle. In addition, police posters/banners also appear on main streets. On many occasions, I took different buses from starting terminals to end terminals and took pictures of various banners along the streets. During several Chinese New Year periods, my research assistants drove me around the city to take pictures of police banners/posters as the police were more likely to post various banners during this period. Besides blanket searches of police posters/banners and crime solicitation posters in urban villages where migrant workers are concentrated, I have also visited numerous neighborhoods where local residents live. Over the past six years, I have acquired a collection of over 20,000 pictures of police posters and banners as well as crime solicitation posters in Guangzhou. Undoubtedly, the police posters and banners provide evidence of what the police have done to promote crime prevention or political propaganda in the public space. Equally important, crime solicitation posters provide evidence of what the police fail to do as these are posted by criminals to solicit partners or victims. The widespread existence of these posters is a signal of public disorder and the "broken windows" of public space (Wilson & Kelling 1982). They also evidence the police failure to control crime.

Police/business posters

Police/business posters refer to posters on which commercial advertisements appear alongside police warnings (see Figures 9.1 and 9.2). The space occupied by business information and police warnings on these posters varies. On some, information from the police covers most of the space, while on others business advertisements dominate. Although I have yet to see any in Hong Kong and Macau, such posters are used widely in Guangzhou and my research suggests that nearly 100 different types of business have provided financial sponsorship for the police enabling them to produce these posters (Xu 2013). For many citizens in Guangzhou, these police/business posters are part of their everyday lives; they see posters on the streets, the walls in their neighborhoods and the doors to apartment buildings. Ordinary people, myself included, usually take the existence of these posters for granted and seldom question their rationale or the symbiotic relationship between businesses and the police embodied in their co-production. These posters are usually designed by the police yet are made and paid for by the businesses. The police post these posters, in the name of crime prevention, in a variety of locations, including inside banks, restaurants and gated communities. On the one hand, in the production of these police/business posters, a business can benefit from legitimately using public space for its advertisements without approval from other government departments, such as the Industrial and Commercial Administration Bureau and Urban Management Departments, which are supposed to regulate outdoor advertisements.

FIGURE 9.1 A poster displayed in an urban village, on the left-hand side of which is an advertisement for the Mary Women's Hospital and on the right-hand side is a call for support for and cooperation with police work, with phone numbers for the local police services

Source: Author

The business can also benefit from expanding its advertising reach and cultivating good relations with the police, which are of vital importance to business success in China. On the other hand, the police can benefit from promoting crime prevention without paying for it.

Most importantly, on these posters, local police offer phone numbers of local police stations and encourage citizens to call them instead of the centralized police hotline at municipal police departments. In doing so, they can reduce the number of crimes recorded on the centralized police hotline system as these calls will be unknown to municipal police departments. Through manipulating crime statistics, the local police officers can receive better performance evaluations and increase their chances of career promotion. Individual police officers might also exploit this opportunity for their private interest. Although police/business posters can be regarded as a 'win–win' game by the police and the business, they also cause much concern regarding the symbiotic relationship between the two. My field research and interviews with citizens revealed that they worry about police impartiality in law enforcement given their receipt of financial support from businesses. This relationship thus damages the image of the police and reduces citizens' trust in them.

FIGURE 9.2   A poster on a wall, the upper part of which consists of police information reminding readers about the risks of theft and robbery and listing typical fraudulent tricks, and the lower part providing the hotline number for McDonald's 24-hour delivery service

Source: Author

While some may regard the production of police/business posters as only a local phenomenon, my research revealed that police at various levels, from community police officers, local police stations, district police bureaus to municipal police departments, are all involved in the creation of police/business posters. And indeed, receiving financial support from business has been a long tradition for the police in China. Not only the police, other government departments also receive regular financial support from private businesses. I argue that an understanding of police/ business posters and the relationship between the two needs to be located in the symbiotic relationships between economic capital and political power in a wider context of crony capitalism in China (Xu 2013). If the police/business posters can reflect the traces of police activities in public space, crime solicitation posters are evidence of what the police fail to do.

Crime solicitation posters

Crime solicitation posters are made by criminals to promote their illegal activities in the public space (see Figures 9.3 and 9.4). They are signals of crime and public disorder. As with police posters, crime solicitation posters are displayed throughout in Guangzhou. In many places, crime solicitation posters appear beside police warning posters. In some extreme cases, crime solicitation posters might appear on top of police posters or police information boards (Figure 9.5). The obvious illegal activities displayed on crime solicitation posters are also part of citizens' everyday life in Guangzhou. These posters usually appear on bus stations, across street overpasses, on the ground of sidewalks and on walls of residential areas. In the past six years, I have identified 22 different types of crime solicitation posters in Guangzhou. The most common advertise the making of various fake documents/certificates such as passports, ID cards, student cards, English level test certificates, marriage certificates and health certificates. Other types of crime solicitation posters include those advertising loan-sharking, debt collection, phone spying, fake invoices, selling gas-pistols, stolen motorcycles and cars, and various frauds related to sex services, credit cards, medical insurance, driver licenses, and so on. These crime solicitation posters are spread unevenly throughout public spaces in Guangzhou. In Guangzhou, there are roughly three different types of residential community. The first is urban villages where most residents are migrant workers. The second is semi-gated former socialist

FIGURE 9.3 Various posters, including those advertising loan shark and fake documentation services and those recruiting male and female sex workers

Source: Author

FIGURE 9.4 A poster for 'women' who are "looking for men to get [them] pregnant" and offering a payment of 1.5 million RMB (a common fraudulent practice)

Source: Author

work unit residential areas containing mostly local residents. The third is gated residential areas where most residents are new, rich and middle class. Data from systematic social observation shows that, while crime solicitation posters are never displayed within gated communities, they are nine times more likely to appear in urban villages than in semi-gated communities (Xu 2015). Further research reveals that the main reason explaining the difference in number of crime solicitation posters displayed in migrant worker communities and local resident communities is the availability and level of private policing or security services. To help make sense of my observations, I relied on some interviews with police (see below), which revealed that public police are largely absent in controlling crime solicitation posters. The most frequently cited reason given by the police to justify this situation was that they were too busy to handle these minor offenses; others believed that the

FIGURE 9.5 A poster displayed on the information board used by police services advertising the production of fake certificates

Source: Author

Urban Management Department should be responsible for them (Xu 2015). The failure of the police to control these self-evident crimes in the public space provides another window through which to examine how public and private policing affect the production of public disorder in urban China.

Reflectivity and research ethics

Although examining the traces of police activities and evidence of what they fail to do in the public space provides a possible method for studying Chinese policing, the difficulty related to study policing in general and the conservative political environment in particular haunted the whole research process, which raises a number of ethical issues in my research.

The first ethical issue concerns relations between researchers and the police. In order to make sense of what I observed in the public space, it was necessary that I interviewed police and ascertained their point of view. For instance, why did the police and businesses cooperate in producing police/business posters? What are the pros and cons for both sides? Or what are the attitudes of police towards crime solicitation posters and how do they control them? Understanding these questions provides the basis for a critical examination of the nature of Chinese policing. However, access to the police is almost impossible without personal connections or Guanxi. Chinese police are particularly vigilant regarding the activities of scholars with overseas backgrounds, allegedly in case they leak state secrets. Although my former identity as a police officer in Guangzhou to some extent reduced such concerns, reluctance on the part of some officers to talk about these issues persisted; those who did talk to me, I could sense were doing me a great favor. Such favors have nothing to do with the significance of my research but result from our Guanxi. People expect to help each other when they are in such relations. However, as other scholars point out, maintaining a good level of Guanxi can be not only time-consuming but also costly (Zhang et al. 2007). For instance, I was once asked by a police officer I had interviewed to write a Master's thesis for him. On another occasion, one police scholar who facilitated the interview asked if I could add his name to my future publications. Although I declined these requests as they were clear violations of research integrity and represented academic corruption, my refusal may also be interpreted as an unwillingness to return a favor, as such practices are widespread throughout mainland China. In addition, police officers I interviewed expressed other concerns, ranging from potential personal trouble caused by talking about sensitive police issues with a scholar from overseas, to the potential tarnishing of the police's image when research findings are published internationally (Xu 2013). My promise of anonymity and maintaining a neutral stance in my writing cannot completely ease these concerns, which may affect my rapport with police and the possibility of cooperation with them in future research. Although institutional review boards have increasingly been regarded as posing many difficulties for ethnographic research in many countries (Cook & Hoas 2011; Hessler et al. 2011) – with some scholars even calling it the "murder of ethnography" in criminology (Hall 2011) – fortunately, the ethical review process for my research at the University of Macau was conducted smoothly.

The second ethical issue relates to the possible consequence of being a critical researcher on Chinese policing. Existing literature on research ethics has explored thoroughly the importance of protecting the research subject (Emanuel et al. 2000; Orb et al. 2001). Undoubtedly, any research should not intentionally cause harm to research subjects, and this is particularly the case when the research subjects are vulnerable populations such as juveniles, migrants, or the poor. If these ethical issues related to protecting vulnerable research subjects are a main concern in democratic countries, there is an added ethical dimension to conducting research in authoritarian societies. For instance, in China where academic freedom is not protected by law, critical researchers themselves may become vulnerable when facing intervention by and even punishment from the government. When researchers run the risk of being punished by the government for political reasons, should they take the consequences of punishment such as losing their job or imprisonment of their family into consideration? Are they taking an ethical stance toward themselves and their families if they know they are running these risks? And to what extent should they worry about these risks? These questions also arise in my research. As a scholar based in Macau, academic freedom is largely protected. However, I have also been friendly reminded by various people that conducting critical research on Chinese policing may mean putting myself in a risky situation because I have to return to mainland China on a regular basis. Worrying about these risks will have an effect on various aspects of research. For instance, I may have to think twice about working on a more challenging topic, such as political and secret policing.

The third ethical issue concerns the publication of findings. Given the political sensitivity of policing research and censorship in academic publications, critical research on Chinese policing can hardly be published in academic journals in China. Scholars based overseas, myself included, who work on Chinese policing may also engage in self-censorship by not submitting articles to Chinese journals. Publication in English journals can not only escape the Chinese censorship regime, but also avoid drawing unfriendly attention from Chinese authorities.[2] However, publication in English also limits its influence among Chinese readers, as most universities do not have access to English journal databases in the social sciences and many scholars are inadequately proficient in English to read articles in it. Research findings can also not be published in the mass media without severe censorship from editors. I was invited by a mainland Chinese national newspaper to write an article on Chinese policing and thus submitted a draft to the managing editor. The editor apologized for the deletion of a particular section that he felt was too politically sensitive and remarked that, without this censorship, the editor in chief may have completely prevented the article's publication. Researchers have to face this dilemma of either accepting certain levels of censorship while publishing their articles or having their voice not heard at all.

Conclusion

In the past three decades, a booming literature on policing studies has emerged. Most of this research focuses on Western countries where empirical research has a long tradition and academic freedom is protected. Empirical research on policing in China is extremely underdeveloped given its political sensitivity and conservative police culture. However, researchers also point out that, although challenging, a rapidly changing Chinese society also creates some room for scholars to maneuver and negotiate with their research subject (Scoggins 2014).

In this chapter, based on a decade of personal research experience on policing in China, I reflected on the possibility of expanding the researchers' 'toolkit' by criminologizing researchers' everyday life and systematically observing traces of police activity on the street and evidence of what they fail to do in the public space. Criminologizing researchers' everyday lives could be especially useful in authoritarian countries where the police are hard to approach for research purposes. It can help to identify research questions and lay the foundation for further ethnographic inquiry on policing. And, indeed, every researcher has a biography that becomes an element in and aspect of the collection and analysis of data (Ragin et al. 2004, p. 15). Despite the advantages of drawing inspiration from lived experiences of studying Chinese policing, researchers still have to face and manage several ethical issues. These ethical issues are more pronounced in authoritarian countries. In democratic societies, relations between the researcher and the police could be less complicated. In China, the conservative police culture and political pressure mean that researchers have to rely on their Guanxi to gain access to the police. Relying on Guanxi could complicate research ethics as the police may have certain expectations of researchers. In democratic countries, the main ethical concern with regard to research is the protection of vulnerable research subjects (De Vries et al. 2004; Marshall 2003). While this concern also applies in China, researchers also have to deal with the problem of protecting themselves from political pressure and even punishment. In China, lack of academic freedom also limits researchers' choice of publication outlet. While publishing research findings in international English journals can avoid censorship by and unfriendly attention from Chinese authorities, it also limits its influence among Chinese readers. Researchers who focus on the police in other authoritarian countries may also encounter similar challenges to those I experienced in China. Criminologizing everyday life means that the dilemma of insider/outsider identity and the unique ethical issues facing researchers in China form an ongoing process through which scholars must advance, negotiate, and compromise in developing policing ethnography.

Notes

1   Hong Kong, a former British colony, was handed over to China in 1997. Currently, Hong Kong and Macau are two Special Administrative Regions within the People's Republic of China.
2   On the one hand, foreign languages present an obstacle for Party officials in terms of tracing critical publications, as their capacity to read in them is limited. On the other hand, publications in foreign languages have less impact on ordinary Chinese citizens, which reduces the party-state's motivation to censor them.

Funding: Multi-Year Research Grants (MYRG2015-00039-FSS) & (MYRG2015-00163-FSS), University of Macau

References

Bakken, B 2000, *The Exemplary Society: Human Improvement, Social Control, and the Dangers of Modernity in China*, Oxford, Oxford University Press.
Bakken, B 2005, 'Introduction: Crime, control, and modernity in China', in *Crime, Punishment, and Policing in China*, ed B Bakken, Lanham, MD, Rowman & Littlefield, pp. 1–26.

Black, DJ 1970, 'Production of crime rates', *American Sociological Review*, vol. 35, no. 4, pp. 733–748.

Carlson, B 2013, '7 things you can't talk about in China', *Global Post*. www.globalpost.com/dispatch/news/regions/asia-pacific/china/130529/censorship-chinese-communist-party.

Chen, A & Zhuang, P 2015, 'Chinese universities ordered to ban textbooks that promote Western values', *South China Morning Post*. www.scmp.com/news/china/article/1695524/chinese-universities-instructed-ban-textbooks-promote-western-values?page=all.

Chen, B 2015, 'Present situation and the strategies of the network public relations in public security organs in new media era', *Journal of Fujian Police College*, vol. 143, no. 1, pp. 43–47.

Cook, AF & Hoas, H 2011, 'Protecting research subjects: IRBs in a changing research landscape', *IRB: Ethics & Human Research*, vol. 33, no. 2, pp. 14–19.

Dai, M 2008, 'Policing in the People's Republic of China: A review of recent literature', *Crime, Law and Social Change*, vol. 50, pp. 211–17.

De Vries, R, DeBruin, DA, & Goodgame, A 2004, 'Ethics review of social, behavioral, and economic research: Where should we go from here?', *Ethics & Behavior*, vol. 14, no. 4, pp. 351–368.

Dutton, M 2005, *Policing Chinese Politics: A history*, Durham, NC, Duke University Press.

Emanuel, EJ, Wendler, D, & Grady, C 2000, 'What makes clinical research ethical?', *JAMA*, vol. 283, no. 20, pp. 2701–2711.

Felson, M & Santos, RB 2010, *Crime and Everyday Life* (4th ed), Thousand Oaks, CA, Sage.

Fraser, A.2013, 'Ethnography at the periphery: Redrawing the borders of criminology's world-map', *Theoretical Criminology*, vol. 17, no. 2, pp. 251–260.

Fu, H 2005, 'Zhou Yongkang and the recent police reform in China', *Australian and New Zealand Journal of Criminology*, vol. 38, pp. 241–253.

Hall, S 2011, 'The murder of ethnography', *Crime Talk*. www.crimetalk.org.uk/library/section-list/38-frontpage-articles/199-the-murder-of-ethnography.html.

Hessler, RM, Donnell-Watson, DJ, & Galliher, JF 2011, 'A case for limiting the reach of institutional review boards', *American Sociologist*, vol. 42, pp. 145–152.

Hu, R 2015, 'Chinese people's political efficacy, political participation and police trust', *Sociological Studies*, vol. 3, no. 1, pp. 76–96.

Hwang, J & Sampson, RJ 2014, 'Divergent pathways of gentrification: Racial inequality and the social order of renewal in Chicago neighborhoods', *American Sociological Review*, vol. 79, no. 4, pp. 726–751.

Jacques, S & Wright, R 2010, 'Criminology as social control: Discriminatory research and its role in the reproduction of social inequalities and crime', *Crime, Law and Social Change*, vol. 53, no. 4, pp. 383–396.

Li, Q 1998, 'The application of public relations among the police', *Journal of Public Security University*, vol. 71, no. 1, pp. 91–93.

Lo, TW 2012, 'Resistance to the mainlandization of criminal justice practices: A barrier to the development of restorative justice in Hong Kong', *International Journal of Offender Therapy and Comparative Criminology*, vol. 56, no. 4, pp. 627–645.

Lo, Y 2010, 'Self image and public image of the police in China', MPhil. thesis, University of Hong Kong.

Loader, I 2011, 'Where is policing studies? A review of democratic policing in a changing world', *British Journal of Criminology*, vol. 51, no. 2, pp. 449–458.

Lumsden, K & Winter, A 2014, *Reflexivity in Criminological Research: Experiences with the Powerful and the Powerless*, Houndmills, Palgrave Macmillan.

Manning, P 2004, 'The police: Mandate, strategies and appearances', in *Policing: Key Readings*, ed T Newburn, Milton, Willan, pp. 191–214.

Manning, PK 2010, *Democratic Policing in a Changing World*, Boulder, CO, Paradigm Publishers.

Marshall, PA 2003, 'Human subjects protections, institutional review boards, and cultural anthropological research', *Anthropological Quarterly*, vol. 76, no. 2, pp. 269–285.

Martin, J 2007, 'A reasonable balance of law and sentiment: Social order in democratic Taiwan from the policeman's point of view', *Law & Society Review*, vol. 41, no. 3, pp. 665–697.

McKinney, JC 1966, *Constructive Typology and Social Theory*, New York, Appleton-Century-Crofts.

Mills, CW 1959, *The Sociological Imagination*, New York, Oxford University Press.

Naughton, M 2014, 'Criminologizing wrongful convictions', *British Journal of Criminology*, DOI: 10.1093/bjc/azu060.

Orb, A, Eisenhauer, L, & Wynaden, D 2001, 'Ethics in qualitative research', *Journal of Nursing Scholarship*, vol. 33, no. 1, pp. 93–96.

Park, RE & Burgess, EW 1921, *Introduction to the Science of Sociology*, Chicago, IL, University of Chicago Press.

Ragin, C, Nagel, J, & White, P 2004, *Workshop on Scientific Foundations of Qualitative Research*, Washington, DC, National Science Foundation. www.nsf.gov/pubs/2004/nsf04219/nsf04219.pdf.

Reiss, AJ 1971a, *The Police and the Public*, New Haven, CT, Yale University Press.

Reiss, AJ 1971b, 'Systematic observation of natural social phenomena', *Sociological Methodology*, vol. 3, pp. 3–33.

Sampson, RJ & Raudenbush, SW 1999, 'Systematic social observation of public spaces: A new look at disorder in urban neighborhoods', *American Journal of Sociology*, vol. 105, no. 3, pp. 603–651.

Scoggins, SE 2014, 'Navigating fieldwork as an outsider: Observations from interviewing police officers in China', *PS: Political Science & Politics*, vol. 47, no. 2, pp. 394–397.

Sun, IY, Wu, YN, & Hu, R 2013, 'Public assessments of the police in rural and urban China: A theoretical extension and empirical investigation', *British Journal of Criminology*, vol. 53, no. 4, pp. 643–664.

Tanner, MS 2005, 'Campaign-style policing in China and its critics', in *Crime, Punishment, and Policing in China*, ed B Bakken, Lanham, MD, Rowman & Littlefield pp. 171–188.

Taylor, RB, Shumaker, SA, & Gottfredson, SD 1985, 'Neighborhood-level links between physical features and local sentiments: Deterioration, fear of crime, and confidence', *Journal of Architectural and Planning Research*, vol. 2, no. 4, pp. 261–275.

Wang, P 2014, 'Extra-legal protection in China: How Guanxi distorts China's legal system and facilitates the rise of unlawful protectors', *British Journal of Criminology*, vol. 54, no. 5, pp. 809–830.

Wilson, JQ & Kelling, GL 1982, 'Broken windows: The police and neighborhood safety', *Atlantic*, March, pp. 29–38.

Wong, KC 2002, 'Policing in the People's Republic of China: The road to reform in the 1990s', *British Journal of Criminology*, vol. 42, no. 2, p. 281.

Wu, YN & Sun, IY 2009, 'Citizen trust in police: The case of China', *Police Quarterly*, vol. 12, no. 2, pp. 170–191.

Xu, J 2009, 'The robbery of motorcycle taxi drivers in China: A lifestyle/routine activity perspective and beyond', *British Journal of Criminology*, vol. 49, no. 4, pp. 491–512.

Xu, J 2012, 'Drive-away policing and situational crime prevention in China: An analysis of motorcycle ban (jinmo) policy in Guangzhou', *International Journal of Offender Therapy and Comparative Criminology*, vol. 56, no. 2, pp. 239–264.

Xu, J 2013, 'Police accountability and the commodification of policing in China: A study of police/business posters in Guangzhou', *British Journal of Criminology*, vol. 53, no. 6, pp. 1093–1117.

Xu, J 2014a, 'Authoritarian policing with Chinese characteristics: A case study of motor-cycle bans in the Pearl River Delta', *Crime, Law and Social Change*, vol. 61, no. 4, pp. 439–460.

Xu, J 2014b, 'Urbanization and inevitable migration: Crime and migrant workers', in *The Routledge Handbook of Chinese Criminology*, eds L Cao, IY Sun, & B Hebenton, London and New York, Routledge, pp. 209–223.

Xu, J 2015, 'Commodification of policing and public disorder in China: A case study of crime solicitation posters in Guangzhou', 7th Annual Conference of the Asian Criminology Society, Hong Kong, June 24–26.

Xu, J & Liu, J 2015, 'Crime and punishment in China', in *The Encyclopedia of Crime and Punishment*, ed WG Jennings, Malden and Oxford, Wiley.

Xu, J, Laidler, KJ, & Lee, M 2013, 'Doing criminological ethnography in China: Opportunities and challenges', *Theoretical Criminology*, vol. 17, no. 2, pp. 271–279.

Young, J 2011, *The Criminological Imagination*, Cambridge, Polity Press.

Zhang, L 2011, 'Transferring Western theory: A comparative and culture-sensitive perspective of crime research in China', in *The Routledge Handbook of International Criminology: An International Perspective*, eds CJ Smith, SX Zhang, and R Barberet, London and New York, Routledge, pp. 77–86.

Zhang, LN, Messner, SF, & Liu, JH 2007, 'Criminological research in contemporary China: Challenges and lessons learned from a large-scale criminal victimization survey', *International Journal of Offender Therapy and Comparative Criminology*, vol. 51, no. 1, pp. 110–121.

Zhou, K & Yan, X 2014, 'The quest for stability: Policing popular protest in the People's Republic of China', *Problems of Post-Communism*, vol. 61, no. 3, pp. 3–17.

PART IV
Emerging areas

10

CARCERAL TOURS AND MISSED OPPORTUNITIES

Revisiting conceptual, ethical and pedagogical dilemmas

Justin Piché, Kevin Walby and Craig Minogue

Introduction

The rise of the modern prison shifted state punishment from public to more clandestine spaces (Foucault 1977), transforming the infliction of pain into a largely invisible phenomenon (Simon 2000). Yet the deprivation of liberty has never been fully out of sight, with tours of operational prisons providing one avenue through which outsiders get a glimpse of life and work behind bars.

Over the past two centuries, carceral tours have been organized for many purposes. In the Canadian context, officials from Upper Canada toured Auburn Prison in New York and Eastern State Penitentiary in Philadelphia, Pennsylvania to decide whether to design Kingston Penitentiary according to the Auburn system of silent communal work or the Pennsylvania system of solitary confinement (Beattie 1977). Tours for observation of system-wide standards, ranging from the conditions of built spaces to the treatment of prisoners, have occurred often in Canada, as documented in government reports (e.g. Ferres et al. 1868) and task forces (e.g. Archambault 1938). Members of the public, including Charles Dickens (1842), took tours of facilities such as Kingston Penitentiary in their first years of operation, though these ceased due to concerns from prison administrators about the zoo-like qualities of the excursions (Miron 2011). Thus, most people interested in entering prison gates today can only do so by visiting one of the dozens of decommissioned carceral facilities that have been transformed into museums or other tourist attractions (Ross 2012) in Australia (Wilson 2008), Canada (Walby and Piché 2015), South Africa (Shearing & Kempa 2004), the US (Brown 2009) and elsewhere (Welch 2013).

While public tours of operational carceral facilities have all but dried-up in Canada and most other jurisdictions around the world, official tours continue along with excursions organized by college and university professors for 'pedagogical' (e.g. Smith 2013) and 'research' (e.g. Pakes 2015) purposes. The fact that the third author of this chapter has been subjected to the objectifying gaze of thousands of carceral tourists in Australian prisons since 1986 attests to the popularity of these academic ventures.

We have problematized such carceral tours (see Minogue 2003, 2009; Piché & Walby 2010, 2012) on two grounds. First, we have drawn attention to the staged, sensational nature of such tours. This conclusion emerged from an analysis of the protocols, regulations and scripts that shape tours of Canadian federal penitentiaries (Piché & Walby 2010). The documents that we obtained using access to information requests demonstrate how carceral tours are staged by placing constraints on tourist interactions with prisoners, the times that they are able to enter these sites and the spaces visitors can access. We argued that where such staging exists, the research and pedagogical value of tours is limited. On the issue of sensationalism, Craig Minogue's (2003) prisoner ethnography describes the many times he had been subject to the gaze of carceral tourists, including one incident where he was viewed and filmed while showering, which highlights the dehumanization these tours can entail in their most extreme manifestations. Second, we sought the viewpoints of prisoners with whom we had been in contact through the *Journal of Prisoners on Prisons* (*JPP*). We asked them whether we should accept Wacquant's (2002, p. 386, emphasis in original) call "*to just do it*" and enter prisons in the midst of a 'curious eclipse of prison ethnography' at the height of mass incarceration even by means of a carceral tour such as the one he took part in. What emerged was a set of peer-reviewed articles by Eugene Dey (2009), Charles Huckelbury (2009), Craig Minogue (2009) and Jon Marc Taylor (2009), who documented the degradation that prisoners experience when they are denied the opportunity to shape the content of these excursions and are reduced to objects deemed unsuitable for human interaction (also see Minogue 2003). For these reasons, the first and second authors of this chapter have never organized carceral tours as part of their criminal justice, criminology or sociology courses.

Our shared position on the shortcomings of and ethical problems with carceral tours has generated three kinds of reaction. Some professors have either ceased to conduct pedagogical and research excursions into prisons due to the issues we raised and/or sought to develop other ways to engage with the penal field (e.g. Minor-Romanoff 2014; Ridley 2014). When the practice has been mentioned during panels and informal discussions at academic conferences, some colleagues who organize carceral tours for their students have told us that they have made our articles mandatory reading and the topic of in-class lectures to ensure prisoners and prison staff are engaged with in a more ethical manner during tours. In a third camp, we find academics who ardently defend carceral tours as an approach to pedagogy that demystifies common assumptions held by students about incarceration and those incarcerated (Boag & Wilson 2013, 2014; Senior 2011; Smith 2013; Wilson et al. 2011), and a research tool that can help scholars understand the dynamics of imprisonment (Pakes 2015).

Drawing on Cohen's (2001) study examining the denial and neutralization of atrocities, this chapter examines how proponents of carceral tours have disregarded critiques of this practice to justify their continued use. In reproblematizing carceral tours, we highlight the conceptual, ethical and pedagogical dilemmas that underpin the justifications for carceral tours and the denial of pain experienced by prisoners when they are subjected to the gaze of outsiders without their consent and voluntary participation. Having raised questions about whether carceral tours for the purposes of teaching or research can be conducted ethically, we conclude by exploring alternative approaches to pedagogy and social inquiry that can build more humane relationships with those living and working behind prison walls, while also fostering in-depth understandings of penality.

On denial

History is rife with small- and large-scale harms that have been normalized and routinized by groups and/or entire societies. For example, Bauman (2000) describes how the Holocaust was the product of modern social engineering that had become bureaucratized and ingrained into the psyches of Germans, to the point that the wrongfulness of the genocide directed toward Jewish persons and other marginalized populations in Europe in which they were engaged was met with indifference.

Whether "individual, personal, psychological and private – or shared, social, collective and organized" (Cohen 2001, p. 9), passive witnessing or active participation in injustices require a denial of troublesome realities one is faced with. For Cohen, denial "includes cognition (not acknowledging the facts); emotion (not feeling, not being disturbed); morality (not recognizing wrongness or responsibility) and action (not taking active steps in response to knowledge)" (p. 9). Denial is also "always partial", as "some information is always registered. This [denial] paradox or doubleness – knowing and not-knowing – is the heart of the concept" (p. 22). There are also literal forms of denial. Such denial can take the form of a "deliberate, intentional and conscious statement which is meant to deceive – that is, lying" where the "truth is clearly known, but for many reasons – personal or political, justifiable or unjustifiable – it is concealed" (p. 4). One can also choose "not to expose ourselves to certain unpalatable information … to switch off the sources of such information" (p. 4), "keeping secret from ourselves the truth we cannot face" (p. 6). Denial can also be legitimate in cases where sufficient facts exist to support such a posture (p. 4) or can be unintentional where knowledge on a given phenomenon remains contested (p. 5). What concerns us here are forms of denial requiring attempts to neutralize knowledge that would otherwise generate thoughts and feelings that would prevent one from acting in a harmful manner, including promoting a damaging practice.

It is only after harms are understood that different ways of thinking about, and institutional arrangements responding to, them can emerge (Cohen 2001, pp. 51–52). Where carceral tours are concerned, we do not appear to have yet entered the realm of such an "acknowledgement phase" (p. 52), as proponents have denied or raised issues distracting their audiences from the harms of the practice to prisoners, which we explore below. To do this, we draw on Cohen (2001), who borrows Sykes and

Matza's (1957) techniques of neutralization, to explain how carceral tours are being defended and even occasionally "praised" (Wilson et al. 2011). These techniques "prepare the ground for the offence [carceral tours] to take place. Afterwards, they also perform the defensive task assigned to denial" (Cohen 2001, p. 61). This is seen as necessary to neutralize or deflect "anticipated social disapproval by significant audiences" that allow one to engage in, rationalize and evade blame – either from oneself or others – for harm inflicted upon othered populations (p. 60). Like Cohen, we explore how denial is being used. We do so not to examine the kinds of deviance that interested Sykes and Matza (1957), but rather the forms of denial that maintain hegemonic practices in both prison and academic settings that would be considered problematic in other contexts, including those characterized by the state monopolization of violence in given territories (Weber 1919). For instance, no one would dare propose tours of "a remote indigenous community with the authority of the local police officer and no community consultation beforehand; no academic who wanted to keep their job would do such a thing" (Minogue 2009, p. 139).

Our main argument is that participating in tours of operational jails, prisons and penitentiaries creates ethical problems when (1) prisoners are gazed upon without their consent and voluntary participation, and (2) tours extend social control in carceral spaces. Defending carceral tours as pedagogical (Smith 2013) or research (Pakes 2015) activities is ends-justifying-the-means reasoning that attributes value to this activity devoid of any serious contemplation of the ethics of the means proposed. Claims to justify ethically unjustifiable carceral tours are discourses of denial, which we examine next.

Appeals to higher loyalties

A central way in which proponents legitimate carceral tours and dismiss concerns raised by critics is to appeal to higher loyalties. Cohen (2001, p. 61) notes that,

> [s]ocial controls are neutralized by playing down the wider society's demands in favour of demands from intimate groups (friends, gang) who are owed more immediate loyalties. If caught in the conflicting demands, delinquents respond to the more pressing ties of subcultural loyalty – thereby, unfortunately, breaking the law.

While this technique of neutralization refers to individual behaviour that transgresses social norms, it also applies to wider institutional(ized) harms. The end goal of our interventions has been to encourage carceral tour supporters to cease their use of the practice or, at the very least, be more mindful of its pitfalls to attenuate the harm that may result from them if they insist on their continued use. Yet critiques of the harms and limits of carceral tours made by academics and prisoners appear to be viewed as mere irritants by tour proponents. The use of prison tours is justified in several ways.

First, some scholars insist that carceral tours are among pedagogical approaches that "have the potential to foster experiential learning" (Smith 2013, p. 53) as they engage the senses of students and connect criminological theory concerning imprisonment to realities on the ground (ibid, p. 54). In an analysis of accounts by students who visited HMP Grendon, a 'therapeutic community', Wilson and colleagues (2011, pp. 350–352) argue that facility tours challenged the views that their students held about imprisonment, prisoners and prison staff, which were largely shaped by media (mis)representations prior to the exercise. It is claimed that these tours also provided an opportunity to engage captors and captives in a relatively unscripted manner. They also suggest the tours allow students to humanize the actors they encountered in ways that convinced some that rehabilitation was viable and they could work toward this end should they pursue careers in the penal system. Senior (2011, p. 1017, emphasis in original) likewise argues that carceral tours provide "criminal justice professionals, who work alongside prisons, to *appreciate the living arrangements*" in a way that helps them become "better sensitized and enable[s] them to have a deeper appreciation" of confinement sites.

In a series of studies, Boag and Wilson examined whether participating in carceral tours that involved engagement with prisoners increased student empathy toward the incarcerated, while decreasing prejudices. Their first collaborative study (Boag & Wilson 2013) involved an analysis of accounts by eight students examining their views prior to, during and after their visits where they "were given a tour of the living quarters of the prison, took part in a debate with and alongside the residents, ate lunch together and were encouraged to interact openly and frankly with the prisoners" (p. 703). It is unclear if and how prisoners consented to the entry of students to their spaces of captivity. Through exposure to the 'therapeutic' prison environment with prisoners who are diligently committed to their programs, the authors concluded that the exercise "leads to increased empathy and reduced prejudice" (p. 707). Having observed this cognitive shift among students, Boag and Wilson argue that such encounters provide "additional skills that are arguably needed" for those pursuing careers in the penal field. For them, such results suggest that developing ways in which the general public can also experience "realistic engagement with serious offenders who are rehabilitated sufficiently to be considered for release should be encouraged" (p. 708).

In another study, Boag and Wilson (2014) examine results from pre- and post-visit questionnaires measuring empathy for and prejudice toward prisoners administrated to 87 students who were randomly selected to participate in a carceral tour and 56 students in the cohort who were not. Having found "experiencing actual engagement with convicted sex offenders and murderers within a prison environment did increase empathy and decrease prejudice towards ex-offenders" (pp. 38–39), the researchers argue that "this domain of research has application potential in the wider field of training people who work with offender populations and in guiding information provided to the general public, employers, etc. regarding offenders who are subsequently released from prison" (p. 40). As they suggest elsewhere, increasing empathy may reduce the potential for recidivism that results in part from a lack of opportunities and exclusion stemming from the stigma of incarceration (Boag & Wilson 2013, pp. 699–701), which, although not "a panacea" can "open up a novel area of research that has the potential to identify ways to increase tolerance in the long term" (Boag & Wilson 2014, p. 40).

Among supporters of carceral tours there are also more classic "implicatory denials" (Welch 2003) that acknowledge potential ethical problems, but minimize them by pointing to ostensive benefits. Beyond pedagogical and broader societal implications, Senior (2011, p. 1018) notes that, "[a]ll visits, nonetheless, have a tone, which denotes the temperature of that prison at that time. By careful observation and appreciation of the environment, you can interpret its context and its current mood and gain useful insights". Pakes (2015, p. 3, emphasis added) similarly argues that:

> prison visits, *if conducted ethically*, can be a useful tool for the comparative researcher. They can inform the visitor on the immediately discernable conditions in prisons. ... They can shed light on the official stance on prisons and issues of punishment, rehabilitation, diversity and culture, and how these ideologies are reproduced on the ground. During visits, informal interactions can at least lift the veil, to an extent, on climate and relations between staff and prisoners. In addition, valuable glimpses can be gained in situations where non-scripted events occur. Thus, prison visits are advisable when getting to know a penal system or a punishment culture, at an early stage. They convey valuable impressions of how the prison presents itself and they can assist in the formulation of hypotheses on penality, culture and prison climate. That said, the prison visitor may be easily fooled.

This is a big 'if' concerning ethics that lacks specificity given Pakes does not clearly define what he considers to be ethical conduct. This is demonstrative of how proponents of these tours push related ethical pitfalls to the margins. While we do not contest that carceral tours can offer some insights into prison life and work, along with the culture of punishment that shapes them (Piché & Walby 2010, 2012), we do take issue with the fact that the appeals to higher loyalties summarized above are rarely weighed against the harms prisoners may experience during the course of this practice in a rigorous manner.

Partial acknowledgement and the denial of injury

Cohen (2001, p. 60) notes that the neutralization of "the wrongfulness of the act by minimizing any resultant hurt or injury" is one technique that can allow the continued perpetration of harm. The denial of injury can occur in a number of ways, including through claims that the harm is an "'isolated incident' ... not systemic or normal" (p. 113), is temporally bound since it "is what used to take place, in the past ... [b]ut ... cannot happen anymore" (p. 114), or that there is an awareness of the problem and those involved "are doing [their] best to deal with it" (ibid). In our reading of the defences of carceral tours advanced by its proponents, the partial denials take the form of spatial isolation (p. 113). This occurs when there is a cognizance that some carceral tours result in harming prisoners, yet proponents make the case that such harms do not occur during the course of pedagogical and research exercises in which they participate. For instance, Wilson and colleagues (2011), Smith (2013) and Boag and Wilson (2013, 2014) argue there are opportunities for dialogue between prisoners and students when pedagogical tours they organize are a part of their courses. Wilson and Boag (2013, p. 709) go further, noting:

> it could be argued that there may be strict behavioural guidelines that influence the experiences that students have with prison staff and prisoners in carceral tours and therefore lack validity (Piché & Walby, 2010). However, we can say with certainty that the residents with whom the participants engaged were not told to behave or respond to the student visitors in a particular way. Rather, the residents were expected to act normally so any restrictions were self-imposed.

We commend colleagues who ensure that there are opportunities for student engagement with prisoners during carceral tours, as opposed to those where prisoners are simply gazed upon (see Dey 2009; Huckelbury 2009; Minogue 2003, 2009), but only to a point. This is because these carceral tour proponents fail to acknowledge that the power relations *inherent* in prisons are reproduced through these excursions. This applies to settings where "the precepts of the therapeutic commitment to honesty and responsibility that the prisoners must adhere to" (Boag & Wilson 2014, p. 39) are at work and where "prisoners [do] not present themselves as victims or in need" (p. 40). As argued elsewhere, the "mere presence and participation of prisoners on a tour does not mean that the power dynamics and ethical dilemmas they engender within penal institutions disappear" (Piché & Walby 2012, p. 414). When Boag and Wilson (2013, p. 709) suggest that if prisoners who are allowed to participate in carceral tours alter their conduct or words they do so by choice, they deny the possibility that it is the coercive power of the prison that shapes such actions. Control and censorship do not have to be explicitly directed for them to be effective or unethical. Prison staff, who control much of the day-to-day life of prisoners, observe the interactions, which can limit the frankness of engagement and potentially result in reprisals should captives veer off-script regarding personal responsibility and accountability that prison living ingrains in them. The lesson that is internalized by the prisoners who are allowed by the prison to participate in tours is one of might is right, even when state violence comes in less visible forms. Omnipresent surveillance and file-keeping that detail the minutia of prisoner behaviour, including during carceral tours, has implications for whether one will be granted a release from prison (Minogue 2011), for example.

The power relations discussed above are evident in the experience of the third author, who has seen the formal and informal scripting involved in such encounters first-hand. Carceral tours in Australia include situations where prisoners are implicitly and explicitly forbidden from speaking. If they are allowed to engage, it is according to a scripted dialogue under tight supervision. As a direct result of his critical resistance to so-called pedagogical tours, which entailed letters of complaint and engagement with tour groups (see Minogue 2003), senior prison staff approached him and threatened to review his privilege of computer access. He was also ordered to never speak to a tour group again or he would be placed in a segregation unit.

Despite these efforts, more secondary and tertiary students, along with their teachers, continue to attend prisons in Victoria, Australia for carceral tours per year than there are prisoners detained in them. This "Schools Program" incorporates a panel of prisoners, who answer questions from students about criminalized harms and punishment, which are highly mediated, controlled and contrived. The policy document, the "Director's Instruction No. 3.16 – Schools Program", provides "Notes for Presenters", both for staff and prisoners, on pages 7–10. These notes cover safety, employment, drugs, reintegration, programs, prison life, suicide and deaths. Typical questions are listed in each section. Under the heading "Discussion Points", the prison provides its official view for the guidance of presenters using the personal pronoun "we" for the institution, thus erasing the boundaries that exist between the different actors inside its walls. The carefully chosen prisoners, who are allowed to participate in the panel discussion, are required, before they are allowed to speak with students and teachers, to read the "Schools Program" policy document and the "Notes for Presenters", and to acknowledge the conditions of their participation by signing an agreement with the prison. Essentially, they agree to stick to the official script of the facility. When these prisoners do speak with students and teachers, they are under the watchful eyes of prison staff. Prisoners know what is expected of them based on prompts regarding the direction and content of the discussion. If students ask 'personal' questions of prisoners, the supervising officers or teachers are to 'intervene' and deflect such questions. The "Schools Program" policy document makes the situation clear: "[A]ny prisoner who raises an issue of personal concern" with students or teachers, or who "deviates from the Notes for Presenters, will be removed from the program." In such circumstances, "issues of authority and (in)justice that can result from carceral tours" that are most often overlooked by their proponents need to be accounted for (Piché & Walby 2012, p. 414).

In another instance of partial acknowledgement, Smith (2013, p. 60) suggests that the thrust of the "ethical quandary" concerning carceral tours "is located in the process itself". Claiming to concur with Craig Minogue's (2009) arguments, Smith (2013, p. 61, emphasis in original) asserts that,

> it is a lack of dialogue between students and inmates coupled with reticent and ill-informed groups of visitors that is offensive to prisoners. Stated differently, it is not looking per se that is pedagogically unethical but rather *it is how one looks*. When dialogue does not occur between students and inmates the social exchange becomes uncomfortable with students left holding the "penal gaze".

This kind of interpretive denial does not refute the ethical problem but, rather, puts a different spin on it to legitimize it in certain circumstances (Welch 2003).

The other main area of the paper where Smith (2013, p. 52) tackles the issue of ethics is in its second footnote, where he notes that during his pedagogical tours "in the Southeast United States (Smith et al. 2009, 2010) we were mandated to receive Institutional Review Board (IRB) approval from the governing University body, including a review process that includes the approval of an inmate advocate". It was during one of these tours that a student, who stood looking through a cell window at a prisoner making a make-shift tent with a bedsheet to hide from the tour group, remarked, "I felt like I was watching an animal coming out of its cave … he just stared at us through the cell window and appeared to be making some sort of sound via his lips, a sort of a 'puh-puh-puh'" (Smith et al. 2009, p. 306). This is a report of a human person who is obviously in a state of distress and is seeking to hide from public view. His dignity has been infringed, when it should have been acknowledged and respected. When a student remarks that prisoners who "looked as if they had mental illnesses … just looked like a *different breed* of person" (ibid, emphasis added) based on carceral tour participation, we question whether one can legitimately claim that this practice promotes ethical engagement even when it receives IRB and prisoner representative approval. In the cases of Smith (2013, p. 52), as well as those of Boag and Wilson (2013, p. 702), it is unclear whether the definition of participant applied to students was extended to prisoners to ensure that their respective IRBs would consider the risks the latter could be exposed to during their criminological travels. Along this line, we question whether the pedagogical or other ends really justify the means. Should the benefits of scholarly endeavours not be balanced against the risks of or documented harm to all participants? We wonder whether what students learn on carceral tours concerns the realities of imprisonment as proponents claim or that subjects of academic inquiry are a 'breed' apart (e.g. prisoners), not to be afforded the same level of consideration as other human beings (e.g. the opportunity to freely consent to participate, to be respected, to be able to opt-out, etc.).

Smith (2013) and others (Boag & Wilson 2013, 2014; Wilson et al. 2011) assert that they go about fostering ethical engagements by ensuring that their students interact with prisoners, yet it is unclear how scholars prepare "for ensuring that the interaction is sensitively handled" (Senior 2011, p. 1017). This is the case when one is confronted with "the spectacle" that "is one of humiliation" and which portrays "prisoners as dangerous animals" or when "security performances" are "the dominating message" (Pakes 2015, p. 10). One can note the need for "an ethical consciousness" and agree with the need for "detailed and profound reflexivity" when comparing punishment practices and impression management in different jurisdictions, which Pakes suggests is a key role carceral tours can play (ibid). However, a clarion call for ethical and reflexive conduct rings hollow when the range of injuries they may inflict during these research and pedagogical encounters with penality are allowed to go on. Benevolent motives and thoughtful conduct of participants aside, one cannot pave-over the production of human suffering that the deprivation of liberty, and thus all carceral tours, entails.

Doublespeak

As noted previously, denial is characterized by a paradox whereby one simultaneously knows and unknows the harms one is perpetrating and perpetuating (Cohen 2001, p. 22). When it takes the form of an argument, denial involves "doublespeak", which involves choosing and shaping "facts selectively, blocking out those that don't fit the agenda or program" (Herman 1992, p. 3). Here, we focus on interventions by Smith (2013) and Boag and Wilson (2013, 2014) to illustrate this point about carceral tours.

One contribution Smith (2013) adds to the debate is conceptual. He argues that sceptics conflate tours of defunct and operational institutions, as well as the purposes of such activities. This kind of literal denial operates as a red herring (see Welch 2003). In our work, we have made an explicit distinction between touring decommissioned facilities (Walby & Piché 2011) and those that continue to confine human beings (Piché & Walby 2010, 2012). While some authors may include these practices under the umbrella of "prison tourism" (e.g. Brown 2009), they do so to account for the similar processes both entail rather than to assert they are exactly the same practice. Instead of acknowledging this, Smith critiques Brown's (2009) concept of penal spectatorship and our use of it that draws attention to the ways in which individuals become consumers of the spectacle of punishment that creates social distance between the authors of pain and prisoners who are on the receiving end of imprisonment. We invoke this concept precisely because the back-stage orchestration of carceral tours by prison authorities can dramatically reduce what is to be learned about prison life. Similar to Wilson and colleagues (2011), Smith (2013) does not delve into much of the back stage of the pedagogical tours that he and his students participate in. As a result, he is not well positioned to reflect upon how his pedagogical excursions into carceral spaces share something in common with leisurely or voyeuristic forms of engagement within defunct carceral settings repurposed as tourist sites (see Ross 2015). More importantly, the claim about alleged conflation distracts from the broader issues we raise concerning ethics and the boundaries of such tours.

Smith (2013) also aims to legitimate carceral tours by taking issue with our mobilization of Goffman's (1959, 1961) work on impression management, and the front and back stages of institutional display. Our argument is that the back stage of carceral tours – embodied in institutional protocols, regulations, scripts and administrative decisions – limit what can be learned from them, casting doubt on their pedagogical usefulness that legitimates the enterprise (Piché & Walby 2010). Smith (2013) suggests that we misunderstand Goffman and he advises that the role of the educator is to expose students to how institutional display happens in practice by providing them with opportunities to directly experience it. He tries to substantiate this position by citing the following from Goffman:

> insofar as the expressive bias of performances comes to be accepted as reality, then that which is accepted at the moment as reality will have some of

the characteristics of a celebration. To stay in one's room away from the place where the party is given, or away from where the practitioner attends his client, is to stay away from where reality is being performed.

Smith attributes this passage to *Asylums* (Goffman 1961, p. 125), where institutional control is indeed a more prominent point of analysis. Yet that page of *Asylums* is blank. The excerpt is actually from *The Presentation of Self in Everyday Life* (Goffman 1959, pp. 35–36), where weddings and other ceremonies are examined. The end of the passage, which Smith opts to leave out, is as follows: "The world, in truth, is a wedding." Why did Smith decide not to include the last line? Could it have something to do with the fact that few if any prisoners, or prison staff for that matter, think of their lives and work as akin to a wedding or celebration? Smith's use of Goffman's work points to a larger gap in the former's theorization of imprisonment within his work on carceral tours as there is little acknowledgement of state violence, control, power or surveillance in prison life. Smith's misattribution aside, our point remains: if control is extended because of an attempt to access the realities of imprisonment through a carceral tour, then it is ethically indefensible. This also applies to carceral tours organized to enable the study of institutional display, as Smith (2013) suggests ought to be done.

Another place where Smith (ibid) takes up part of our arguments and sows confusion is his claim that we are opposed to carceral tours in all their manifestations *and* experiential learning. We revisit both points in turn. First, our argument is that the ways in which tours of jails, prisons and penitentiaries are commonly organized erect barriers that limit what students can learn (Piché & Walby 2010). While we leave open the possibility that such tours can potentially overcome some of the barriers by promoting meaningful contact with prisoners and staff before, during and after tours, we maintain that the time constraints of the practice in which researchers and/or students briefly enter these carceral spaces are significant (ibid). Smith (2013) does not acknowledge this limit in his reading of our work. Second, he misconstrues critiques of carceral tours as attacks on experiential learning. We are not opponents of experiential learning. Elsewhere we have outlined alternative pedagogical approaches that can be used to connect scholars to the realities of incarceration in a sustained manner that largely avoid the ethical pitfalls of carceral tours, while also promoting dialogue with prisoners and staff in some cases (see Piché & Walby 2012, pp. 415–416).

While the points by Smith (2013) noted above distract readers from a discussion of the planks of our problematization of carceral tours, Boag and Wilson (2013, 2014) significantly distort our arguments. In one breath they quote our passage, "the tours' objectification of prisoners violates a central tenet of both research and teaching: that the dignity of individuals should be respected" (Piché & Walby 2010, p. 573), and in the next state "their argument appears to be more focussed on the lack of transparency of regulations set for prisoners' behaviour to negatively impact on the interpretation of results obtained on carceral tours, rather than the impact of carceral tours per se" (Boag & Wilson 2013, p. 701). We concede that a carceral tour that does not place additional "behavioural restrictions to residents taking part in the carceral tour" (ibid, p. 702) and prison staff (Boag & Wilson 2014, p. 39) beyond those that already exist in a prison setting is a step in the right direction. Yet it needs to be underscored that prisoners and prison staff continue to be subjected to institutional rules, both formal and informal, that shape their conduct (Piché & Walby 2012). One such rule in the case of Boag and Wilson's (2014, p. 39) carceral tour is that the "(prison)'s compulsory requirements for honesty and personal accountability" be observed by prisoners. One wonders whether such a requirement prevents prisoners from pointing to structural injustices that have shaped their lives or places significant constraints on possibilities for them to critique the penal system and prison conditions in their 'therapeutic' environment. Moreover, our argument was not only about how regulations shape the conduct of captives and captors, but also about tourists who are constrained with regards to their behaviour inside prison walls in ways that limit the humanity of their encounters with criminalized others. Indeed, we remain concerned about the impact that institutional regulatory frameworks have on the results of carceral tours, but also their consequences for ethical and humane interactions. Boag and Wilson (2013) are silent on both fronts and thus avoid inconvenient questions about a practice they engage in.

Alternatives to carceral tours

We have examined how proponents of carceral tours have defended the necessity and denied the harms of this practice in ways that occasionally verge on deceit (Shilling & Mellor 2014). In denying their limitations and harms, carceral tour champions have failed to entertain whether alternative means exist to meet their research and pedagogical objectives. As we have discussed elsewhere (Piché & Walby 2012), there exist alternatives to carceral tours that do not reproduce the ethical issues prisoners and others have raised concerning the practice. Below, we discuss how these approaches can position scholars and students closer to the realities of imprisonment and bring the voices of prisoners into academe in ways that are not possible through the most common forms of carceral tours, which are tightly regulated and scripted.

In terms of advancing research inside spaces of confinement, there are numerous ways in which academics can work with prisoners to make visible their experiences of incarceration. Prisoner ethnography, defined as "the application of ethnographic and participant observation research methods to carceral settings by those held captive within them" (Piché et al. 2014, p. 393), can be facilitated by academics. Such work involves "(a) creating a space to publish ethnographic works written by prisoners" such as the *Journal of Prisoners on Prisons* (see www.jpp.org), "(b) developing relationships with prisoners and encouraging their research and writing pursuits, (c) using the peer-review process to collaborate on the development of their situated knowledge, and (d) publishing their contributions" (ibid, p. 395).

As noted by Ross and colleagues (2014), prisoners who wish to conduct research while behind bars encounter numerous barriers to producing knowledge (also see Gaucher 1999, 2002; Huckelbury 1999; McMaster 1999; Piché 2008; Wright 1999). Some challenges faced by imprisoned writers include policies and practices in place that may restrict one's ability to conduct fieldwork and compile data, a lack of basic resources such as access to scholarly works and writing materials, being situated in an environment where it is difficult to sustain scholarly endeavours, and the stigma they face when submitting works to publications that may not be receptive to their contributions (Ross et al. 2014). Among the suggestions advanced to navigate these barriers is collaborative research and writing between prisoners and academics (ibid, p. 8; also see Bosworth et al. 2005). Involving prisoners in action-research initiatives to improve their living conditions, while challenging imprisonment more broadly, can also provide opportunities to produce scholarship that resists the penal status quo (e.g. Mathiesen 2014).

As prison sentences come to an end, academics can serve as mentors to former prisoners who are interested in pursuing their studies. Convict Criminologists are among those who have merged their prison experiences, whether as captives or captors, with academic training to make contributions to criminology and related fields (Ross & Richards 2003). They have gone on to mentor numerous colleagues with similar lived experiences over the years who strive to join academe. This work involves assistance with navigating obstacles related to community re-entry (e.g. finding housing), obtaining an education (e.g. gaining admission into university and accessing financial support) and finding related employment (e.g. obtaining an academic position and tenure) stemming from the stigma associated with having come into conflict with the law, up to and including support for legal action (Richards 2013, pp. 381–383). Such efforts ensure the growth of auto-ethnographic as well as other grounded accounts of criminalization and punishment produced under Convict Criminology (Richards & Lenza 2012).

While qualitative work by researchers behind bars is "usually temporally and corporeally detached from carceral settings" in the sense that academics enter and exit prison walls, and can decouple themselves from what they hear and see during the course of their work (Piché et al. 2014), there needs to be a continued commitment to building knowledge with current (Irwin 2009) and former (Ricciardelli 2014) prisoners, as well as staff (Ricciardelli & Spencer forthcoming), through qualitative research. Such work is vital to illuminating what would otherwise be kept invisible inside institutions characterized by opacity (Simon 2000; Wacquant 2001).

As there are numerous approaches available to academics who wish to advance research on the experiences of prison life, there are also avenues available to advance their pedagogical goals. Helping students connect theory to lived realities in the punishment sphere is challenging. One way to do this is to provide opportunities for students to have sustained, meaningful encounters with those who live and work inside prisons. This can be achieved through the creation of voluntary groups like "the Infinity Lifers Group, a collective of mostly undergraduate students that has met with prisoners at Collins Bay Institution [Kingston, Ontario] … on a regular basis for over a quarter century" (Piché & Walby 2012, p. 415).

Offering prison-based work placements has also been touted by Ridley (2014) as a way to demystify dehumanizing portrayals of prisoners and sensational aspects of imprisonment circulating in popular culture and political debates. Ridley became uncomfortable with carceral tours. On the kinds of tour advocated by Wilson and Smith, Ridley (2014, p. 21) writes:

> the gaps in this approach still outweigh the positives. The carceral tour began to concern me in that it still felt very much like a staged event where prison staff could select the areas to visit and the prisoners with whom the students would have the opportunity to speak.

Prison-based work placements are a better alternative, she argues. By exposing students to the mundane aspects of incarceration in a sustained, immersed manner, the researcher and educator asserts that students can work towards their academic and professional objectives, while engaging with prisoners in a more ethical manner than carceral tours allow for.

An example of a course-based pedagogical approach that bridges the gap between perceptions and realities of prison life is the *Inside-Out Prison Exchange*. Operating in some universities in the US and Canada, courses offered inside carceral institutions through this initiative "bring college students and incarcerated individuals together as peers in a classroom setting that emphasizes dialogue and critical thinking" (Shomaker et al. 2014, p. 41). Several of these courses have focused on prison-related issues, while others examine topics such as creative writing. Where such opportunities are not available, academics have found creative ways of exposing students to prison experiences such as producing videos featuring interviews with prisoners that touch upon themes such as institutionalization, their participation in programs and other challenges encountered during their sentences, as well as the dilemmas they face as they ponder their eventual release from prison (see Miner-Romanoff 2014).

These options allow researchers to continue their work in more ethical ways. We challenge proponents of pedagogical and research tours to be reflexive concerning the ethical issues that arise within the context of these excursions. Given the considerable ethical limits associated with carceral tours, and the existence of viable alternative approaches to research and pedagogy, it is not acceptable "*to just do it*" (Wacquant 2002, p. 386, emphasis in original). In the face of scholarship that appeals to higher loyalties, denies injury and engages in 'doublespeak' that muddies the content of our original arguments to ensure that carceral tours continue unabated, we maintain

> that greater reflexivity is needed in this debate about penal tourism, research and pedagogy. After all, the stakes are high. Respect for the dignity of human beings rests in the balance. (Piché & Walby 2012, p. 417)

Participating in tours of operational jails, prisons and penitentiaries for research or for class trips might be popular or impart some knowledge, but that does not make them ethical, whether sanctioned by university ethics boards or not.

References

Archambault, G 1938, *Report of the Royal Commission to Investigate the Penal System of Canada*, Ottawa, Queen's Printer.

Bauman, Z 2000, *Modernity and the Holocaust*, Ithaca, NY, Cornell University Press.

Beattie, JM 1977, *Attitudes towards Crime and Punishment in Upper Canada, 1830–1850*, Toronto, Centre of Criminology, University of Toronto.

Boag, EM & Wilson, D 2013, 'Does engaging with serious offenders change students' attitude and empathy towards offenders? A thematic analysis', *Journal of Forensic Psychiatry & Psychology*, vol. 24, no. 6, pp. 699–712.

Boag, EM & Wilson, D 2014, 'Inside experience: Engagement empathy and prejudice towards prisoners', *Journal of Criminal Psychology*, vol. 4, no. 1, pp. 33–43.

Bosworth, M, Campbell, D, Demby, B, Ferranti, S.M. & Santos, M 2005, 'Doing prison research: Views from inside', *Qualitative Inquiry*, vol. 11, no. 2, pp. 249–264.

Brown, M 2009, *The Culture of Punishment: Prison, Society, and Spectacle*, New York, New York University Press.

Cohen, S 2001, *States of Denial: Knowing about Atrocities and Suffering*, Cambridge, Polity Press.

Dey, E 2009, 'Prison tours as a research tool in the golden gulag', *Journal of Prisoners on Prisons*, vol. 18, no. 1&2, pp. 119–125.

Ferres, JM, O'Neill, TJ, & Tassé, FZ 1868, *First Annual Report of the Directors of Penitentiaries of the Dominion of Canada for the year 1868*, Ottawa, I.B. Taylor.

Foucault, M 1977, *Discipline and Punish: The Birth of the Prison*, New York, Vintage Books.

Gaucher, B 1999, 'Inside looking out: Writers in prison', *Journal of Prisoners on Prisons*, vol. 10, no. 1&2, pp. 14–31.

Gaucher, B ed 2002, *Writing as Resistance: The Journal of Prisoners on Prisons Anthology (1988–2002)*, Toronto, Canadian Scholars' Press.

Goffman, E 1959, *The Presentation of Self in Everyday Life*, New York, Anchor Books.

Goffman, E 1961, *Asylums: Essays on the Social Situation of Mental Patients and Other Inmates*, New York, Anchor Books.

Herman, E 1992, *Beyond Hypocrisy: Decoding the News in an Age of Propaganda*, Boston, MA, South End Press.

Huckelbury, C 2009, 'Tour de farce', *Journal of Prisoners on Prisons*, vol. 18, no. 1&2, pp. 126–128.

Irwin, J 2009, *Lifers: Seeking Redemption in Prison*, New York, Routledge.

Mathiesen, T 2014, *The Politics of Abolition Revisited*, London, Routledge.

McMaster, G 1999, 'Maximum ink', *Journal of Prisoners on Prisons*, vol. 10, no. 1&2, pp. 46–52.

Minogue, C 2003, 'Human rights and life as an attraction in a correctional theme park', *Journal of Prisoners on Prisons*, vol. 12, pp. 44–57.

Minogue, C 2009, 'The engaged specific intellectual: Resisting unethical prison tourism and the hubris of the objectifying modality of the universal intellectual', *Journal of Prisoners on Prisons*, vol. 18, no. 1&2, pp. 129–142.

Minogue, C 2011, 'Is the Foucauldian conception of disciplinary power still at work in contemporary forms of imprisonment?' *Foucault Studies*, vol. 11, pp. 178–192.

Minor-Romanoff, K 2014, 'Student perceptions of juvenile offender accounts in criminal justice education', *American Journal of Criminal Justice*, vol. 39, no. 3, pp. 611–629.

Miron, J 2011, *Prisons, Asylums, and the Public: Institutional Visiting in the Nineteenth Century*, Toronto, University of Toronto Press.

Nagelsen, S & Huckelbury, C 2009, 'The prisoner's role in ethnographic examinations of the carceral state', *Journal of Prisoners on Prisons*, vol. 18, no. 1&2, pp. 111–118.

Pakes, F 2015, 'Howard, Pratt and Beyond: Assessing the value of carceral tours as a comparative method', *Howard Journal of Criminal Justice*, Online First. DOI: 10.1111/hojo.12127.

Piché, J 2008, 'Editor's introduction. Barriers to knowing inside: Education in prisons and education on prisons', *Journal of Prisoners on Prisons*, vol. 17, no. 1, pp. 4–17.

Piché, J & Walby, K 2009, 'Dialogue on the status of prison ethnography and carceral tours: An introduction', *Journal of Prisoners on Prisons*, vol. 18, no. 1&2, pp. 88–90.

Piché, J & Walby, K 2010, 'Problematizing carceral tours', *British Journal of Criminology*, vol. 50, no. 3, pp. 570–581.

Piché, J & Walby, K 2012, 'Carceral tours and the need for reflexivity: A response to Wilson, Spina and Canaan', *Howard Journal of Criminal Justice*, vol. 51, no. 4, pp. 411–418.

Piché, J, Gaucher, B, & Walby, K 2014, 'Facilitating prisoner ethnography: An alternative approach to "doing prison research differently"', *Qualitative Inquiry*, vol. 20, no. 4, pp. 392–403.

Ricciardelli, R 2014, *Surviving Incarceration: Inside Canadian Prisons*, Waterloo, Wilfrid Laurier University Press.

Ricciardelli, R & Spencer, D Forthcoming, 'Correctional officers, sex offenders, and emotions', *Theoretical Criminology*.

Richards, SC 2013, 'The new school of Convict Criminology thrives and matures', *Critical Criminology*, vol. 21, no. 3, pp. 375–387.

Richards, SC & Lenza, M eds 2012, 'A special issue commemorating the 15th anniversary of Convict Criminology', *Journal of Prisoners on Prisons*, vol. 21, nos. 1&2, pp. 1–204.

Ridley, L 2014, 'No substitute for the real thing: The impact of prison-based work experience on students' thinking about imprisonment', *Howard Journal of Criminal Justice*, vol. 53, no. 1, pp. 15–30.

Ross, JI 2012, 'Touring imprisonment: A descriptive statistical analysis of prison museums', *Tourism Management Perspectives*, vol. 4, pp. 113–118.

Ross, JI 2015, 'Varieties of prison voyeurism: An analytic/interpretive framework', *Prison Journal*, vol. 95, no. 3, pp. 397–417.

Ross, JI & Richards, SC eds 2003, *Convict Criminology*, Belmont, CA, Wadsworth.

Ross, JI, Zaldivar, M, & Tewksbury, R 2014, 'Breaking out of prison and into print? Rationales and strategies to assist educated convicts conduct scholarly research and writing behind bars', *Critical Criminology*, vol.23, pp. 73–83.

Senior, P 2011, 'In and out of the belly of the beast', *International Journal of Offender Therapy and Comparative Criminology*, vol. 55, no. 7, pp. 1015–1019.

Shearing, C & Kempa, M 2004, 'A museum of hope: A story of Robben Island', *Annals of the American Academy of Political and Social Science*, vol. 35, no. 2, pp. 62–78.

Shilling, C & Mellor, P 2014, 'For a sociology of deceit: Doubled identities, interested actions, and situational logics of opportunity', *Sociology*, vol. 49, no. 4, pp. 607–623.

Shomaker, RD, Willis, B, & Bryant, A 2014, 'We are the products of our experiences: The role higher education plays in prison', *Journal of Prisoners on Prisons*, vol. 23, no. 1, pp. 31–55.

Simon, J 2000, 'The "society of captives" in the era of hyper-incarceration', *Theoretical Criminology*, vol. 4, no. 3, pp. 285–308.

Smith, HP 2013, 'Reinforcing experiential learning in criminology: Definitions, rationales, and missed opportunities concerning prison tours in the United States', *Journal of Criminal Justice Education*, vol. 24, no. 1, pp. 50–67.

Smith, HP, Koons-Witt, BA, & Meade, B 2011, 'Demystifying prisons through the use of experiential learning', *Corrections Compendium*, vol. 35, no. 2, pp. 1–5.

Smith, HP, Meade, B, & Koons-Witt, BA 2009, 'The utility of the correctional tour: Student perceptions and the propensity for academic growth', *Journal of Criminal Justice Education*, vol. 20, no. 3, pp. 292–311.

Sykes, G & Matza, D 1957, 'Techniques of neutralization', *American Sociological Review*, vol. 22, pp. 664–670.

Taylor, JM 2009, 'Diogenes still can't find his honest man', *Journal of Prisoners on Prisons*, vol. 18, nos. 1&2, pp. 91–110.

Wacquant, L 2002, 'The curious eclipse of prison ethnography in the age of mass incarceration', *Ethnography*, vol. 3, no. 4, pp. 371–397.

Walby, K & Piché, J 2011, 'The polysemy of punishment memorialization: Dark tourism and Ontario's penal history museums', *Punishment & Society*, vol. 13, no. 4, pp. 451–472.

Walby, K & Piché, J 2015, 'Making meaning out of punishment: Penitentiary, prison, jail and lock-up museums in Canada', *Canadian Journal of Criminology and Criminal Justice* vol. 57, no. 4, pp. 475–502.

Weber, M (2005 [1919]), 'Politics as a vocation', in *Weber: Selections in Translation*, ed WG Runciman, trans E Matthews, New York, Cambridge University Press, pp. 212–225.

Welch, M 2003, 'Trampling human rights in the war on terror: Implications for the sociology of denial', *Critical Criminology*, vol. 12, no. 1, pp. 1–20.

Welch, M 2013, 'Penal tourism and a tale of four cities: Reflecting on the museum effect in London, Sydney, Melbourne, Buenos Aires', *Criminology and Criminal Justice*, vol. 13, no. 5, pp. 479–505.

Wilson, D, Spina, R, & Canaan, JE 2011, 'In praise of the carceral tour: Learning from the Grendon experience', *Howard Journal of Criminal Justice*, vol. 50, no. 4, pp. 343–355.

Wilson, JZ 2008, *Prison: Cultural memory and dark tourism*, New York, Peter Lang.

Wright, P 1999, 'The history of *Prison Legal News*: The Samizdat of the American gulag', *Journal of Prisoners on Prisons*, vol. 10, nos. 1&2, pp. 53–62.

11

ILLUMINATING THE DARK NET

Methods and ethics in cryptomarket research

James Martin

Introduction

The online trade in illicit drugs has expanded dramatically in recent years. This growth is due in large part to the emergence of cryptomarkets – anonymous online forums "where goods and services are exchanged between parties who use digital encryption to conceal their identities" (Martin 2014a, p. 356). These peculiar 'dark net' websites are a recent innovation, with the first massively popular cryptomarket, the infamous and now defunct Silk Road, commencing operations in 2011 (Barratt 2012). Since then dozens of other cryptomarkets have emerged that trade in all manner of illicit goods and services, from computer hacking and stolen credit card information to pornography and unlicensed firearms. By far the largest product category traded on cryptomarkets is illicit drugs (Christin 2013; Dolliver 2015).

Aside from the illegality of goods and services typically traded on cryptomarkets, these websites function in much the same way as legitimate 'surface web' trading sites, such as eBay and Amazon Marketplace. They provide virtual meeting places for tens of thousands of drug dealers to spruik (advertise) their wares and connect with potential customers, thereby facilitating a vast global network of illicit exchange. Online drug deals are carried out using an intriguing combination of both low and high technologies, with user identities and locations concealed from authorities through the use of digital encryption and electronic currencies, while goods are delivered to customers with deceptive simplicity via traditional 'snail mail' postal networks or courier services (Martin 2014a, 2014b).

The proliferation of cryptomarkets presents a fascinating area of inquiry for criminologists and other scholars seeking to understand how new technology is impacting the global drugs market. There is now a growing repository of cryptomarket-focused studies showcasing a diverse range of research methodologies, from quantitative surveys (Barratt, Ferris et al. 2013a; Barratt, Lenton et al.

2013b), qualitative, in-depth interviews conducted with online drug vendors, consumers and site administrators (Lavorgna 2014;Van Hout & Bingham 2014, 2013b) to theoretical and conceptual analyses based on direct, unobtrusive observation of the sites themselves (Martin 2014a, 2014b; Phelps & Watt 2014). Academics with programming skills are also innovating sophisticated technical solutions to gathering data online, most notably through the development of software 'crawlers' (Aldridge & Décary-Hétu 2014; Christin 2013; Dolliver 2015). Crawlers are computer programs that automatically collect and sort publicly available information that is hosted on cryptomarkets. They are increasingly popular in cryptomarket studies and essentially 'vacuum up' a range of data listed on the various webpages that comprise a cryptomarket (e.g. vendor names, product prices, textual and numerical customer reviews). Regardless of whether online data is gathered manually or through the use of automated crawlers, a range of similar ethical issues are likely to be encountered.

In addition to piquing interest amongst scholars, the rapid expansion of the online drugs trade is, unsurprisingly, also attracting the attention of law enforcement. Policing agencies tasked with enforcing drug prohibition have significantly increased their efforts to combat the online drugs trade, with largely mixed results. While prominent cryptomarkets, including Silk Road, Silk Road 2 and Pandora have been shut down, new sites continue to emerge, quickly filling any void left by successful site closures. While the ongoing failure on the part of law enforcement to stamp out the online drugs trade may surprise some observers, the reality is that the dynamic and technologically sophisticated realm of cyberspace is not a comfortable operating environment for law enforcement. Online investigations are complex and resource intensive, particularly when compared to standard counter-narcotics operations, and they require a high degree of technical proficiency amongst investigators. This specialist expertise is, at best, atypical within law enforcement agencies that have limited organizational experience in combating crime committed on the digital frontier.

The various challenges associated with investigating cryptomarkets have prompted some law enforcement agencies to seek out the assistance of the academic community. While academics are incentivized to work with law enforcement in a variety of ways, such collaborations also raise ethical concerns, including risk of harm to both research subjects and scholars. Perhaps the most serious of these is the risk of gathering incriminating ethnographic data that may subsequently be seized by law enforcement and used to prosecute research subjects (see, for example, Garrett 2014). A related issue that further complicates academic work in this area is an absence of consensus regarding appropriate online research methodologies and applied ethics practices. As a novel area of scholarly inquiry involving the use of new and unfamiliar research methods, academics who are involved with cryptomarket research have had relatively limited opportunity to reflect upon the real-world application and implications of their work. This chapter is intended to help address this gap in understanding regarding ethical research practices when conducting cryptomarket research. It provides a reflective rather than prescriptive exploration of some of the practical methodological and ethical complexities associated with researching the online drugs trade. The principal aims are to analyze some of the different online data sources available, and to explore how different harms may result from new forms of academic inquiry. Finally, the broader political implications of collaborating with law enforcement are discussed and assessed within the context of the global War on Drugs.

Reflections on cryptomarket data

A variety of data sources are immediately available to researchers seeking to conduct either manual or crawler-based observation of cryptomarkets. Particularly valuable are the many thousands of individual 'seller pages' that comprise the retail sections of these sites and are used by drug vendors as online storefronts. Seller pages list numerous details about the vast cornucopia of illicit products sold online, including product types, prices, quantities and the geographical regions to which goods may be delivered. They also display up-to-date textual and numerical feedback from customers, providing semi-independent and readily comparable perspectives regarding the perceived quality of the service and products provided by each vendor. Cryptomarket discussion forums offer a further, important source of information regarding user perspectives concerning diverse topics, from site security and smuggling strategies to harm reduction measures, vendor scams and debates about the philosophy of cryptomarket trading and resistance to state crime (Barratt, Lenton et al. 2013; Martin 2014b).

The sheer abundance, variety and ready accessibility of primary data available on cryptomarkets is quite simply unparalleled in the history of illicit drug market research. Never before have so many detailed, up-to-date sources of information regarding the operation of illegal marketplaces and the people who use them been so freely and immediately accessible to any researcher equipped with a computer and internet connection. The newfound availability of this data has important implications for a variety of academic disciplines and fields of inquiry, from computer science and network analysis to digital sociology and the study of online communities. For criminologists (and members of law enforcement) interested in the criminal aspects of the online drugs trade, the differences to conventional illegal drug markets are particularly stark; it is as if drug offenders have suddenly started to keep detailed notes about the various deals that they make before instantaneously volunteering these details online (with carefully redacted names and addresses). The unprecedented depth and breadth of information regarding cryptomarkets therefore represents an exciting and novel opportunity for scholars to track and analyze in real-time the development of complex and transnational criminal phenomena.

More broadly, the ready availability of cryptomarket data points to the transformational potential of contemporary online communication and encryption technologies. In what must be a sobering realization for state authorities already struggling to enforce global drug prohibition, the proliferation of free yet incredibly powerful encryption software indicates that, for a growing number of drug dealers and their customers, the benefits of maintaining a public presence online now outweigh the risks of arrest and incarceration. Drug vendors are increasingly prepared to share information about their business activities online because it is both profitable and relatively safe to do so (Lavorgna 2014; Van Hout & Bingham 2014). Unlike conventional illicit transactions that place dealers at risk of immediate arrest by undercover law enforcement agents, online drug traders are insulated by several protective factors, including geographical separation – with buyers and sellers often located in different countries – as well as multiple layers of digital encryption. These conceal vital evidence such as Internet Protocol (IP) addresses, user identities, addresses and the financial details of transactions involving electronic currencies.

In addition to highlighting the limited power of contemporary law enforcement to disrupt online drug trading, the public visibility of cryptomarket data reveals an intriguing and superficially contradictory symbiosis between anonymity and transparency on the dark net. Naturally, online dealers and their customers do not share information about their illegal activities for the benefit of outside observers. Rather, publicly available data is integral to the operation and self-regulation of a unique virtual trading environment that relies simultaneously upon both real-world anonymity and online reputation. In contrast to conventional illicit drug markets, which operate in at least a minimally covert manner in order to maintain security, cryptomarkets function with purposive openness. Online dealers routinely provide detailed information in order to advertise illicit products, establish their online reputation or 'brand' and compete with one another for limited custom (Christin 2013; Martin 2014a, 2014b; Van Hout & Bingham 2013a, 2013b). The anonymity and geographical separation inherent in cryptomarket drug trading also frees drug dealers from the threat of violent competition and criminal predation that is characteristic of conventional illicit drug markets (Aldridge & Décary-Hétu 2014; Lavorgna 2014; Martin 2014a, 2014b). This latter point has particular relevance to questions regarding scholarly cooperation with law enforcement and is elaborated upon at the end of the chapter.

The capacity to access vast amounts of online data is similarly empowering for drug consumers, who have traditionally suffered from a persistent (and sometimes fatal) lack of information regarding the composition and purity of illicit drugs. It is not unusual for online dealers to provide detailed product and service information of a kind more commonly associated with legal retailing. These include lengthy terms and conditions of sale and refund policies for goods that are lost in transit, as well as comprehensive chemical analysis of various drugs (Martin 2014b). Particularly important in terms of validating claims to quality made by drug vendors is customer feedback, which is provided in the form of a five-star rating and brief textual comments. If vendors sell products that are noticeably different from what they have advertised, customers are able to express their dissatisfaction publicly and the vendor's business is likely to suffer accordingly. Automated systems also collate customer feedback and rank vendors competitively on the basis of numerical reviews, further amplifying the effects of both positive and negative feedback.

The routine provision of customer feedback witnessed on cryptomarkets is part of a more general trend that is also impacting legal retailing on the surface web. Whether reviewing pizza from a local restaurant or hashish from an international drug trafficker, consumers located in both the licit and illicit economies are increasingly engaging with each other as well as with retailers in a multidirectional exchange of information. This kind of active participation on the part of consumers stands in stark contrast to earlier modes of consumption, where end-users were constrained as passive recipients of corporate advertising or similarly tightly controlled, unidirectional messaging from traditional media. By enfranchising consumers and empowering them as active participants in the exchange process, cryptomarkets have come to embody some of the transformational organizational characteristics of an increasingly interconnected digital age (Castells 2011).

The transparency that is integral to cryptomarkets is yet to be fully appreciated and utilized by the academic community. Part of the problem is methodological in nature and concerns the somewhat bewildering effect of dealing with exceptionally large sets of data – the so-called 'big data' problem. Put simply, there is so much cryptomarket-related information available online that scholars are still in the process of determining exactly what questions this data can be used to answer. A further, related problem concerns the discrete disciplinary silos within which academics traditionally operate. In the context of cryptomarket research, this poses a particular challenge for criminologists and others who may lack the technical skills and knowledge necessary to gather and interpret online data. This means that criminologists with advanced discipline-specific knowledge may be impeded in conducting or contributing to research that is otherwise relevant to their spheres of expertise (such as the operation of organized crime groups and modes of conventional drug distribution). Likewise, computer scientists and other academics with high-level technical proficiencies may lack the detailed criminological or other knowledge that is necessary to make full use of the online data that is more easily accessible to them.

Finally, scholars may be reluctant to conduct cryptomarket research due to the unfamiliar ethical terrain associated with this unique, opaque and occasionally threatening digital research environment. Amongst researchers presently engaged in the study of cryptomarkets there appears to be some latent trepidation about the current lack of consensus regarding appropriate and ethically sound research methods. This presents a significant challenge to scholars concerned about risks both to themselves and to prospective research subjects. As the following sections will illustrate, concerns about the ethical appropriateness of certain kinds of cryptomarket research may be justified in some circumstances; in the few short years in which scholars have undertaken cryptomarket research, a range of potential risks and harms have emerged. These highlight deficiencies in the process of institutional ethical review and signpost important issues for future research. The next section first presents a general critique of institutional ethical review, and then analyzes its relevance to both cryptomarket research and the broader field of criminological inquiry.

Identifying and managing direct and indirect harms

It is an oft-repeated and axiomatic claim that scholarly research should benefit both the broader public and the academic community. Research institutions are, quite rightly, expected to contribute to the public good. Statements reflecting this sentiment are written into university charters, the ethical codes of academic and professional associations and the mission statements of government funding institutions. Transforming this high-minded rhetoric into reality can be problematic, however, and there are myriad ways in which scholarly inquiry can negatively impact research subjects and scholars, as well as others not directly involved in the research process. Guarding against this is a difficult and complex task, and processes specifically intended to promote ethical conduct and prevent harm may even prove counter-productive if they fail to take into account specific disciplinary challenges and the broader socio-political context of research.

On other occasions, research is undertaken with the knowledge that certain minor forms of harm will be encountered. Studies such as these, in which high degrees of risk are pre-emptively identified, must be justified on a utilitarian basis, whereby the dangers associated with research are calculated against potential benefits. Accurately assessing these risks is, however, often problematic, particularly given the perpetually morphing exigencies associated with cryptomarket research, combined with the typically glacial pace inherent in institutional ethical review. By the time ethical approval for a particular research project is eventually granted, there is no guarantee that any cryptomarket listed on an application will necessarily resemble an earlier iteration (e.g. in terms of size or type of goods and services traded) or even remain in operation at all.

The two general mechanisms by which harm results from scholarly research are either: direct, through inappropriate research practices or methodological design, or indirect, through research that promotes, informs or legitimizes harmful ideologies, social movements or public policies. Instances of direct harm would include events such as death, injury or incarceration that resulted from, for example, asking traumatized research subjects emotionally damaging questions, or storing incriminating ethnographic data that was subsequently subpoenaed by law enforcement. Examples of indirect harm, by contrast, could result from scholarly reports being used as an intellectual justification for a government violation of human rights, or promoting theories that rationalize the imposition of cruel and ineffective carceral policies upon vulnerable populations. In both cases, harm is caused, either by the researchers themselves, or by proxy in facilitating the harmful activity of others.

Responsibility for preventing harms associated with academic research lies with individual scholars, as well as with university ethics review committees and other institutional review boards. These powerful gatekeepers exercise control over how studies involving human subjects are to be conducted, and they may allow, disallow or demand changes to any program of research submitted to their scrutiny. Institutional review boards are guided in their determinations by legislation and state directives concerning the legal limits of acceptable research, and also by more detailed codes of conduct and discipline-specific ethics statements developed by professional academic associations. In Australia, for example, scholarly research must be carried out in accordance with the principles articulated by the federal government in the *National Statement on Ethical Conduct in Human Research* (2007), while in the US scholarly inquiry should align with statements articulated in the *Belmont Report* (1979).

Ideally, institutional ethical review provides a valuable opportunity for those seeking expert feedback and advice regarding the appropriateness of their research. Under the constructive scrutiny of learned colleagues with advanced disciplinary and applied ethical knowledge, criminologists and other scholars may test the ethical integrity of their proposed research and reflect critically upon the aims and likely implications of their work. Forearmed with their collective insights, they may then venture forth into the field confident in their practice and intent and newly attuned to some of the previously unanticipated risks to themselves and their research subjects (although it should be noted that institutional review boards only advise – they do not assume any legal liability for approved research). In reality, unfortunately, as many who have been through this process would readily confirm, the progression through institutional ethical review often fails to live up to this ideal. Indeed, institutional review boards routinely come under criticism from social scientists in particular who become frustrated with seemingly inconsistent, illogical or ill-informed determinations that appear to have little or no relevance to the applied reality of their research (Dingwall 2008; Haggerty 2004; Roberts & Indermaur 2003; Schrag 2011; van den Hoonaard 2011).

Much of the criticism leveled toward institutional review boards concerns the awkward imposition of ethical principles developed within a specific context of clinical research (Schrag 2011; van den Hoonaard 2011). While useful in the natural and biosciences, such principles often have limited applicability for humanities-based inquiry. A prominent example of this kind is the Hippocratic dictum of 'doing no harm'. This is a valuable and largely unproblematic guiding principle in both medical research and practice, and is intended to protect the wellbeing and agency of research subjects. Exactly how this principle would apply to a criminologist conducting research into cryptomarkets or other criminal phenomena is often difficult to determine. This is because a critical difference between medical and some criminological research is that criminologists may seek to compromise the agency of their research subjects and expose and disrupt harmful, criminal activities committed on their part.

There are obvious reasons underlying why the agency of people involved in criminal activity, which also is assumed – sometimes incorrectly – to be harmful, should not be afforded the same levels of consideration as, for example, a cancer patient involved in the study of a trial medicine. For example, an academic assisting the authorities in developing a better online policing strategy would presumably hope that their research findings would contribute to a reduction in online drug trading. Such an outcome would, at the very least, harm the cryptomarket as well as the lifestyle of anyone involved with this kind of criminal enterprise, and may even increase the chance that individual 'offenders' will be incarcerated. However, despite intentionally violating a touchstone medical principle, one would be hard-pressed to argue that criminological research of this nature is *inherently* unethical on the basis that it could result in potential harm to 'offenders'. Indeed, if this were the case, then practically all criminological research that actively sought to combat or reduce other forms of crime, for example police corruption, serial killing or corporate crimes, would also be considered unethical.

This is not to argue that criminological research should be either free from ethical scrutiny or not adhere to certain established ethical principles. Far from it – criminologists regularly work with vulnerable and dangerous groups, including offenders and victims of crime. Their involvement with illegal activity contributes an additional degree of risk to the health, liberty and wellbeing of all parties and makes good ethical research practice absolutely essential. However, abstract and simplistic principles developed for biomedical research may not always be useful or appropriate in complex criminological research that necessarily involves balancing the agency and welfare of different groups.

The tension between ethical principles such as 'beneficence' and 'doing no harm' and the investigation of criminal activity results in criminologists often walking a fine and somewhat contradictory line between avoiding research practices that could *directly* harm research subjects, whilst simultaneously pursuing research aims that may be intended to cause *indirect* harms. Institutional review boards do not assist researchers in reconciling these tensions, or even prompt consideration of the harmful indirect social impacts of their research. Instead, they tend to focus exclusively on managing direct harms associated with research methodologies. While it should be noted that there are exceptions to methodology-focused ethical review (see, for example, Connelly & Reid 2007), these alternative models do not represent the majority approach, meaning that researchers are largely unsupported in navigating broader, non-methodological ethical issues. For inexperienced researchers not yet cognizant of the practical limitations of institutional ethical review, obtaining ethical approval may therefore result in a false sense of confidence in the appropriateness of one's research. In satisfying the narrow requirements of an institutional review board concerned only with short-term, direct harms, researchers risk entering into the field without undertaking a genuinely self-critical and reflexive assessment of the aims and likely impacts of their research.

Some of the dangers inherent in criminological research, such as the inadvertent gathering of incriminating data, are heightened further in an online research environment, where ethical norms and practices are still in a process of development. Institutional review boards that are staffed with researchers from outside of criminology and other social science disciple nes are not necessarily well-equipped to assess research methodologies that involve complex social interactions and processes outside of a clinical environment. Even in instances where review boards are represented by experienced criminologists, the complexities and novelty associated with online research may still prove confounding. Regardless of the precise cause, the consequences of ineffective institutional review are profound and may result in researchers lacking meaningful ethical guidance precisely when they need it.

Rather than relying solely on the efficacy of institutional ethical review, criminologists and other researchers would do well to develop their own sense of ethical awareness and responsibility (Connelly & Reid 2007; White 2009). In this, a useful first step is to develop a familiarity with the various legislation and state directives concerning the legal limits of acceptable research, and also to examine more detailed codes of conduct and discipline-specific ethics statements developed by professional academic associations. While their relevance to criminological inquiry, particularly for so distinctive and novel a field as cryptomarket studies, is sometimes questionable, they do articulate standard ethical principles and prompt a number of considerations with which one may at least begin to assess the ethical appropriateness of one's research.

Of more immediate and practical use to scholars seeking to investigate the online drugs trade are insights revealed in the limited body of existing studies that comment on ethical considerations in cryptomarket research. For example, studies conducted by Christin (2013) and Barratt and Maddox (forthcoming) discuss a range of ethical concerns encountered when investigating cryptomarkets; these include the gathering and publication of potentially incriminating data, obtaining informed consent, differentiating between public and private data sources, and respecting the confidentiality of research subjects through the use of encrypted communications. The following section offers an analysis of how these various sources may be utilized to inform ethical considerations when conducting cryptomarket research.

Managing direct harms – informed consent and public vs. private

Obtaining informed consent from research participants is a foundational ethical practice in scholarly research. This process involves first disclosing to prospective participants the nature of the research to which they will be subject, and subsequently affording them the opportunity to decline or withdraw at any stage. Informed consent is ubiquitous in both biomedical and social science research and plays an important role in protecting the agency and interests of research subjects. It is not an inalienable right, however, and there are a variety of circumstances in which researchers may legitimately argue that it is either unnecessary or inappropriate. With regard to the study of illegal activity, the *National Statement* distinguishes between research that may result in potential harm to subjects and that which "uses collections of non-identifiable data and involves negligible risk" (National Health and Medical Research Council 2007, p. 3.5). In cases of the latter, studies may be exempted from the usual requirements to obtain either the consent of research subjects or even formal approval by an institutional review board. This is a similar process to that observed in the US, where government legislation formally recognizes research subjects only in instances involving interaction with researchers or when obtaining data through the observation of "identifiable private information"

(Code of Federal Regulations (CFR) 1991, 46.102(f)). Here, private information is defined as that which "occurs in a context in which an individual can reasonably expect that no observation or recording is taking place, and information which has been provided for specific purposes by an individual and which the individual can reasonably expect will not be made public" (ibid).

How to determine whether websites (including cryptomarkets) and associated online discussion forums are 'public' or 'private' is a topic generating considerable debate within the academic community. This issue also neatly demonstrates some of the complexities involved in applying ethical processes developed in a physical as opposed to virtual research environment. Eysenbach and Till (2001) suggest that several factors should be considered when determining whether or not an online space should be regarded as private, including whether a subscription or other barrier (e.g. membership or group approval) must be negotiated before a researcher may gain access to relevant data. They also suggest assessing the 'publicness' of the group on the basis of the total number of members included in communications, noting that "a posting to a mailing list with 10 subscribers is different from a posting to a mailing list with 100 or 1000 subscribers" (ibid, p. 1104). Small groups that tightly regulate their membership through significant barriers to entry naturally have a greater claim to privacy when compared to larger groups that are open for anyone to join.

These recommendations may be usefully applied to the various sources of data available on cryptomarkets. Factors in favor of considering seller and customer feedback pages as private include the presence of a barrier to entry – one must register a user account before the retail sections of a cryptomarket may be accessed (by contrast, cryptomarket discussion forums typically do not impose barriers to entry when simply observing rather than posting messages). Also, while seller and feedback information is intended for a wide viewership, people who post these kinds of information almost certainly do not intend for them to be used for the purposes of academic analysis. Indeed, some users may actively resent the presence of academics and other outsiders, particularly law enforcement. Users have even posted statements specifically addressed to police officers who are assumed to be constantly monitoring communications (Martin 2014b).

While some users demonstrate hostility to external observation, such sentiments also reveal a grudging awareness that external observation and recording is likely to be taking place at any given time. Ironically, this lends credibility to the perspective that communications in these spaces are essentially public in nature and may therefore be observed without violating user privacy.

In response to the issue of barriers to entry, Christin (2013) notes the lack of exclusivity associated with the registration process, which involves simply providing a user name and password, and the input of a CAPTCHA code.[1] No personal or other identifiable information is required, nor is there any requirement to agree to terms and conditions, for example to refrain from using data contained therein for other purposes.

Another argument in favor of considering cryptomarket data public is the large number of users to which the retail sections and cryptomarket and discussion forums are available. These sites often maintain a large number of registered users, sometimes numbering in the tens or even hundreds of thousands (Christin 2013; Dolliver 2015). It seems logical to conclude that communications knowingly visible to so large a group could not meaningfully be considered 'private', particularly when the user base is widely known to include both researchers and representatives from law enforcement who are working undercover (Martin 2014b).

While arguably public in nature, determining whether cryptomarket data is identifiable or not is more complicated than it may initially seem. For obvious reasons, drug traders who use cryptomarkets are typically scrupulous in maintaining their anonymity and avoid posting any details online that are likely to reveal their real-world identities. Anonymity may therefore be considered a general, even defining characteristic of practically all publicly available cryptomarket data, whether posted on a seller or customer feedback page or a discussion forum. On this basis, it is arguable that unobtrusive research methodologies involving automated data collection or the manual observation of publicly available cryptomarket data fall into a category of negligible risk, and therefore ethically unproblematic and appropriate research. Indeed, most studies utilizing these methodologies (Aldridge & Décary-Hétu 2014; Christin 2013; Dolliver 2015; Martin 2014a, 2014b) make no reference to seeking the consent of cryptomarket administrators or users, with the respective researchers presumably able to justify this approach when initially seeking institutional ethical approval.

However, while users of cryptomarkets have a strong incentive to maintain their online anonymity, there is no guarantee that this is observed or achieved by all users at all times. Consumers may, for example, mistakenly upload identifiable information including names, email or postal addresses to public forums or feedback pages. Alternatively, identifiable information may be revealed deliberately and maliciously in a practice known colloquially online as *doxxing*. Doxxing is the publication of private information for the purposes of public shaming, intimidation or incrimination (Brenner 2010). Several high-profile cryptomarket-related doxxing incidents have now been documented, targeting suspected scammers and, more controversially, the US district court judge presiding over the trial of convicted Silk Road administrator, Ross Ulbricht (Maréchal 2015). Despite the imposition of specific anti-doxxing policies on some cryptomarkets, the practice continues to present a real threat to the safety of identified parties.

Whether deliberate or inadvertent, the posting of identifiable information online has significant implications when conducting cryptomarket research. For scholars, a potential ethical problem arises if such data is inadvertently captured and stored – an occurrence that seems especially likely if utilizing an automated crawler that, unlike a researcher conducting manual observation, cannot distinguish between identifiable and non-identifiable data. While it appears as though such cases are relatively rare, the potential for incriminating evidence to be revealed online presents a slim but plausible risk to research subjects if scholarly databases that contain identifiable data are subpoenaed by law enforcement.

Given the vast amounts of data collected by automated crawlers, it may be difficult to design processes that safeguard against the automated, inadvertent gathering and collection of identifiable and therefore incriminating user information. On the other hand, scholars undertaking manual observation, and those who wish to make datasets publicly available have a greater opportunity to ensure that identifiable information is not captured. Researchers who have acquired large data sets through the use of crawlers therefore arguably bear some responsibility for ensuring they do not contain identifiable information before they are made public.

Hostile research populations and potential harms to researchers

A further ethical problem that is more frequently encountered in cryptomarket research concerns the attitudes of research populations for whom the prospect of academic or other outsider scrutiny is either unwelcome or actively resented. Suspicion of or resistance to external observers – otherwise known as the insider–outsider dilemma – is a common and well-understood phenomenon affecting ethnographic work across the entire academic spectrum (Lindvall & Rueda 2014; Paechter 2013). This has particular salience within criminological research, given the need for people involved in illegal activity to maintain a sufficiently low profile in order to avoid attracting attention from law enforcement. Other reasons for resistance include prejudicial attitudes, such as stereotypes of academics as "social justice warriors" (as the author was pejoratively described in one online forum post) or, in the case of criminological research in particular, the common misperception that researchers necessarily function as extensions or constituent parts of the criminal justice system.

Hostile perceptions amongst research populations may be compounded by the research practices of scholars. For example, conducting observational research may contribute to feelings of unwelcome surveillance, even if informed consent is sought and attained. Potentially negative attitudes towards scholars are likely to be aggravated further if the aims or findings of research are perceived to work against the interests of unwilling subjects. For example, Christin's (2013) study into the original Silk Road concluded with a section outlining several strategic options that law enforcement may use to crack down on the online drugs trade. This study was carefully designed to ameliorate direct harms resulting from unobtrusive, crawler-based observation (such as publication of identifiable, incriminating data), though in informing policing strategy it is implicitly linked to the potential for longer-term, indirect harms. While Christin outlined several compelling reasons why law enforcement agencies should at least consider a laissez-faire approach and allow the trade to continue unregulated, such nuance may be lost amongst a research population who may, understandably, exhibit heightened sensitivity towards threats posed by law enforcement. Alternatives to enforcement-led approaches may similarly be ignored by government agencies that are beholden to outdated and counter-productive War on Drugs ideology and policing strategies, and are determined to simply 'take down' a perceived criminal enemy.

Scholarly collaboration with law enforcement

Efforts on the part of law enforcement to disrupt or shut down cryptomarkets have stepped up markedly in recent years (Greenberg 2014, 2015). Recognizing the limitations inherent in local and national approaches to what is essentially a global phenomenon, policing and security agencies are increasingly working together with their foreign counterparts. Contemporary large-scale anti-cryptomarket operations, such as the recently executed Operation Onymous, now involve cooperation between some of the world's most powerful national and transnational law enforcement agencies. These include the FBI, DEA, Europol and the US Department of Homeland Security, as well as dozens of other smaller national police forces (EUROPOL 2014).

Despite this increase in international cooperation, the online drugs trade continues to flourish. More drug users than ever report sourcing their drugs online (Winstock 2015), yet cryptomarket-related arrests remain infrequent, to date numbering only around 300 globally (Gwern 2015). Customs agencies are reporting some success in intercepting larger numbers of small-volume drug consignments concealed in postal messages (Australian Customs and Border Protection Service 2013), which is consistent with the modus operandi of online vendors. However, these interceptions rarely result in arrests, and analysis of cryptomarket data (for example, positive customer feedback or details of generous refund policies for intercepted goods) indicates that many online vendors are both willing and able to smuggle illicit goods across even the most heavily policed national borders, such as Australia's (Martin 2014b). Anti-cryptomarket operations also produce limited returns in terms of large-scale seizures of goods, particularly when compared to conventional counter-narcotics operations that result in the seizure of large quantities of illicit drugs valued in the tens or even hundreds of millions of dollars. This lessens the newsworthiness and propaganda value of online drug busts, and further diminishes their attractiveness to law enforcement agencies seeking to maximize returns on scarce investigative resources.

In short, existing law enforcement strategies are failing to contain the growth of the online illicit drugs trade. Given the daunting complexities associated with this task, it is natural that law enforcement agencies would seek scholarly assistance in designing more effective approaches to the policing of cryptomarkets. The prospect of collaborating with law enforcement is likely to be attractive to academics for a variety of reasons. First, they are well placed to contribute valuable expertise to this fascinating endeavour. The complex and dynamic interplay between policing agencies and shadowy cyber-offenders is ideal intellectual fodder for criminologists and others who relish the challenges associated with the strategic, 'cat and mouse' aspects of law enforcement. Researchers with expertise in, for example, the operations of organized crime groups or the dynamics of drug trafficking networks are capable of making a valuable contribution to the development of more effective cryptomarket policing strategies.

Second, working with law enforcement is likely to be beneficial for individual scholars. Invitations to present research findings to law enforcement agencies, and informing the development of real-world law enforcement policy and practice, is useful for academics who are required to justify research allocations and demonstrate the real-world application, social utility and impact of their studies. Also relevant in this regard is the potential of securing external research funding from state institutions. In aligning one's research interests with those of the state, academics are in a favourable position to seek external financial support, either through government-funded competitive grants – with criteria often related to 'national security' or 'safer communities' – or through direct partnerships with well-resourced police or national security agencies. Scholarly collaboration with law enforcement therefore represents a valuable and potentially career-enhancing avenue to both external recognition and all-important research funding.

Finally, and perhaps most pertinently, scholars may believe that collaborating with law enforcement is in the best interests of the general public. This perspective aligns with a popular view that cryptomarkets are an unambiguously dangerous phenomenon that should be opposed by whatever means available. The arguments underpinning this perspective were articulated by the US district court judge presiding over the trial of Ross Ulbricht. In handing down a sentence of two life sentences plus an additional 30 years – a custodial sentence even in excess of what was requested by state prosecutors – Judge Forrest declared that Silk Road (and, by extension, other cryptomarkets) constituted "an assault on the public health of our communities" (Hong 2015). She concluded that Silk Road expanded access to dangerous illicit drugs, enriching dealers at the expense of addicts and directly resulting in fatal overdoses and increases in drug-related crime.

It is intriguing that Judge Forrest should emphasize the threats that cryptomarkets pose to public health, rather than the safer rhetorical ground of 'public morality' or 'law and order'. As is often noted by scholars critical of government policies associated with the War on Drugs (Moore & Elkavich 2008; Wood et al. 2009), prohibition results in serious damage to public health. Nonetheless, this line of reasoning is compelling (particularly when articulated by the parents of young people who have died tragically as a result of drug overdoses), and it fits neatly within the standard narratives associated with War on Drugs propaganda. It is not, however, necessarily accurate or reflective of the nuances associated with the growth of the online drugs trade. Of course, illicit drugs – like many legal narcotics, such as alcohol and tobacco – are potentially dangerous. To varying degrees, they are addictive, they alter the mental faculties of users, thereby affecting mood and decision-making, and they are also sometimes fatal. Many of these harms are compounded further by the absence of a legal market. A lack of regulation in their production and distribution means that organized crime groups are free to produce or adulterate drugs using sub-standard and potentially toxic ingredients. This results in end users often having little idea about what they are actually consuming, with limited knowledge about what might constitute safer levels of consumption.

Aside from harms to drug users, the other major danger associated with illicit drugs is their association with systemic violence. Organized crime groups involved in the drug trade regularly use violence for a range of purposes that are necessary to ensure success within this most profitable of black markets. These include: the protection of assets and personnel; enforcing 'business contracts' and internal group discipline; intimidating or using violence against members of the general public who may be opposed to their activities or witness crimes; bribery and corruption of police officers, customs officials, judges, politicians and other state representatives; and the elimination of competitors in order to seize and maintain control of drug dealing territory and trafficking routes (Martin 2013a, 2014b). Again, many of the systemic harms associated with illicit drugs either result from or are amplified by the illegality of the drugs trade. Denied the protection of the state, suppliers of illicit drugs use some of the vast monies at their disposal to innovate their own defensive (and offensive) capabilities.

It is an intriguing and counter-intuitive development in the history of the War on Drugs that a criminal innovation – cryptomarkets – may actually help ameliorate some of the many dangers associated with illicit drugs. A new body of scholarship is finding that cryptomarkets, as opposed to conventional drug distribution organizations, may actually reduce a range of drug-related harms, both to individual users as well as those that result from systemic violence (Aldridge & Décary-Hétu 2014; Barratt et al. 2013b; Martin 2014a, 2014b; Van Hout & Bingham 2014, 2013). This is not necessarily due to greater moral or ethical responsibility on the part of online drug traders when compared to their terrestrial counterparts, but rather concerns the operation of virtual systems of exchange that maintain real-world anonymity and physical separation between buyers and sellers, while also emphasizing the importance of personal reputation and accountability.

From a user perspective, customer feedback systems and detailed product information that is regularly provided online increases knowledge about the potency and chemical composition of various drugs. This information is not necessarily completely accurate – customer feedback represents consumer perceptions, rather than rigorous chemical analysis, and vendors seeking to drum up business may also post misleading 'fake' reviews. However, the existence of large amounts of at least semi-independent product data is invaluable for consumers who wish to use illicit drugs whilst minimizing risks to their personal health.

Cryptomarket discussion forums also host information about harm reduction measures and safer levels of use, and provide further opportunity for drug users to anonymously seek advice regarding safer methods of drug use. Potential harms to users are reduced further through the method of delivery. Drugs purchased online are posted directly to the home, thereby removing the potential for violent interactions with dealers or others who may be prepared to steal drugs or cash. This simplified method of distribution also bypasses many of the links in a conventional drug distribution chain of supply, such as retail, mid-level dealers, and sometimes even wholesalers and international traffickers. The involvement of fewer parties means that drugs may be delivered more cheaply and with fewer opportunities for adulteration (Martin 2014a, 2014b). These arguments are also supported by ethnographic research that indicates that drug consumers are attracted to cryptomarkets due to perceptions of high product quality (Barratt et al. 2013b; Van Hout & Bingham 2013; Winstock 2015).

With regard to systemic drug violence, cryptomarkets produce an arguably beneficial effect by altering the structure of drug distribution networks and minimizing opportunities whereby violence may be useful. Online anonymity not only protects dealers from law enforcement, it also insulates them from the threat of violent competition and criminal predation. As one cryptomarket dealer explained to Lavorgna (2014, p. 267), "if you try to take over a [conventional] route for cocaine or heroin delivery, you are going to get killed. … But you can create your own new market over the Internet and [operate] in a semi-anonymous fashion." The safety that is characteristic of online dealing also enables wholesalers to sell directly to end users – a practice that is both logistically unfeasible and prohibitively risky in conventional drug markets. In bypassing these stages, and rendering the involvement of associated organized crime groups redundant, online drug trading limits the possibility for criminal entities to control drug retailing territory and trafficking routes.

Further research is required to investigate these and other potential harm reduction benefits associated with cryptomarkets. However, despite the unanticipated benefits associated with the growth of online drug trading, it is not a panacea. Many drug-related problems – such as violence in source countries such as Mexico and Afghanistan – will persist regardless of whether a greater proportion of the illicit trade moves online (Martin 2014a, 2014b). However, the perspectives outlined above indicate that scholars and indeed law enforcement should be wary of the unintended consequences of a crackdown on cryptomarkets. The most obvious result of this course of action would be the re-routing of illicit drugs back into the hands of conventional dealers, with all the associated problems that that entails.

Proactive and critical engagement

The above section sought to articulate some of the long-term, indirect harms that may be encountered if researchers choose to collaborate with law enforcement in their efforts to eliminate cryptomarket-facilitated drug distribution. However, a similar range of indirect harms may also be encountered if researchers avoid engaging with law enforcement altogether. These include the risk of contributing to a false 'us' vs. 'them' dichotomy, whereby academics are isolated from the legitimate needs and concerns of state representatives and law enforcement agencies are deprived of alternative, nuanced and critical perspectives regarding the potentially negative consequences of their work. This too is an ethically problematic outcome that could hinder the development of less harmful, evidence-based policing strategies.

Of course, if a cryptomarket researcher decides *not* to collaborate in the design of more robust online policing strategies, this does not necessarily preclude other forms of constructive engagement with law enforcement. One alternative 'middle way' that may be useful for all parties – researchers, law enforcement agencies and the general public – is to respond to requests for assistance from law enforcement agencies by offering to provide critical knowledge regarding the relative risks and benefits of cracking down on cryptomarkets when compared to allocating similar investigative resources towards conventional, violence-prone drug distribution organizations (or indeed other, arguably more serious, online criminal threats, such as those posed by cyber-terrorists or distributors of child exploitation material). In the author's experience, law enforcement and other government representatives are often prepared to at least consider harm reduction arguments. Even if law enforcement agencies do not formally endorse such a perspective (which is likely given the political implications of being publicly perceived to 'green light' any form of criminal enterprise), harm reduction arguments may prove influential during internal deliberations regarding how to best prioritize the allocation of scarce investigative resources.

This form of critical engagement on the part of criminologists is similarly important with regard to working with researchers from other scholarly disciplines who are also involved in the study of cryptomarkets. As outlined earlier in the chapter, the multi-faceted nature of cryptomarket research necessitates cross-disciplinary collaboration between scholars located across the breadth of the academy. Through the formation of multidisciplinary collaborative partnerships, researchers of all stripes may benefit from the sharing of discipline-specific knowledge and expertise including, from a criminological perspective, critical understandings regarding the growth of the online drugs trade and its impact upon conventional drug distribution networks and organized crime groups, and the potential consequences – intended or otherwise – of different policing strategies. This cross-disciplinary perspective is valuable in terms of informing ethical considerations regarding both short-term direct harms and longer-term indirect harms associated with the broader socio-political context of cryptomarket research.

Finally, academics have an ethical as well as a professional responsibility to communicate their research findings to the broader public. Internet crime and illicit drugs are both topics about which many sections of the polity often have little understanding. For too long public discourse surrounding illicit drugs in particular has been dominated by sensational, ill-informed and self-serving War on Drugs propaganda (Benson 2009; Benson et al. 1995; Wood et al. 2009). In the absence of objective, evidence-based criminological perspectives, cryptomarkets represent prime sites for the creation of moral panic. Popular misunderstanding regarding the various harms associated with illicit drugs is dangerous, and risks lending public support to the formation of reactionary and counterproductive law enforcement strategies. It is therefore incumbent upon researchers who are engaged in the study of both cryptomarkets and illicit drugs more generally to communicate their perspectives to the general public and to inform public debate through productive engagement with both old and new forms of media.

Conclusion

This chapter has sought to explore some of the ethical and methodological issues associated with cryptomarket research and to highlight problems associated with the process of institutional ethical review. Existing ethics processes emphasize the importance of appropriate methodological design in ameliorating harms to research subjects. However, this chapter has argued that a broader and more inclusive approach to the ethical implications of one's studies is necessary when engaged in criminological and, specifically, cryptomarket research. All scholarly inquiry, to a greater or lesser extent, has political significance and is, in the words of Wetzell (2000, p. 11), "full of both emancipatory and repressive potential". Cryptomarkets and the growth of the online drugs trade represent at least one area of criminal innovation that counter-intuitively may benefit the general public. Criminologists should therefore resist, or at the very least question, the various institutional and normative pressures to assist law enforcement in combating the online drugs trade, and be mindful of whose interests our scholarly endeavours may ultimately serve. Through productive and ethical engagement with other researchers and with law enforcement agencies, and by communicating research findings to the broader public, criminologists and other cryptomarket researchers may help realize lofty yet worthwhile scholarly aspirations to contribute to the public good.

Note

1   Completely Automated Public Turing tests to tell Computer and Humans Apart (CAPTCHA) are commonly used on cryptomarkets as well as legitimate websites to prevent automated 'bots' from entering forums and distributing spam. They typically take the form of a set of numbers and letters that are blurred or otherwise visually distorted and are difficult for automated programs to interpret.

References

Aldridge, J & Décary-Hétu, D 2014, ' 'Not an "eBbay for drugs": The cryptomarket "Silk Road" as a paradigm shifting criminal innovation'. http://papers.ssrn.com/sol3/Papers. cfm?abstract_id=2436643.

Australian Customs and Border Protection Service 2013, *Australian Customs and Border Protection Service Annual Report 2012–2013*, Canberra, Australian Customs and Border Protection Service.

Barratt M 2012, Letters to the editor. 'Silk Road: eBay for drugs', *Addiction*, vol. 107, pp. 683–684.

Barratt, MJ & Maddox, A Forthcoming, *Dark Net Ethnography: Conducting Sensitive Research in Volatile Digital Spaces*, Sydney, Australia, National Drug and Alcohol Research Centre.

Barratt, MJ, Ferris, JA, & Winstock, RA 2013a, 'Use of Silk Road, the online drug market-place, in the UK, Australia and the USA', *Addiction*. DOI: 10.1111/add.12470.

Barratt, MJ, Lenton, S, & Allen, M 2013b, 'Internet content regulation, public drug web-sites and the growth in hidden Internet services', *Drugs: Education, Prevention, and Policy*, vol. 20, no. 3, pp. 195–202.

Benson, BL 2009, 'Escalating the war on drugs: Causes and unintended consequences', *Stanford Law & Policy Review*, vol. 20, p. 293.

Benson, BL, Rasmussen, DW, & Sollars, DL 1995, 'Police bureaucracies, their incentives, and the war on drugs', *Public Choice*, vol. 83, nos. 1–2, pp. 21–45.

Brenner, S 2010, *Cybercrime: Criminal Threats from Cyberspace*, Santa Barbara, CA, Praeger.

Castells, M 2011, *The Rise of the Network Society: The Information Age: Economy, Society, and Culture*, New York, John Wiley & Sons.

CFR 1991, *Code of Federal Regulations, Title 45*, Washington DC, Government Printing Office.

Christin, N 2013, *Traveling the Silk Road: A Measurement Analysis of a Large Anonymous Online Marketplace*, Proceedings of the 22nd international conference on the World Wide Web. www.andrew.cmu.edu/user/nicolasc/publications/Christin-WWW13.pdf.

Connolly, K & Reid, A 2007, 'Ethics review for qualitative inquiry adopting a values- based, facilitative approach', *Qualitative Inquiry*, vol. 13, no. 7, pp. 1031–1047.

Dingwall, R 2008, 'The ethical case against ethical regulation in humanities and social science research', *Twenty-First Century Society*, vol. 3, no. 1, pp. 1–12.

Dolliver, DS 2015, 'Evaluating drug trafficking on the Tor network: Silk Road 2, the sequel', *International Journal of Drug Policy*, vol. 26, no. 11, pp. 1113–1123.

EUROPOL 2014, 'Global action against dark markets on the Tor network', The Hague, EUROPOL.

Eysenbach, G & Till, JE 2001, 'Ethical issues in qualitative research on internet communities', *British Medical Journal*, vol. 323, no. 7321, pp. 1103–1105.

Garrett, B. 2014, 'Access denied: Place-hacker Bradley Garrett: Research at the edge of the law', *Times Higher Education*, 5 June.

Greenberg, A 2014, 'Global web crackdown arrests 17, seizes hundreds of dark net domains, *Wired*, 11 July.

Greenberg, A 2015, 'German police just made a gigantic dark-web drug bust', *Wired*, 12 March.

Gwern 2015, 'Tor black-market-related arrests'. www.gwern.net/Black-marketarrests.

Haggerty, K 2004, 'Ethics creep: Governing social science research in the name of ethics', *Qualitative Sociology*, vol. 27, no. 4, pp. 391–414.

Hong, N 2015, 'Silk Road founder Ross Ulbricht sentenced to life in prison', *Wall Street Journal*, 29 May.

Hoonaard, WC van den 2011, *The Seduction of Ethics: Transforming the Social Sciences*, Toronto, University of Toronto Press.

Lavorgna, A 2014, 'Internet-mediated drug trafficking: Towards a better understanding of new criminal dynamics', *Trends in Organized Crime*, vol. 17, no. 4, pp. 250–270.

Lindvall, J & Rueda, D 2014, 'The insider–outsider dilemma', *British Journal of Political Science*, vol. 44, 02, pp. 460–475.

Maréchal, N 2015, 'Gabriella Coleman, hacker, hoaxer, whistleblower, spy: The many faces of anonymous', *International Journal of Communication*, vol. 9, p. 5.

Martin, J 2013, 'Informal security nodes and force capital', *Policing and Society*, vol. 23, no. 2, pp. 145–163.

Martin, J 2014a, 'Lost on the Silk Road: Online drug distribution and the "cryptomarket"', *Criminology and Criminal Justice*, vol. 14, no. 3, pp. 351–367.

Martin, J 2014b, *Drugs on the Dark Net: How Cryptomarkets are Transforming the Global Trade in Illicit Drugs*, Basingstoke, Palgrave Macmillan.

Moore, LD & Elkavich, A 2008, 'Who's using and who's doing time: Incarceration, the war on drugs, and public health', *American Journal of Public Health*, vol. 98, no. 5, 782–786.

National Health and Medical Research Council 2007, *National Statement on Ethical Conduct in Human Research*, Canberra, Australian Government.

Paechter, C 2013, 'Researching sensitive issues online: Implications of a hybrid insider/outsider position in a retrospective ethnographic study', *Qualitative Research*, vol. 13, no. 1, pp. 71–86.

Phelps, A & Watt, A 2014, 'I shop online–recreationally! Internet anonymity and Silk Road enabling drug use in Australia', *Digital Investigation*, vol. 11, no. 4, pp. 261–272.

Roberts, L & Indermaur, D 2003, 'Signed consent forms in criminological research: Protection for researchers and ethics committees but a threat to research participants?', *Psychiatry, Psychology and Law*, vol. 10, no. 2, pp. 289–299.

Schrag, ZM 2011, 'The case against ethics review in the social sciences', *Research Ethics*, vol. 7, no. 4, pp. 120–131.

Van Hout, MC & Bingham, T 2014, 'Responsible vendors, intelligent consumers: Silk Road, the online revolution in drug trading', *International Journal of Drug Policy*, vol. 25, no. 2, pp. 183–189.

Van Hout, MC & Bingham, T 2013, '"Silk Road", the virtual drug marketplace: A single case study of user experiences', *International Journal of Drug Policy*, vol. 24, no. 5, pp. 385–391.

Wetzell, RF 2000, *Inventing the Criminal: A History of German Criminology, 1880–1945*, Chapel Hill, University of North Carolina Press.

White, L 2009, 'Challenge of research ethics committees to the nature of operations research', *Omega*, vol. 37, no. 6, pp. 1083–1088.

Winstock, AR 2015, *The Global Drug Survey 2015 Findings*. www.globaldrugsurvey.com/the-global-drug-survey-2015-findings/.

Wood, E, Werb, D, Marshall, BD, Montaner, JS, & Kerr, T 2009, 'The war on drugs: A devastating public-policy disaster', *The Lancet*, vol. 373, no. 9668, pp. 989–990.

CONCLUSION

Fostering the development of an ethical imagination

Rose Ricciardelli and Michael Adorjan

In drawing on the applied and lived experiences of our expert contributors, we, in this edited collection, revealed how ethical considerations shape each of the various phases of conducting research, liaising with research participants, review boards, academic publishers and journal reviewers, as well as practitioners in the criminal justice system. We strove to centre on the *realpolitik* of conducting criminological research by drawing attention to the lived experiences of researchers as they try to overcome ethical issues and dilemmas; to include a range of international experiences and contributors in order to show the universality yet geographically distinct nature of ethical concerns – researchers are always affected by social and political conditions and exigencies; and to be inclusive of a wide range of areas of criminology and criminal justice. Indeed, ethical considerations are unique yet similar in the ways in which they 'play out' in practice and in the field.

In this context, a universal truth emerged. Quite simply put: our contributors found their chapters difficult to write. Writing is an ethical act, and writing about ethics doubles down on this bet. Many of our contributors expressed just how difficult it was to write their chapters; naturally not due to lack of academic skill or insight (quite the opposite). Many found it challenging to introspectively explore ethical considerations yet stay true to their participants, maintain anonymity or navigate their research intentions versus the lived intentions of those they study. Clearly, how do you write about the ethical considerations of doing research that concerns, for instance, vulnerable or dispossessed people who may harbour their own fears about the ramifications of even participating in said research? When collaborating with criminal justice institutions, to what extent is a research project steered by their goals and expectations for research outcomes? How does one respond when conducting reviews for certain criminology journals with criteria suggestive of the screening of 'politically correct' interpretations of data? What are the unanticipated and indirect harms that emerge during the course of research as blind spots to initial research ethics board (REB) screening of direct harms? Our contributors write about these and other related ethical concerns and dilemmas that are encountered in every phase of research, well beyond formal ethical approval.

Keeping an international focus, we set out in this edited collection to highlight both shared experiences and local idiosyncrasies. Our contributors invoked the *realpolitik* of engaging in criminological research today within their unique fields and areas of study, which range from research involving vulnerable and subaltern criminalized populations, policing in mainland China, victimology and trauma resulting from victimization, the politics and ethical implications of carceral tours, and 'cryptomarkets' in cyberspace. The underlying theme is the simple fact that doing criminological research is laced with ethical challenges that involve many layers, which in turn affect researchers, participants, administrations, universities and diverse groups across the public sphere. Challenges can start before the research ever begins, as a researcher can be barred access to the population they wish to study, or have access but be refused ethical clearance from their institution. In some cases, researchers may be granted access with full ethical approval to proceed, but refuse funding for a project based on ethical concerns (see Carlen, this volume). We sought to write this book about the realities of doing research that one will not necessarily learn in traditional methods textbooks, where ethics may be a discrete chapter focused on generic issues relating to obtaining informed consent, maintaining confidentiality, and so forth. Recognizing that the field is where researchers learn about all that goes right and all that may go wrong when doing research, and the fact that fieldwork is unscripted, we sought to capture the applied experiences of doing criminological research. Indeed, we never know what we will find in the field and as researchers we need to trust in ourselves and our training to negotiate the field, protect the persons under study and, at the end of the day, protect our colleagues and ourselves. Our contributors' experiences as a whole reveal the importance of developing an ethical imagination related to conducting criminological research (see Adorjan, this volume); an imagination that moves beyond tired critiques of university REBs to a more fluid and dynamic adjustment to the 'going concerns' (Hughes 1971) of ethical challenges encountered, often in unexpected areas, and that considers how individual decisions may bear longitudinal consequences for researchers, participants and wider social groups alike.

Ethics on paper: navigating research ethics boards

Criticisms levied at institutional REBs (equivalent to institutional review boards) are abundant amongst sociologists and criminologists, particularly qualitative researchers such as ethnographers who must often forge relationships with strangers in order to conduct their research. Even the process of introducing participants to a letter providing information or a consent form can be a challenge that may hamper the research process given the length of time it takes to review, and assumptions regarding literacy and comprehension of what 'consent' entails (especially regarding youth and/or vulnerable populations). This applies even more so if the research is explicitly geared to investigate victimization experiences or criminal behaviour. Some maintain that the original impetus for increased ethical regulation is an outdated biomedical model that bears little resemblance to the exigencies of ethnographic or interview-based research with people, and argue that sociological and criminological research will never pose the same risks to human participants as those posed in the biomedical and natural sciences. As Dingwall (2006, p. 52) sardonically suggested:

> We have no research technique that carries an inherent risk of immediate death or serious physical damage. We have no power to impose ourselves on people. Social scientists are guests in other people's lives – if anything, the power lies with our informants who oblige us to behave with circumspection in exchange for the privilege of accessing information that they control. ... At no point are we going to forcibly inject dependent patients with irreversibly toxic green stuff.

Carlen, this volume, similarly states, "this is social, not medical, research. Loss of life or limb is not usually at stake" (p. 54).

These critiques are buttressed by Haggerty's (2004) argument (reproduced in this volume) that, borrowing from the idea of 'mission creep', ethical protocols and bureaucratic procedures have infiltrated unanticipated areas. Drawing on his time as an insider, serving on a Canadian REB, he suggests that the movement of REBs toward increasingly scrutinizing and restricting the boundaries within which researchers can conduct their studies is found to constrain both scholarly research and, more problematically, what knowledge researchers are 'allowed' to make known. Haggerty recognizes this as one outcome of the "ethical 'creep'" where researchers have no choice but to adhere to suggestions made by REBs – or they will not be granted clearance to conduct said research – that arguably, unintentionally "complicate, hamper, or censor certain forms of nontraditional, qualitative, or critical social scientific research" (p. 14). Moreover, and with potentially wider implications, criminologists may react to increasing "bureaucratic oversight" (p. 15) through self-censorship of their own research ideas. As Haggerty suggests,

> An unfortunate consequence of these developments will likely be that researchers will choose to employ certain types of unproblematic and often predictable research methodologies rather than deal with the uncertainty and delays associated with qualitative, ethnographic, or critical scholarship which do not fit easily into the existing research ethics template. The more ethical roadblocks are installed for innovative and critical research, the more we risk homogenizing inquiry and narrowing vision, as scholars start to follow what they perceive to be the path of least institutional resistance. (p. 32)

Tierney and Corwin (2007) highlight the ways in which they observe REBs undergo institutional review that potentially infringes on the academic freedom of researchers. Specifically, they see this as occurring as a result of review boards regulating (a) "who is required to consent to research, (b) by stipulating the type of questions allowed and location of research interactions, and (c) by limiting research design" (p. 388). Their arguments here are clearly informed by their prior study, where they drew on colleagues' experiences with REBs to show how ethics boards can delay research – or impede researchers from ever getting started (Tierney & Corwin 2004). In some circumstances researchers may not be able to fulfil their obligations to the granting agency since they cannot proceed with their funded project, which may lead to consequences in terms of their ability to receive another grant or contract. Examples exist of researchers, due to the extreme micro-management of methodological processes by REBs, being unlikely to successfully complete funded projects and therefore jeopardizing their likelihood of receiving further funding for follow-up research (e.g. the case of Laurie Thompson, involving institutional review board monitoring of a project involving children and technology (see Tierney & Corwin 2004, p. 226)).

Critics also point to the constantly changing nature of study designs and contexts that renders initial ethics approvals arguably meaningless (and where modifications would have to be submitted so frequently they would stymie the ability to proceed) (Dingwall 2006; van den Hoonaard 2001). What does this suggest about researchers? Indeed, knowing that research rarely takes the predicted course and only so many amendments can be filed before a project is permanently stymied, we may ask, are all researchers inherently somewhat unethical? Ferrell and Hamm (1998, cited in Feenan 2002, p. 774) provocatively suggest that "acting illegally or unethically may be necessary to achieve criminal 'verstehen'". Similarly, Israel (2004, p. 732) astutely argues, "integrity does not necessarily mean that researchers follow every law or rule. Indeed, maintaining integrity may mean that they break some rules". REBs do not monitor if a researcher does what they say they will be doing or how far from said processes they are forced or choose to stray, yet ethics are awarded only at the start of a project rather than throughout the lifetime of the study – outside of amendments and annual updates until the closure of the file (see Calvey 2008).

While institutions, on the one hand, and research participants, on the other, are protected from harm, the protection of researchers themselves is often insufficiently prioritized; a concern perhaps more prescient among criminologists. We may ask, should ethics boards offer the researcher some degree of protection as they do research participants? By going through the ethics review processes, adhering to institutional regulation and garnering clearance, should researchers not be guaranteed support if something is to go wrong? Instead, researchers are accountable and can only request, with hopes of it being granted, legal or other types of support from their universities when they are subpoenaed to provide information or if a problem arises over the course of their study. Criminological researchers engaged in ethnography, for instance, may experience violence as part of group initiation and gaining access to particular criminal subcultures; moreover, harassment and threats may follow when covert researchers reveal themselves to be academics (see Winlow et al. 2001). Criminologists conducting covert research may have more difficulties passing through ethics screening, and may have to be more careful when justifying the merit of their study based on the increased risk for themselves and their institutions. Calvey (2008, p. 913), conducting covert research as a bouncer, writes:

> Some would view my role as problematic in terms of collusion, which is only an issue if one retains a traditional conception of fieldworker objectivity. Obviously, these encounters could have put me in an ambiguous legal position, as I had acquired a type of deviant knowledge … but fortunately that never happened. In a way, it was a type of "fingers crossed ethnography" where my luck might have run out.

In Canada, legal decisions have strengthened the protection afforded to criminological researchers. The recent case of University of Ottawa criminologists Dr Chris Bruckert and Dr Colette Parent is considered precedent-setting by many. Here, Quebec Superior Court Justice Sophie Bourque decided to deny the Montreal police access to a taped interview with Luka Magnota, who was at the time accused of the murder and dismemberment of Chinese student, Lin Jun. The researchers' lawyer, Peter Jacobsen, called the decision the "first court recognition of researcher–participant privilege". Justice Bourque further stated that,

> The evidence demonstrates that much of the research involving vulnerable people can only be conducted if human participants are given a guarantee that their identities and the information that they share will remain confidential. (Fine 2014)

The court decision is a reminder of the importance of protecting criminological researchers and the risks they themselves face in conducting their research (see also Dingwall 2007, p. 788).

It should of course be recognized that REBs are not immune from 'ethics creep' and as such are under scrutiny regarding their composition; for example, number of community and Aboriginal members, lawyers, and so on (see Walter, this volume). We may consider the many ways in which REB members are themselves subject to the same wider processes of governance and regulation that affect researchers (e.g. the movement towards REB accreditation and further institutional oversight (Haggerty, this volume, p. 32). Alongside researchers, they are also subjected to growing bureaucratization and techniques of accountability and regulation (Guta et al. 2013); board members and researchers seem to be caught up in wider institutional concerns with litigation and risk minimization (Hammersley 2009, p. 218). Where some sort of process appears to be in place to govern compliance, members of review boards have described ethics becoming more about 'risk management' than ethical reviews and their roles becoming centred on enforcing compliance or administrative tasks like paperwork (Guta et al. 2013). Given this context, REB members may thus feel undervalued and underutilized. This tends to be compounded by the fact that many ethics offices are also under-resourced and members bear heavy workloads; this is especially the case considering that any study that does not use secondary data sources *must* have approval to proceed. Another permutation REBs may be increasingly concerned with is the publication of REB decisions in peer-reviewed journals that highlight, perhaps unfairly, individual decisions as representative of wider malaise (even where anonymized, some rudimentary deduction may reveal the identities of specific board members).

Our own position is that, despite ongoing critiques and concerns we feel have merit, REB oversight is an essential process that should not be dismantled (indeed to suggest this is rather absurd). Review processes are imperfect, yet required. We take issue with critiques that, in broad brush stroke, suggest that ethics boards should not involve themselves in methodological matters. There should be oversight over procedures that by their nature have ethical implications for how participants are involved in research. For example, research involving students, especially adolescents and children, must carefully address how participants receive information about the study (especially if schools are involved) and how potential coercion is to be minimized (i.e. ensuring students participate without concern that their academic performance will be negatively affected). Some scholars, such as Charles Bosk (2004), writing in response to Kevin Haggerty (this volume), suggest a pragmatic approach with which we agree:

> [W]e should not waste our energies resisting a process that has an enormous amount of both bureaucratic momentum and social consensus behind it. Instead we should focus our energies on reforming and revising procedure; we should fix the system where it is broken. Our constant whining that we are somehow the targets and victims of intrusive regulation is not only tiresome; it is inappropriate. (p. 417)

A more productive notion is to think about institutional review processes as a discourse rather than a fixed set of governing practices which would, ultimately, encourage more flexibility for researchers as they hone their craft (Halse & Honey 2007). Further, as Hammersley (2009) has noted, there is much to be gained by researchers focusing on ethical reflection when designing projects rather than learning the craft of filling out protocols in ways that maximize the possibility of acquiring approvals quickly (see also Israel & Hay 2006).

Of course, despite any animosities that may exist between researchers, institutions and review board members, researchers all share the same long-term objective: ensuring that their research does not harm our participants in any way, shape or form (Guta et al. 2013). Different scholars have made suggestions about how to make the ethics board and review processes more effective. A number have called for more active participation by researchers of different stripes to populate boards and help provide input and discipline-specific knowledge to help contextualize proposals. Some have argued that REBs would benefit from having members who understand qualitative research methods and who could provide insider insights through reviewing existing rules and protocols (Bosk 2004; Connolly & Reid 2007;

Tierney & Corwin 2004, 2007), which is a common practice in many institutes (see Hedgecoe, 2008). Or, as van den Hoonaard (2001) advocates, board members could use more flexibility in how they treat protocol forms, a flexibility that recognizes the multitude of approaches to data collection used, especially by qualitative (and we would add criminological) researchers. In short, researchers and board members, it has been suggested, should both be involved in the review process (Connolly & Reid 2007; Librett & Peronne 2010). Bosk (2004) suggests that one way to facilitate this involvement is for researchers to carefully draft a cover letter that outlines what standard of review is most appropriate for their research study and what alternative procedures may be necessary (i.e. verbal rather than signed consent). This may also include a reminder that a REB is to 'audit' ethical concerns, particularly surrounding perceived harms and/or risks, and not the researcher's methodology or research questions (see Connolly & Reid 2007, pp.1035–1036).

We would agree with those advocating for a more interactive researcher–reviewer process tied to gaining ethical clearance. Instead of researchers passively waiting for the 'verdict' on their application, they should be informing and shaping their study to resolve any ethical concerns and create the most suitable study processes feasible (Connolly & Reid 2007; Librett & Peronne 2010). We argue also that a broader institutional culture needs to be cultivated that supports such positive and productive interactions. For instance, some researchers report that ethics offices, instead of becoming increasingly accessible to researchers, have moved in the other direction, which distracts from any opportunities to work through ethical concerns interactively (see Guta et al. 2013).

Some of the contributors in this book make reference to their experiences of initial ethics review. Adorjan, a Canadian writing of experiences conducting criminological research in Hong Kong, encountered a relatively smooth ethics review process for his collaborative project on fear of crime and perceptions of police. This may be due to the adoption, in Hong Kong, of ethical protocols and processes from the UK academic system during its colonial period. Xu reports a similar 'smooth' process of institutional ethics review in Macau, which like Hong Kong is a Special Administrative Region of China.

Spencer, writing his chapter on ethical dilemmas related to research on victimized persons, recalls receiving varied responses from REBs "ranging from informative to odd" (p. 110). He found one suggestion regarding his recruitment strategies very useful, especially when considering that his participants came from marginalized and 'hidden' populations. On the other hand, for one study interviewing police officers, he was required to stipulate on a consent form that he needed to report to police any disclosure by police regarding child sexual victimization. Spencer also reports experiencing different responses to the same application across REBs in different Canadian universities. He argues that, when researching victimized persons, ethics goes well beyond receiving institutional approval, abiding to ethical guidelines and "making good decisions" (p. 111). He advocates for an ethics specifically geared to researching victims and vulnerable populations, and in his chapter proceeds to outline "ethics as witnessing", offering a conceptualization of what such an ethics may look like. Spencer's chapter suggests productive directions are possible if REBs are viewed not as static but interactive processes that can be altered through researcher input. For instance, he argues that an ethics of witnessing has the potential to enable the researcher to experience a vicarious trauma "which, arguably, challenges the myopic concern of research ethics boards (with participants and risk), to a much broader evaluation of how victim-related research is a thoroughly traumatic endeavor" (p. 114).

Relatively new areas of criminological inquiry offer their own particular challenges for REBs. The Hippocratic oath to do no harm is greatly problematized, Martin writes in his chapter, when approaching REBs to review research on the 'dark net' and online 'cryptomarkets' where illicit drugs are bought and sold, among other criminal activities. Unlike biomedical research, Martin writes, criminologists "may seek to compromise the agency of their research subjects and expose and disrupt harmful, criminal activities committed on their part" (p. 198). REBs, in rendering decisions on cryptomarkets research, may draw assumptions about harm in their assessments of risks and benefits (i.e. assumptions regarding criminal activity assumed to be harmful, which may not be deemed so to potential research participants). As Haggerty (this volume, p. 30) argues, "the epistemological and political difficulties of speaking for other groups, combined with an awareness of the marginal status of such research participants, has fostered a tendency to view all research participants as vulnerable, lacking power, and needing protection". REBs are geared largely to the management of *direct* harms associated with research methodology, Martin writes, but not to assessing or ameliorating the more concomitant *indirect* harms related to issues outside the purview of methodological processes. Furthermore, criminologists conducting research online must contend with the possibility of unintentionally acquiring incriminating data that raise significant questions about participant vulnerability as well as researcher susceptibility to law enforcement requests for their data (see below). Many REBs, Martin notes, are not populated by those familiar with criminological research in cyberspace, "where ethical norms and practices are still in a process of development" (p. 199). Here, too, those with such knowledge would benefit REBs through their active participation on such boards.

The notion that REBs should be informed by the exigencies and situated realities facing the populations being studied becomes arguably even more prescient in research involving Aboriginal populations, as explicated by Walter in her insightful contribution to this book. In her survey of ethical review protocols and procedures in four first-world settler states, Walter highlights not only sensitivity on the part of institutional review boards to the idiosyncratic ethical issues involving particular Aboriginal peoples (including Aboriginal and Torres Strait Islander people in Australia, the Māori of New Zealand, First Nation groups in Canada, and Native Americans), but often the need for researchers to simultaneously acquire direct approval from groups being researched. Moreover, REBs often acknowledge the existence of a spectrum of ethical behaviour ranging from 'minimal compliance' to 'best practice', and encourage researchers to adopt the latter. 'Best practices' include, in the context of Aotearoa New Zealand, conducting research in line with Aboriginal methodologies and with tangible outcomes benefitting Aboriginal communities. However, even those who strive to achieve research in line with best practices face challenges associated with potentially unacknowledged social positions (especially if researchers are part of the dominant majority in first-world settler states). "Even if the researcher is fully cognizant of Indigenous ethical dimensions, the outcome is not necessarily ethical research," Walter astutely points out (p. 88). Very similarly, Piché and his colleagues argue in their chapter on carceral tours (i.e. tours of operational jails, prisons and penitentiaries for research or class visits) that while such tours may offer some insight and knowledge, "that does not make them ethical, whether sanctioned by university ethics boards or not" (p. 189).

As these highlights suggest, the ethics of doing research only begins with receiving clearance from an REB. The contributors in this book wrote most explicitly about their encounters and dilemmas during the course of conducting research, as well as issues related to the dissemination of research findings after the completion of data collection. We highlight some of the major themes they trace in the following two sections.

Ethics in the field: self-governance during data collection

The contributors to this book were encouraged to reflect on ethical concerns and dilemmas encountered during the course of conducting criminological research in the 'field'; to push beyond their take on research ethics boards (REBs) and to mine the ethical *realpolitik* of encounters in practice during the course of data collection and dissemination of research findings at academic conferences and through peer-reviewed journals.

Mark Israel, in his chapter examining research on prisoners in the US, argues that consent procedures have been systematically evaded; the ironic effect of correctional institutions being protected at the expense of prisoners. Ethics approval 'on paper' may well be granted, though the very presence of the researcher within a prison evokes several ethical issues primarily related to the vulnerability of the prisoners being studied. On the one hand, there is the general issue of how to approach prisoners in order to acquire informed consent, with the challenge being to clearly communicate research goals and procedures. However, research in "total institutions" (Goffman 1961) (or indeed across a range of penal contexts at varying security levels) needs to begin with the recognition that the very nature of the setting and context of incarceration reifies structural inequalities that endow researchers with much greater power than the prisoners being researched. No amount of effort to minimize harms is able to ameliorate this power dynamic; criminological research must begin with this understanding of positionality. Such research renders inappropriate the 'data raid' model of consent, Israel writes (p. 71, quoting Grounds and Jamieson 2003), "whereby consent is obtained from participants only at the beginning" of a research study.

Israel highlights the experiences of criminologists who witnessed attempts by prison staff to coerce prisoners into participating in research, sometimes threatening sanctions if they chose to decline. Penologists must also consider whether prisoner participation will be noted at the time of parole review. In such circumstances prisoners may feel compelled to participate or face negative feedback sent to parole boards; a punishment over and above the sentence already being served. Israel's chapter proceeds to document historical abuses targeting American prisoners as *subjects* of largely biomedical research, not research *participants*. While subsequent guidelines and regulations were put in place granting some recognition of prisoner vulnerability, the focus on biomedical research meant that most research within prisons in the US did not require REB review and oversight. Israel goes on to show how the eventual development of research ethics regulations needs to be understood alongside a developing 'institutional protectionism' (Hannah-Moffat 2011) in corrections, whereby "the principles and structures of research ethics have been used to protect correctional institutions from external scrutiny and it is this lack of external scrutiny that makes it far more likely that abuse of prisoners might occur" (p. 79). Ironically, Israel argues, research ethics regulations permit the denial of access to researchers on the grounds of the protection of prisoners. A lack of transparency exacerbates this further, he writes, enabling prisons to be run relatively free of oversight, unlike systems in the UK and Australia.

Given this context, Israel concludes by advocating for the greater use of covert research to challenge the "images powerful groups wish to project" (p. 80; cf. Erikson 1967). He points to several national codes offering support for covert research in exceptional circumstances. Israel concludes by noting that, "criminology has said little about the exploitation of prisoners by researchers" (p. 81), due in part to criminologists not yet engaging with the general literature of research ethics. No doubt Israel's contribution helps to craft stronger links between criminology and research ethics, while illuminating ongoing challenges for those seeking to capture the lived experiences of incarcerated populations.

Pat Carlen, in her contribution, reflects on her four decades of research on female ex-prisoners and poverty to show how ethical dilemmas are often encountered throughout, rather than just when seeking formal institutional approval at the beginning of a research project. The particular dimensions of ethical challenges may change whether one is researching 'subaltern' populations or crime among elites, though what stays constant is the need for the researcher to engage ongoing positioning of the self in relation to research participants. Carlen recalls encountering, during her graduate research on the proceedings of London magistrates' courts, the "daily parade of inequality and poverty … in and around Central London's lower courts [which] ignited within me an anger which fuelled not only the courts' research, but all my social investigation for the next 40 years" (p. 53). Carlen experienced the intertwining of ethics and epistemology and their inextricable connection to politics. While institutional ethics boards are essential in their capacity as "watchdogs" and advisors, Carlen argues that, "it is impossible to tease out in advance a hierarchy of ethical and other principles which ought to be, might be or will be situationally operative during the conduct of qualitative empirical research" (p. 54). Among her varied recollections, Carlen discusses the marketization of research in universities, especially those subject to assessment exercises, which, she argues, inhibits smaller-scale ethnographic or library-based research projects (Wacquant 2002), and may lead researchers to alter their choice of topic, method and outlet for publication of findings alongside considering how to present 'permissible' findings (Hope 2004). While universities operate under a "bureaucratic pragmatism" that provides the appearance of a judicious and consistent distribution of research funding along sound ethical lines, this, Carlen argues, "encourages violation of researchers' own ethical principles as shaped by their professional culture and ethical code" (p. 59).

Recalling research during which she interviewed women about their criminal careers, while Carlen initially decided to analyze their experiences along the lines of gender and class (all were experiencing poverty), she decided to inform her analysis by including race, because all of the black women interviewed mentioned experiencing racism. "The problem for me," Carlen writes, "came when black women argued that black men in general treated their women worse than white men treated theirs. They argued that it was part of their culture" (p. 60). Carlen decided to omit references to such comments, despite this issue being raised by several of the women she interviewed. Indeed, the problem rested with how to write ethically, in a publication, given the fear "that if I repeated comments that made comparisons between white men and black men that favoured white men I would be accused of racism against black men" (p. 60). Is this a failure of ethics, of theory or of both? Carlen admits to wrestling with this question for nearly 30 years. She decides that it was in fact an unethical decision, not based on theoretical, methodological nor even ethical principles, but simply due to an avoidance strategy, as well as a concern regarding politics at her research institution at the time. This issue – wrestling between personal convenience and ethical principle – is one that Carlen repeatedly underscores in her chapter and demonstrates ethical arenas that are well outside the institutional 'gaze' of REBs. Decisions here involve, ultimately, self-governance in actions made during every facet of research. These decisions resonate long after findings are published.

A number of our contributors, including Israel and Carlen, examine ethical issues relating to research with vulnerable and/or subaltern populations. In his chapter, Dale Spencer advocates a post-structural "ethics of witnessing" appropriate to the study of crime victims, especially those who have been subjected to extreme violence. Spencer's chapter reflects on the politics of victimology research, challenging any simplistic positioning of researcher as neutral (and omniscient) observer in the witnessing of victims' lived experiences. He criticizes the ways in which, especially in "some positivistic approaches", victimization is reduced to a category of experience which "connotes a universal acceptance of the category of 'the victim'" (p. 112). In some cases, Spencer writes, interviewers and people who have experienced an event of victimization "enter into an encounter whereby the victimized *survives to tell their story but also tells their story to survive*" (p. 113, emphasis in original). Spencer argues that the ethical challenge here involves how to reproduce the encounter "in ways that ensure they do not lose their impact, and that does not reduce them to clichés or turn them into versions of the same story" (p. 113; see Caruth 1995). Moreover, while writing, the victimization researcher must recognize that the victimization event is never revealed in its totality. Writing thus becomes, in Spencer's words, a "work of mourning", which simultaneously recognizes "that the task of comprehending the past always ahead" (p. 113; see Derrida 1995). Spencer's "ethics of witnessing" is also geared to highlight the "polyvocality" of victims' traumatic experiences, and which reside beyond the often monolithic victimization discourses presented through mass media. His chapter proceeds to offer examples from his own research on homeless masculinities and victimization and he reproduces excerpts of interviews that capture the arguments he raises regarding the ethics of witnessing. Indeed, the reader becomes a witness – rather than a neutral observer – and part of the ethical imagination Spencer's chapter inspires.

Beyond the ethics of research with vulnerable and/or criminalized populations, our contributors also examine ethical issues related to research on policing or with police as collaborators, as well as research examining tours of correctional facilities. These criminal justice institutions are gatekeepers that hold a degree of power and control over questions of access and the ways in which they seek representation in research collaborations. Jianhua Xu, for instance, illuminates some of the challenges of researching policing in mainland China. What is striking is the recognizability of many of the issues he raises as transferrable to other nations, such as Western liberal democracies, yet he underscores the socio-political specificities that augment how ethical issues are experienced and responded to. For instance, Xu writes about the secret nature of much police work, which instills an often conservative culture that deincentivizes the sharing of knowledge with researchers. This is an issue frequently encountered by policing scholars (Manning 2004). The state of policing scholarship in China aggrandizes this situation, especially through researchers who "seldom question the philosophy, method and consequences of policing strategy" (p. 155; see Lo 2010). He also discusses the putatively debased state of academic freedom in China, arguing that the authoritarian Chinese Communist Party "actively preempts any possible challenges to its rule" (p. 155), and a critical criminology challenging the police – a natural extension of the state – would simultaneously raise a challenge to the legitimacy of the state itself. Censorship from the top down is also likely coupled, in terms of policing research, with scholars' own self-censorship to avoid negative consequences (i.e. to research funding and perhaps to their own personal security). Xu also underscores the lack of experience and skill scholars possess for conducting empirical inquiry. This is again related back to historical factors such as the Chinese Communist Party's banning of all social science disciplines in the 1950s, after it first came to power. He thus finds obtaining access to police in China to be the most challenging aspect of his work. Given these challenges, he discusses his approach to ethnographic inquiry that studies "the traces left behind by police activity or the evidence of what the police fail to do in public space" (p. 158), specifically the production of policing posters aimed at crime prevention and posters soliciting crime (e.g. creating fake documents and certificates, advertising and recruiting sex workers, promoting loan sharking, etc.). Xu describes the curious "symbiotic relationship" (p. 161) that exists in urban villages where both types of poster can be found, often displayed side by side. Moreover, he argues that this situation derives from the "symbiotic relationships between economic capital and political power in a wider context of crony capitalism in China" (p. 163; see Xu 2013).

To make sense of his observations, Xu relied on some interviews with police but, he notes, this presented several challenges. He was born and raised in mainland China where he received his Master's degree and also worked as a police officer, after which he pursued graduate and post-doctoral research in Hong Kong before moving to the University of Macau – both Special Administrative Regions of mainland China. Xu writes about his simultaneous insider–outsider status as relevant to his experiences of conducting research on policing in mainland China. He reflects that, "access to the police is almost impossible without personal connections or Guanxi" (p. 167), a Chinese form of personal connection, and felt his former police officer status helped him attract some participants, but with some notable reluctance (i.e. their concern that publication of findings in international journals may tarnish the image of the police). Those police officers he did interview also gave Xu the sense that they were doing him a "big favor", which, he writes, had "nothing to do with the significance of my research but to our Guanxi" (p. 167). He subsequently had to deal with a number of requests to return 'the favour' (i.e. to reconcile the balance of Guanxi), such as one police officer who asked him to write his Master's thesis for him. He writes that he declined such requests "as they were clear violations of research integrity and represented academic corruption" but also noted that his "refusal may also be interpreted as an unwillingness to return a favor, as such practices are widespread throughout mainland China" (p. 167). Such declines could well have ramifications not only for Xu but also other scholars seeking access to the police (especially those based in Hong Kong, Macau or abroad), who may in the future be denied formal access. This issue, here given a particular cultural and geopolitical flavour, is also, we argue, related to the importance of criminologists fostering an ethical imagination regarding the longer-term consequences of their actions. The irony is that the 'right decision', ethically speaking, may lead to unavoidable negative consequences. Making those decisions, we argue, is at the heart of an ethical imagination and both broader integrity and scholarly legitimacy that impacts the self and society. Xu's chapter addresses issues familiar to criminologists conducting research generally, yet it underscores the importance of situating ethical dilemmas within their cultural and socio-political context.

In his chapter reflecting on researching Hong Kong citizen perceptions of crime and police, Adorjan writes about being variably positioned as an 'external-outsider' and 'internal-outsider', arguing that insider and outsider roles are not static orientations taken on throughout the course of research, but often projections on the part of research participants that researchers need to situate themselves within. Not speaking Cantonese and coming to Hong Kong from Canada as a relatively naïve newcomer, Adorjan highlights the value of collaborating with those who are insiders in relation to Hong Kong (i.e. who understand its language, culture and socio-political context). This approach helps identify a number of ethical issues during the course of data collection, such as the way in which the presence of foreign researchers (e.g. an English-speaking white male) may affect focus group discussions, and whether or not to include groups whose views regarding crime and police are affected by political leanings or prior contact with police. Similar to Xu, ethical issues are related to positionality along a continuum of insider–outsider status. The ethical issues encountered by Adorjan are, again similar to Xu, at times relatively generic ones related to qualitative research. Yet ethical issues take on contextualizing local exigencies that suggest both similarities and differences when compared with conducting research in the 'Anglo-Global North'.

In addition to addressing ethical issues involving research *on* police, contributors to this book also explored experiences of research *with* police. Ricciardelli, Huey, Crichton (criminological researchers) and Hardy (a retired Assistant Commissioner and former-Commanding Officer of the Royal Canadian Mounted Police (RCMP)) challenge unilaterally cynical attitudes towards the potential for researchers and police to develop meaningful collaborations. Shared understandings of the objectives of research, methodology and ultimate policy-related goals are often misunderstood and/or mismatched. "Different professional cultures, ethical considerations, systems, and organization," Ricciardelli and colleagues write, "have also compromised potentially successful and ongoing research relationships between police and academics" (p. 143; see Cordner & White 2010). The benefits of successful collaborations, however, are considerable for both policing practice and academic research. The chapter offers shared auto-ethnographic reflections regarding a collaborative partnership among academic researchers and police officers (i.e. the RCMP). The project, in broad terms, seeks to inform the policing of youth and relations between youth and police during a period when an Eastern Canadian province is aiming to implement extra judicial measures (under Canada's Youth Criminal Justice Act).

To instill trust and transparency, the collaborators developed a memorandum of understanding early on, which acted to "ensure that the findings produced were immune from censorship and always protected the participants using methodologies that were in line with agreed upon objectives" (p. 144). An evidence-based, applied model of research was identified at the start as mutually beneficial (i.e. practically applied by the police and serving academics' need for publishable results and the advancement of theory and methods). The value of the chapter is its inclusion of the voices of both a high ranking police officer and the primary investigator on the research project, which consistently underscores the importance of developing shared objectives through transparent dialogue. The authors identify some early misunderstandings related largely to the role academics play in and their motives for conducting research (e.g., the principal investigator recalls how some police officers did not understand that she was motivated to do the research because of her research interests). The academics also found navigating and understanding ranks within the police hierarchy challenging. "What researchers often encountered were officers concerned with how they might be viewed by their superiors" (p. 147), they write. A similar experience is recalled by Rowe (2007) in his ethnographic research with police. He observed,

> demonstrating that formal access was agreed at a high level might have been counterproductive when trying to convince junior staff that I was trustworthy, since they were sometimes concerned that I had been "planted" by senior managers to report on them. (p. 38)

For Ricciardelli and her research team, it became evident that officers were concerned about obeying the orders of their superiors and also avoiding reprimand. Ironically, the relatively close, collegial and trusting relationship between Assistant Commander Hardy and Ricciardelli "also meant that researchers sometimes had to work harder to convince lower ranking officers that what they said and did would be treated confidentially, and would not be reported back to the Commanding Officer" (p. 147–148). Researchers eventually assuaged participating officers' concerns through open discussions about confidentiality, consent and the scope of the project. However, the main challenge for the research team centred on their status as 'outsiders' who suddenly find themselves on the 'inside' in a way incommensurate with the institutional hierarchy of the RCMP.

The auto-ethnographic reflections offered by Ricciardelli and colleagues suggest the importance of leadership and that a certain charismatic authority at the 'top' of criminal justice hierarchies helps cement promote successful collaborations. This issue is highlighted in Erin Gibbs Van Brunschot's chapter, where she examines the "mixed investments" that are inherent in research collaborations with police. Gibbs Van Brunschot explores what may be defined as 'useful' research involving police and academics who may hold varying expectations regarding research. She frames her analysis by considering the development of policing paradigms and the changing nature of policing and policing philosophies (i.e. the gravitation from traditional 'law enforcement' to 'community policing'). Collaborations may be attractive for both academics and police in order to examine the implications of community policing practices and policies. Moreover, policing organizations that embrace community policing may recognize academics as important community stakeholders who may generate valuable and actionable knowledge. Gibbs Van Brunschot productively argues that, "rather than viewing the 'research dissonance logic' between academics and police as a barrier to collaboration, such dissonance may be a means of leveraging the respective impact that collaborators can have on each other" (p. 130). Where research may reveal findings ostensibly unfavourable to policing organizations, it is important to begin the process, Gibbs Van Brunschot argues, by framing collaborative research as 'solution-oriented', whereby "research findings that might otherwise be seen as unfavorable can be interpreted as part of a solution-based approach rather than as a means of placing blame" (p. 130).

Usefully, Gibbs Van Brunschot explicates reasons why collaborations may be beneficial for both police and academics. Among the reasons highlighted, following the findings of academic research may enable the police to create a more effective organization and thus cut costs; they may also foster increased legitimacy with the public vis-à-vis greater 'cooperative transparency' (Engel & Whalen 2015, p. 106). Academics, likewise, benefit from leaving the proverbial ivory tower and engaging with police directly, developing more intimate knowledge of 'on the ground' practices. "It would be difficult for an academic to truly appreciate citizen–police encounters without ever having witnessed a citizen–police encounter first-hand" (p. 132), Gibbs Van Brunschot argues. The chapter then turns to highlighting her experiences with both successful policing collaborations and those where unanticipated challenges emerged. One project involved various 'advisory' stakeholders (including those outside of the police), through which terms of reference for a project were drafted and approved. Difficulties arose when one of the stakeholders desired changing the terms of reference, including the agreed-upon notion that "decisions will be reached through a consensus" (p. 133). Academics on the project, Gibbs Van Brunschot writes, felt this interfered with academic freedom and, moreover, that it undercut the ability of the research team to effectively advise the police. She explores potential reasons for this, including issues early on in the project related to how stakeholders were identified and approached. There were also misunderstandings related to the 'deliverables' of the project, including frustration from stakeholders regarding the "lengthy list of limitations" (p. 133) that often qualify research results. Comparable to Ricciardelli and colleagues, Gibbs Van Brunschot also found "support at the executive level" (p. 134) to be a critical factor in successful collaborations. While in one project support from the chief translated to support at all levels below, there was only enthusiasm and support "at the unit level" (p. 134), not above, and the project did not progress. Staff turnaround, moreover, complicated the process, and related to issues regarding 'ownership' of the project. Here, too, reliance upon the retention of 'charismatic authorities' was central to the efficacy of research collaborations with police. Gibbs Van Brunschot also turns to a range of external pressures on police in particular, such as antagonistic public perceptions of crime and police, especially in the Canadian 'tough on crime', penal populist context (under the now former Conservative government), and a debasement of stable funding support from government for policing research (see Griffiths 2014).

Both chapters that explore academic–police collaboration underscore the potential to foster 'public criminology' (i.e. knowledge exchange; see Loader & Sparks 2011; Uggen & Inderbitzin 2010) and bring research findings to a wider audience beyond academics and practitioners alike. In another chapter, Justin Piché and his colleagues examine the ethical dilemmas inherent in carceral tours – tours often organized for criminology students but also members of the general public. These tours, in a sense, can also be seen as a venue for the transmission of public criminology, insofar as they have the potential to transmit insights to various publics regarding corrections and the experiences of prisoners. Piché writes the chapter with fellow criminologist Kevin Walby, and Craig Minogue, currently a prisoner and active academic who writes about his personal experience of carceral tours. These tours have been advocated by criminologists as a result of their pedagogical benefits (e.g. Smith 2013); they have also been suggested to benefit researchers (e.g. Pakes 2015). Piché and colleagues do not deny these arguments, but suggest that continuing to engage in them based on such arguments alone is unethical. Their critique rests on the arguments that such tours are often "staged", scripted and "sensational" (p. 176; see also Piché & Walby 2010). They also argue that these tours "extend social control in carceral spaces" (p. 178), such that prisoners who refuse to participate in being 'gazed upon' (in a rather zoological sense) may face negative repercussions administered by correctional officers and even parole boards (i.e. revocation of privileges, reports of uncooperative behaviour). They draw these conclusions not only from their own assessments, but also through soliciting the viewpoint of prisoners themselves. They acquired prisoners' perspectives through the *Journal of Prisoners on Prisons*, which is an explicit venue for public criminology with a focus on corrections, and is a prescient example of how ethical issues in criminology may be insightfully examined through the inclusion of multiple voices, including those of academics, practitioners and, in this case, prisoners themselves.

The chapter traces the various responses to the critiques offered by Piché et al., which include those of professors who have ceased to conduct such tours altogether, those who find alternative exercises for students and those who continue to defend the tours "as an approach to pedagogy that demystifies common assumptions held by students about incarceration and those incarcerated" (p. 176) and on the basis of the knowledge they reveal for research purposes. Their argument here is similar to Walter's, as described in her chapter; i.e., that although, that although research with vulnerable populations may be granted permission to proceed as ethically sound (that is, through the approval of REBs), this does not mean that such protection is sufficient. Here, too, an ethical imagination must consider the longer-term consequences that will likely accrue based on more narrowly 'ethical' encounters with vulnerable populations.

Some have argued that carceral tours can, if one is careful, be conducted ethically. Piché and colleagues describe this argument as an appeal to higher loyalties and a denial of harm (drawing from Cohen (2001) and Skyes and Matza (1957)) that is, moreover, "rarely weighed against the harms prisoners may experience during the course of this practice in a rigorous manner" (p. 180). Relatedly, there is also the denial of injury; that is, some negative encounters experienced by prisoners in the course of carceral tours are exceptions within what are seen as accepted and routinized events. Piché and colleagues argue that this stance, also used to justify the continuing practice of carceral tours if done 'better' (e.g. with greater interaction with prisoners), also fails "to acknowledge that the power relations *inherent* in prisons are reproduced through these excursions" (p. 181). They add that when proponents of tours point to the 'free choice' of prisoners to interact and veer from any script provided to them, "they deny the possibility that it is the coercive power of the prison that shapes such actions" (p. 181), including the omnipresence of prison staff who hold the power to negatively sanction transgression. Here, too, the longer-term implications of tours connects with the potential of prisoners to receive positive reviews from parole boards, which ultimately affects their potential release date from prison (here, the chapter benefits from the personal insights of the third author, reflecting on his experience of Australian prison tours as a prisoner; see also Minogue 2003, 2011). Piché and colleagues argued forcefully that, "if control is extended because of an attempt to access the realities of imprisonment through a carceral tour, then it is ethically indefensible" (p. 165).

The chapter concludes by offering some alternatives to carceral tours that retain the possibility for experiential learning, including engaging in prisoner ethnography. Examples include the creation of outlets in which prisoners themselves can publish their work, such as the *Journal of Prisoners on Prisons* (see www.jpp.org), and prison-based work placements for students that expose them "to the mundane aspects of incarceration in a sustained, immersed manner" (p. 188), which better protects the ethical obligations of all parties. The collaboration between Piché and his colleagues, alongside that of Ricciardelli and her colleagues, serve as good examples of public criminology that can result in writing reflectively about shared experiences with criminological implications.

The chapters in this book thus examine ethical dilemmas from various standpoints and phases of research, which, despite taking on particular 'glocal' forms (Bauman 1998), suggest certain recurring patterns across national and more local contexts. One may still ask whether the ethical dilemmas examined thus far apply in the realm of cyberspace, and more specifically to the area of online cryptomarkets, defined as anonymous online forums "where goods and services are exchanged between parties who use digital encryption to conceal their identities" (Martin 2014, p. 356). Are ethical issues here old wine in new bottles or genuinely novel permutations generated through criminological research into the 'dark net'? James Martin, one of the few criminologists examining cryptomarkets, asks the following questions in his chapter: what methods are appropriate for conducting online research; how does one deal with encrypted and anonymized transmissions of information, especially those dealing with the buying and selling of illicit substances online; and how does a researcher 'do no harm' when working with the perpetually shifting landscape of cryptomarkets? The ephemeral nature of dark net websites, such as the Silk Road (which, before it was shut down, specialized in the trafficking of illicit drugs), pose particular challenges when applying for REB approval. For example, a researcher may receive approval to examine a particular dark net site, though the site may itself be shut down by policing agencies before research can be undertaken. As Martin suggests,

> By the time ethical approval for a particular research project is eventually granted, there is no guarantee that any cryptomarket listed on an application will necessarily resemble an earlier iteration (e.g. in terms of size or types of goods and services traded) or even remain in operation at all. (p. 197)

As noted above, Martin argues that the biomedical model governing REBs, centred on addressing direct harms associated with criminological research, is not geared to addressing the various indirect harms that may emerge and affect both researcher and subjects in the area of cryptomarket research. For instance, he writes about the various challenges facing law enforcement agencies investigating cryptomarkets that may seek out the assistance of academics. Such collaborations raise ethical concerns related to both researchers and research subjects (i.e. cryptomarket users), Martin argues, including "the risk of gathering incriminating ethnographic data that may subsequently be seized by law enforcement and used to prosecute research subjects" (p. 193; see, for example, Garrett 2014). Martin also observes how cryptomarkets enable certain 'affordances' for sellers and buyers of illicit drugs, such as anonymity and geographic separation, which "also [free] drug dealers from the threat of violent competition and criminal predation that is characteristic of conventional illicit drug markets" (p. 195). Violence is most notably minimized through the elimination of the role of the 'middle man' in offline drug transactions, though Martin notes that it is not entirely ameliorated (especially at the source of drug production, such as Mexico and Afghanistan).

Researchers, and police, are also behooved to consider how cryptomarkets enabling illicit drug transactions may ultimately be "empowering for drug consumers who have traditionally suffered from a persistent (and sometimes fatal) lack of information regarding the composition and purity of illicit drugs" (p. 195). Product information supplied by dealers is comparable to that provided on Amazon and eBay, including customer feedback that holds sellers accountable for the quality (and, by proxy, safety) of their drugs. Added to this, cryptomarket researchers must contend with the indirect harms that can result when published findings are appropriated by police, government and others used to justify and "rationalize the imposition of cruel and ineffective carceral policies upon vulnerable populations" (p. 197). Here, Martin refers to the US War on Drugs in particular, and the broader permutations of the Hippocratic oath individual researchers must consider. "It is an intriguing and counter-intuitive development in the history of the War on Drugs that a criminal innovation – cryptomarkets – may actually help ameliorate some of the many dangers associated with illicit drugs" (p. 206), Martin argues compellingly, citing a range of studies suggesting that cryptomarkets, rather than conventional drug distribution organizations, may reduce harm to end users and to those who may suffer the consequences of violence related to drug transactions 'in real life'. Equally problematic, Martin argues, would be cryptomarket researchers who refuse to collaborate with law enforcement, which may also lead to a range of indirect harms, such as the reinforcement of an 'us' versus 'them' dichotomy, whereby police would be deprived of critical insights and alternative perspectives. Martin shares his experience demonstrating that policing agencies and government are often ready to at least consider arguments for harm reduction in the area of drug enforcement and crime prevention.

While the majority of the experiences contributors wrote about took place during data collection, some also made reference to ethical issues that were subsequently encountered during research dissemination (including conference presentations and the publication of research findings in peer-reviewed journals). We highlight some of their points in the following section, which again demonstrates the need to consider long-term impacts of ethical practices and policies.

The ethics of research dissemination

In her chapter in this volume, Pat Carlen discusses the work of Jill McCorkel (2013), which details the experiences of incarcerated women in a facility that evidences "a saga of verbal abuse, disrespect, mental torture and the attempted brainwashing of poor black women" (p. 62–63). McCorkel's decision to anonymize the identity of the institution in question is critiqued in a book review by Meda Chesney-Lind (2014), who argues that the egregious conditions warrant, on ethical grounds, 'naming names'. Carlen is direct in her disagreement with this suggestion. While not denying that researchers may feel obliged to breach confidentiality under certain circumstances "in the interests of justice" (p. 63), she argues that such actions may lead to future researchers being denied access to similar institutions. Indeed, as Van Maanen (1983, cited in Israel 2004, p. 718), wrote, "if fieldworkers were to reveal their personal sources of information … it would not be long before they had no personal sources of information left". An end result of this is the debasement of trust (Lofland 1984, cited in Israel 2004, p. 724) that applies not only to the individual but also a wider collective body of researchers over a protracted period of time. An ethical imagination is needed here, where ramifications of decisions conducted during the course of research, and subsequent to publication, are considered regarding both the short-term impact on the researcher and participants, and the longer-term impact on researchers and social groups as a whole. Individual battles may be won, but lost are opportunities to engage with a wider and more ambiguous conflict.

Maggie Walter's critiques of publications examining Aboriginal criminality also suggest the importance of fostering this sense of an ethical imagination. Her critique centres on the publication of Don Weatherburn's (2014) book, *Arresting Incarceration: Pathways out of Indigenous Imprisonment)*. The book rests on the argument (see also Weatherburn et al. 2003) that "the primary reason for over-representation of Australian Indigenous people in the criminal justice system is widespread criminality among Australian Indigenous peoples" (p. 99). Weatherburn's analysis acknowledges the impacts of colonization but, according to Walter, dismisses these "as weak inadequate explanations" (p. 99). Rather than critiquing Weatherburn's thesis directly, Walter suggests that the research is not ethically sound based on its lack of adherence to the six values proscribed by *Values and Ethics: Guidelines for Ethical Conduct in Aboriginal and Torres Strait Islander Health Research* (described in detail in her chapter). This leads Weatherburn to rather tautologically conclude that Aboriginal offending is based on high levels of violence among Aboriginal people. Comparisons are made to non-Aboriginals "but pejoratively", in a practice Walter describes as "the orthodoxy of the dichotomy" (p. 100; see also Walter 2010), which instills negative comparison "whereby the explanation to an intractable social problem, in this case high Indigenous arrest rates, is to be found in the Indigenous peoples themselves. Criminality, in this research, is raced" (p. 100). There are also socio-legal implications to consider, which require an ethical imagination regarding how policy makers may be influenced by research findings. Walter highlights

Weatherburn's thesis that "not only is there no evidence that lack of legal representation was a major cause of Indigenous over-representation in prison, there is no evidence to suggest such services reduce Indigenous over-representation" (p. 101; see Weatherburn 2014, p. 35). Walter adds that though no direct connection can be made, "research such as this provides a rationale for policy actions such as the 2014 cutting of $13.4 million from Indigenous legal services" (p. 101). The 'case studies' offered by both Carlen and Walter should be read not only as critiques of individual pieces of research or reactions to research but also as suggestive of the significance of pushing individuals to think beyond the immediate locales of research and to consider the wider effects on both researchers and research participants.

Some of our contributors offer reflections on ethical issues related to the publication of criminological research outside of the 'West', or more specifically the 'Anglo-Global North'. Jianhua Xu, for instance, writes about research conducted in mainland China, where "a critical discourse is largely absent" (p. 154), and where many academics are characterized as 'worshippers' and 'flatterers' of the Chinese party-state's ideology. Xu recalls his personal experience reviewing Chinese journal articles on crime and policing, where reviewers solicit feedback based on whether articles are "politically correct or not" (p. 156); that is, not critical of the mainland Chinese government, in particular the Chinese Communist Party. While his personal strategy for dealing with such instructions is to simply agree that an article is, indeed, 'politically correct', he rightly acknowledges that "other reviewers may act differently" (p. 156). He adds that, "the existence of this political criteria itself illuminates the lack of academic freedom in China, which greatly affects the formation of a critical analysis of policing among Chinese scholars" (p. 156). Xu also writes about the advantage of publishing findings in international English-language journals whereby Chinese authorities are unlikely to discover dissension; however, this approach simultaneously limits the impact of findings for Chinese students and scholars working in universities without access to English-language journals. He was also once invited to write an article for a mainland Chinese newspaper whose editor apologized to him for deleting a section deemed too politically sensitive. Xu's chapter raises the question of whether or not researchers should themselves be protected to some degree, even if not to the same extent as research participants. He shows how criminologists in China, especially those engaging in politically sensitive areas, are vulnerable to the threat of censorship or punishment.

Xu's ethical dilemmas are based on his ongoing navigation as an insider–outsider in mainland China. Adorjan presents an alternative perspective on this issue, and writes that the fostering of an ethical imagination is crucial from the inception of research design to final publication and the dissemination of findings. Like other qualitative examinations of fear of crime, participants in Hong Kong discussed a range of concerns that sometimes resided in wider issues related to social order, not crime *per se*. Communicating such findings is difficult at international conferences, where the complex post-colonial context of Hong Kong needs to be considered before research findings are discussed in detail. International audiences are also likely to have seen reports in the international media regarding protests in China (e.g. the

'Umbrella revolution' in September 2014 involving clashes between protestors and the Hong Kong police), which may lead some to hold expectations regarding what focus group discussions reveal regarding citizen anxieties and concerns. For Adorjan, developing an ethical imagination as an outsider conducting research with citizens of Hong Kong requires paying careful attention to how findings are written up in publications and presented at academic conferences and dissemination events. The chapter underscores how findings evidenced much more than "orthodoxy of the dichotomy" in terms of high or low levels of fear of crime or high or low levels of satisfaction and trust in police. Even after the official end of such a research project, the ethical challenges for Adorjan reside in the need to represent the lived experiences and voices of participants in their full complexity, recognizing his positionality and privilege as an (internal- and external-) outsider in Hong Kong.

Related to the issues and concerns raised by our contributors are questions about what can, should or must be disclosed to public audiences. We recognize that censorship is a real ethical challenge: some data must be censored yet censorship is ethically problematic (as is not censoring data, clearly a circular argument). How do we determine what can versus what cannot be disclosed? As avid researchers in the field, we have learned that our 'best stories' will often never make it to press because each may leave participants, as well as academic colleagues and criminal justice collaborators, much too identifiable. Even where anonymity is secured in publication, individual identities may be gleaned by others familiar with the social contexts written about. Despite best efforts to anonymize setting and other contextualizing factors, published findings may also threaten seemingly benign or fundamental processes in a community. Further, criminological researchers may opt to refrain from writing papers that, although revealing important findings that could fill lacunae in our academic knowledge, may impinge upon public safety, which always trumps reporting of practices. While criminologists cannot have their work published when their findings are rendered too ambiguous for an academic audience, at the same time they must also consider how publications (and public presentations, dissemination events, symposia, etc.) may negatively impact a range of audiences, research participants, colleagues and collaborators, and may have wider unintended consequences beyond their immediate horizon. Across our contributors we see how clearly each strives to protect participants, maintain the integrity of their work, and, with success, advance their collective fields.

Concluding thoughts: on the going concerns of ethics

Across this edited collection, we strove to stay true to our objective: to centre on the *realpolitik* of conducting criminological research in practice. In bringing together a collection of international expert contributors, each with a unique focus on the trials, tribulations and successes experienced during criminological research we have shown how ethics are an organizing reality shaping research, underpinning methods and even inadvertently restructuring our research questions, programs and studies.

Rather than discreet topics, we exemplify how ethical considerations in practice are ongoing dilemmas when conducting criminological research – dilemmas that can and do arise at all stages of research, from gaining entry into the field, when in the field, to well after results are published. Ethics has become a topic of research in itself at times, changed the entire scope of a study or highlighted new areas in need of inquiry. Centrally, however, we also reveal how researchers, in dealing with ethical considerations, can shed light on their personal attributes. In this context we strove to personalize the researcher by paying attention to how ethical challenges impact researchers, who must manage vicarious trauma and overcome their personal limitations and apprehensions to give their participants voice. Ethics are personal, public and political. The impacts are vast, yet at times intangible, while at other times omnipresent.

In many respects, how one chooses to conduct criminological research involves assumptions and orientations towards power: from the framing of the research problem, selection of certain participants, choice of methodology and accompanying theoretical framework. These are all interrelated and yet constitutive elements that impact greatly on the ethical issues experienced and the manner through which researchers seek to resolve them. Holding closely guarded assumptions regarding who constitutes 'vulnerable' populations and what can be defined as 'elite and powerful' institutions only further entrenches and reifies presumptions about where power resides and in what capacity. It is not novel to demonstrate that subaltern populations, including the criminalized and socioeconomically marginalized, possess agency and power (i.e. to resist negative labelling) (Kitsuse 1980). It is perhaps more challenging to consider the ways in which power operates among agents of social control, including correctional and policing institutions. We advance here the argument that one of the single largest challenges for ethics in criminological research is to develop an empirical program of research examining the permutations of power that is sensitized to ambiguity, discord and the unexpected. Power is, after all, as power does.

References

Bauman, Z 1998, 'On glocalization: Or globalization for some, localization for others', *Thesis Eleven*, vol. 54, no. 1, pp. 37–49.

Bosk, C 2004, 'The ethnographer and the IRB: Comment on Kevin D. Haggerty, "Ethics creep: Governing social science research in the name of ethics"', *Qualitative Sociology*, vol. 27, no. 4, pp. 417–420.

Calvey, D 2008, 'The art and politics of covert research: Doing "Situated ethics" in the field', *Sociology*, vol. 42, no. 5, pp. 905–918.

Caruth, C 1995, 'Introduction', in *Trauma: Explorations in Memory*, ed C Caruth, Baltimore, MD, Johns Hopkins University Press, pp. 3–12.

Chesney-Lind, M 2014, 'Review of Jill McCorkel, *Breaking Women: Gender, Race and the New Politics of Imprisonment*', *Punishment & Society*, vol. 16, no. 1, pp. 126.

Cohen, S 2001, *States of Denial: Knowing about Atrocities and Suffering*, Cambridge, Polity Press.

Connolly, K & Reid, A 2007, 'Ethics review for qualitative inquiry: Adopting a values-based, facilitative approach', *Qualitative Inquiry*, vol. 13, no. 7, pp. 1031–1047.

Cordner, G & White, S 2010, 'The evolving relationship between police research and police practice', *Police Practice and Research*, vol. 11, no. 2, pp. 90–94.

Derrida, J 1995, *Points... Interviews, 1974–1994*, trans P Kamuf, Palo Alto, CA, Stanford University Press.

Dingwall, R 2006, 'Confronting the anti-democrats: The unethical nature of ethical regulation in social science', *Medical Sociology Online*, vol. 1, pp. 51–58.

Dingwall, R 2007, '"Turn off the oxygen…" (comment on the Presidential Address)', *Law & Society Review*, vol. 41, no. 4, pp. 787–795.

Engel, RS & Whalen, JL 2010, 'Police–academic partnerships: Ending the dialogue of the deaf, the Cincinnati experience', *Police Practice and Research: An International Journal*, vol. 11, no. 2, pp. 105–116.

Erikson, K 1967, 'A comment on disguised observation in sociology', *Social Problems*, vol. 14, no. 4, pp. 366–373.

Feenan, D 2002, 'Legal issues in acquiring information about illegal behaviour through criminological research', *British Journal of Criminology*, vol. 42, no. 4, pp. 762–781.

Fine, S 2014, 'Researcher's taped interview with alleged killer Magnotta off-limits to police', *Globe and Mail*, National Section, 22 January. www.theglobeandmail.com/news/national/researchers-magnotta-tape-off-limits-to-montreal-police-judge-says/article16443842/.

Garrett, B 2014, 'Place-hacker Bradley Garrett: Research at the edge of the law', *Times Higher Education*, 5 June. www.timeshighereducation.com/features/place-hacker-bradley-garrett-research-at-the-edge-of-the-law/2013717.article.

Goffman, E 1961, *Asylums: Essays on the Social Situation of Mental Patients and Other Inmates*, New York, Doubleday.

Griffiths, CT 2014, 'Economics of policing: Baseline for policing research in Canada', *Public Safety Canada*, Cat. No. PS14-30/2014E-PDF.

Guta, A, Nixon, SA, & Wilson, MG 2013, 'Resisting the seduction of "ethics creep": Using Foucault to surface complexity and contradiction in research ethics review', *Social Science & Medicine*, vol. 98, pp. 301–310.

Haggerty, K 2004, 'Ethics creep: Governing social science research in the name of ethics', *Qualitative Sociology*, vol. 27, no. 4, pp. 391–414.

Halse, C & Honey, A 2007, 'Rethinking ethics review as institutional discourse', *Qualitative Inquiry*, vol. 13, no. 3, pp. 336–352.

Hammersley, M 2009, 'Against the ethicists: On the evils of ethical regulation', *International Journal of Social Research Methodology*, vol. 12, no. 3, pp. 211–225.

Hannah-Moffatt, K 2011, 'Criminological cliques: Narrowing dialogues, institutional protectionism, and the next generation' in *What is Criminology?*, eds M Bosworth & C Hoyle, Toronto, University of Toronto Press, pp. 440–455.

Hedgecoe, A 2008, 'Research ethics review and the sociological research relationship', *Sociology*, vol. 42, no. 5, pp. 873–886.

Hoonaard, W van den 2001, 'Is research-ethics review a moral panic?' *Canadian Review of Sociology and Anthropology*, vol. 38, no. 1, pp. 19–36.

Hope, T 2004, 'Pretend it works: Evidence and governance in the evaluation of the burglary initiative', *Criminology and Criminal Justice*, vol. 4, no. 3, pp. 287–308.

Hughes, EC 1971, *The Sociological Eye: Selected Papers*, Chicago, IL, Aldine/Atherton.

Israel, M 2004, 'Strictly confidential? Integrity and the disclosure of criminological research and socio-legal research', *British Journal of Criminology* vol. 44, no. 5, pp. 715–740.

Israel, M & Hay I 2006, *Research Ethics for Social Scientists*, London, Sage.

Kitsuse, J 1980, 'Coming out all over: Deviants and the politics of social problems', *Social Problems*, vol. 28, no. 1, pp. 1–13.

Librett, M & Peronne D 2010, 'Apples and oranges: Ethnography and the IRB', *Qualitative Research*, vol. 10, no. 6, pp. 729–747.

Lo, Y 2010, 'Self image and public image of the police in China', MPhil thesis, University of Hong Kong.

Loader, I & Sparks R 2011, *Public Criminology?*, London, Routledge.

Manning, P 2004, 'The police: Mandate, strategies and appearances', in *Policing: Key Readings*, ed T Newburn, Cullompton, UK, Willan, pp. 191–214.

Martin, J 2014, 'Lost on the Silk Road: Online drug distribution and the "cryptomarket"', *Criminology and Criminal Justice*, vol. 14, no. 3, pp. 351–367.

McCorkel, J 2013, *Breaking Women: Gender, Race and the New Politics of Imprisonment*, New York, New York University Press.

Minogue, C 2003, 'Human rights and life as an attraction in a correctional theme park', *Journal of Prisoners on Prisons*, vol. 12, pp. 44–57.

Minogue, C 2011, 'Is the Foucauldian conception of disciplinary power still at work in contemporary forms of imprisonment?', *Foucault Studies*, vol. 11, pp. 178–192.

Pakes, F 2015, 'Howard, Pratt and beyond: Assessing the value of carceral tours as a comparative method', *Howard Journal of Criminal Justice*, Online First. DOI: 10.1111/hojo.12127.

Rowe, M 2007, 'Tripping over molehills: Ethics and the ethnography of police work', *International Journal of Social Research Methodology*, vol. 10, no. 1, pp. 37–48.

Smith, HP 2013. 'Reinforcing experiential learning in criminology: Definitions, rationales, and missed opportunities concerning prison tours in the United States', *Journal of Criminal Justice Education*, vol. 24, no. 1, pp. 50–67.

Sykes, G & Matza, D 1957, 'Techniques of neutralization', *American Sociological Review*, vol. 22, no. 6, pp. 664–670.

Tierney, W & Corwin, Z 2004, 'Qualitative research and institutional review boards', *Qualitative Inquiry*, vol. 10, no. 2, pp. 219–234.

Tierney, W & Corwin, Z 2007, 'The tensions between academic freedom and institutional review boards', *Qualitative Inquiry*, vol. 13, no. 3, pp. 388–398.

Uggen, C & Inderbitzin, M 2010, 'Public criminologies', *Criminology and Public Policy*, vol. 9, no. 4, pp. 725–749.

Wacquant, L 2002, 'The curious eclipse of prison ethnography in the age of mass incarceration', *Ethnography*, vol. 3, no. 4, pp. 371–397.

Walter, M 2010, 'The politics of the data: How the statistical indigene is constructed', *International Journal of Critical Indigenous Studies*, vol. 3, no. 2, pp. 45–56.

Weatherburn, D 2014, *Arresting Incarceration: Pathways out of Indigenous Imprisonment*, Canberra, Aboriginal Studies Press.

Weatherburn, D, Fitzgerald, J, & Hua, J 2003, 'Reducing Aboriginal over-representing in prison', *Australian Journal of Public Administration*, vol. 62, no. 3, pp. 65–73.

Winlow, S, Hobbs, D, Lister, S, & Hadfield, P 2001, 'Get ready to duck: Bouncers and the realities of ethnographic research on violent groups', *British Journal of Criminology*, vol. 41, no. 3, pp. 536–548.

Xu, J 2013, 'Police accountability and the commodification of policing in China: A study of police/business posters in Guangzhou', *British Journal of Criminology*, vol. 53, no. 6, pp. 1093–1117.

INDEX